To Nana,
Happy Summer!
Love,
Beth

IMAGES
of America

BELTON

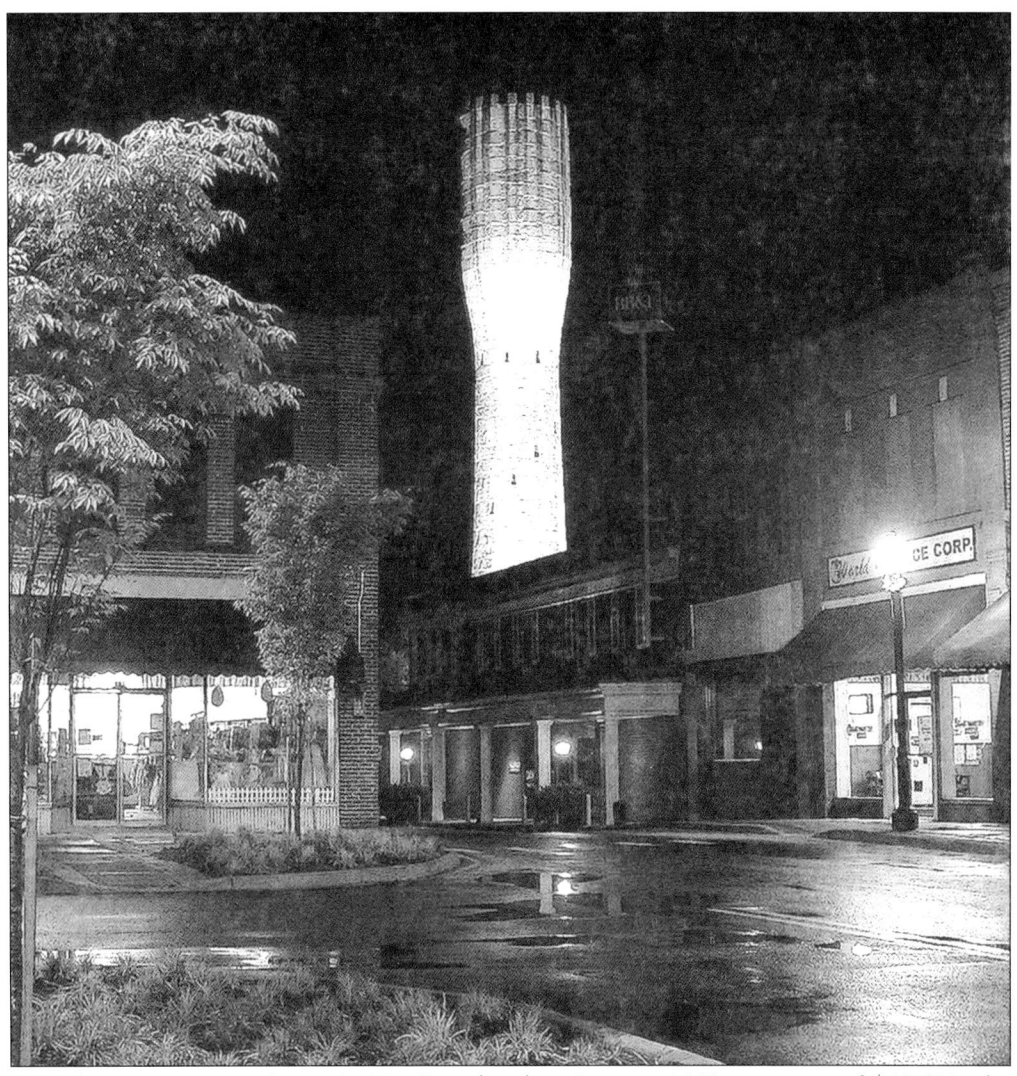

THE SYMBOL OF THE CITY, 2003. Completed in January 1909 at a cost of $12,500, the Standpipe rises 155 feet over the southeast corner of the Square in Belton. Originally the Standpipe provided artesian well water and pumped over 165,000 gallons daily to the growing city, but now it is used only as a storage tank for supplemental needs. Listed on the National Register of Historic Places in 1987 and restored in 1990, the Standpipe boasts a brightly lit star, which shines every Christmas season. In May of 2003, a new lighting system was installed to draw attention to this historic structure at night. (Photo by Bobby Johnson.)

On the Cover
TENNIS ANYONE? The Blake family rests after a late summer game of lawn tennis in 1914. They are, from left to right, as follows: father Lewis Blake, secretary of the Belton Mill; his wife Annie, daughter of Capt. Ellison Smyth; and their seven children, Lewis (Bootsie) Blake Jr.; Julius Blake; Sadie Blake (Rogers); Smyth Blake; Ed Blake; Julia Blake; and Nancy Blake (Haynie). Tennis has been a popular recreational sport for the townspeople of Belton since 1892, when the first court was placed between the separating train lines at the present site of the depot.

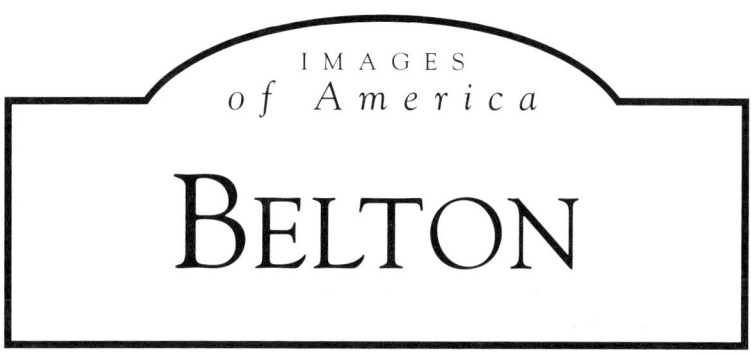

BELTON

Images of America

Alison Ashley Darby

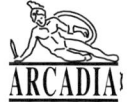

Copyright © by Alison Ashley Darby
ISBN 0-7385-1606-6

First published in 2003
Reprinted in 2004

Published by Arcadia Publishing
Charleston, SC; Chicago, IL; Portsmouth, NH; San Francisco, CA

Printed in Great Britain

Library of Congress Catalog Card Number: 2003114170

For all general information contact Arcadia Publishing at:
Telephone 843-853-2070
Fax 843-853-0044
E-mail sales@arcadiapublishing.com
For customer service and orders:
Toll-Free 1-888-313-2665

Visit us on the internet at http://www.arcadiapublishing.com

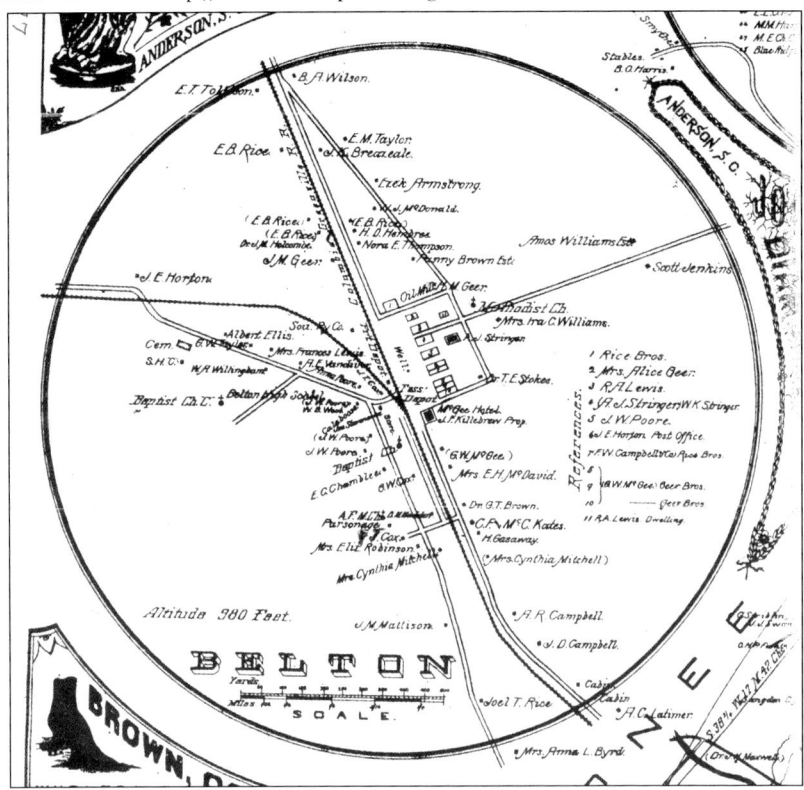

OVER 40 YEARS OF GROWTH, 1897. The layout of the square appears in this 1897 map that was published as part of an advertisement. The businesses noted include Rice Oil Mill; the mercantile companies of R.A. Lewis, A.J. Stringer, J.W. Poore, F.W. Campbell, and the Geer Brothers; the post office run by J.E. Horton; the railroad depot; and main home sites.

Contents

Introduction		7
1.	A Child of the Railroad	9
2.	Business Pursuits	15
3.	Beltonians at War	39
4.	School Days	53
5.	Arts, Entertainment, and Civic Organizations	69
6.	Government and Politics	89
7.	Churches and Religious Activities	99
8.	Mill Life	113
Acknowledgments		127

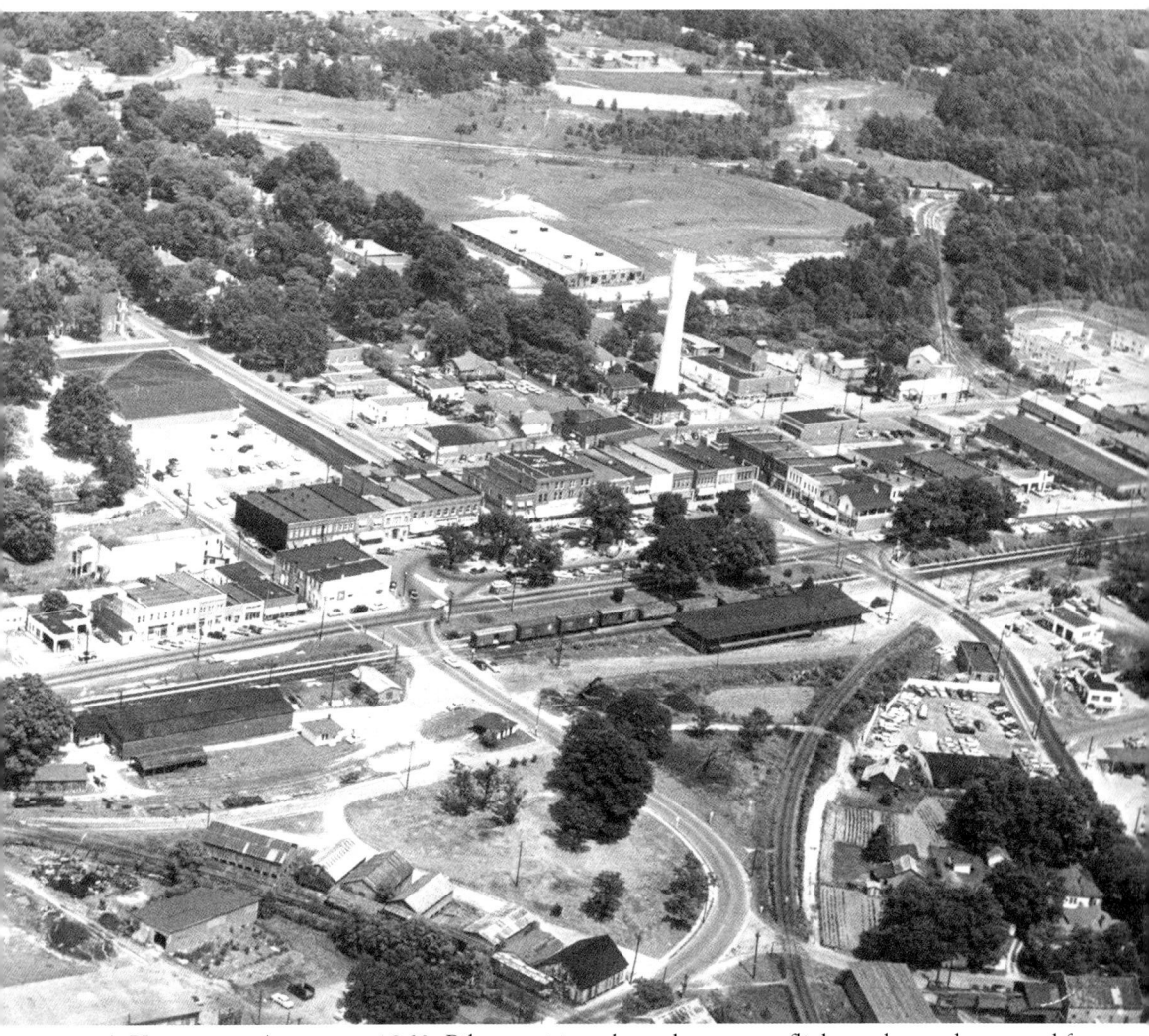

A VIEW FROM ABOVE, C. 1960. Pilots cruising along the eastern flight path stood on guard for the Belton Standpipe as their mark to turn westward to reach Atlanta. Many of the buildings seen in this photo have been torn down, such as the Geer Hotel, the Wertz Building, the Merchants Grocery building, and the P&N Depot on South Main Street; the warehouses along the railroad tracks; the south-facing block of buildings on the Square; and Mitchell-Cox Lumber Company on North Main.

INTRODUCTION

The City of Belton shines like the newly lit standpipe itself in preparation for its 150th anniversary in December of 2005. In recognition of this milestone, Arcadia Publishing Company contacted the Belton Area Partnership with the offer to produce a book of pictures depicting Belton's illustrious history. This volume is the result.

Belton has been called a "Child of the Railroad." In 1845, prominent citizens of Greenville, Anderson Courthouse, Abbeville, Columbia, and Charleston met to establish the Columbia and Greenville Railroad Company. In 1847, when the work on the railway bogged down, Chief Engineer Mills proposed that $100,000 could be saved if the rails ran over the high ridge west of the Saluda River. After much consideration, land owned by Dr. George Brown, James Telford, G.R. Telford, and J.B. Lewis was chosen as the most direct route, and construction resumed immediately.

To appease investors from Anderson Courthouse who disapproved that the railway wouldn't run through their town as originally proposed, a spur line was added to connect this new route to Anderson. Naturally, a town was needed to provide rest and refreshment for the weary traveler on this railway stop. Dr. Brown had his brother-in-law survey the area and lay out town lots. The lots were sold at public auction and the town sprang up around the tracks. By 1853, there was a hotel, mercantile shop, post office, and depot. The town received its charter in December of 1855. The Presbyterian Church (previously known as the Bradaway or Broadaway Presbyterian Church) moved to town in 1851, and the First Baptist Church was established in 1861. The 1860 census recorded 213 residents in the city limits.

After the Civil War, to which Belton contributed a number of gallant soldiers, the town began to thrive as money poured in from the sale of cotton and other cash crops that grew abundantly on the surrounding farms. Taking advantage of the need for cotton processing in the area, Enoch and Joel Rice bought a cotton gin, which was placed above the north end row of stores. By 1899 the first cloth mill (Belton Mill) was established. Two other mills specializing in terry cloth production and finished products were begun in the next four decades. Infrastructure was enhanced by the establishment of phone service (1902), the availability of electricity (1905), and the erection of a public water tower (1909). The square was paved in 1924 to accommodate increasing automobile traffic.

By 1877, the city was prospering. A.J. Stringer built a three-story brick structure that boasted an opera house on the top two stories. Dramatic productions were performed for the town's entertainment there. At the turn of the century, a skating rink, bowling alley, silent movie theater, and water park were all available for enjoyment. Tennis has always been a favorite pastime for the local young people, and a town court was constructed in 1892 at the site of the present depot. In addition to beautifying the town, the Belton Civic League founded the first public library in 1914 and maintained it until the 1930s when the city government took over its management.

After World War II, the city drew in many other industries, and existing mills prospered. In response to the growing need for labor in the area mills, the population of Belton reached its peak in 1980 with over 5,283 residents. The prudence of its citizenry and business leaders is evident in that Belton has suffered no bank failures in its history, even during the volatile period of the Depression.

In 2003, corporations that employ the citizens of Belton and those in its environs include Milliken-Peerless Plant, Hydro-Aluminum, LoomCraft, Rice Mill, Blair Mill, Rockwell Automation, Goodman Conveyor, Service Laundry Machinery, and Belton Metal Company. Two national grocery chains (one of which has its beginnings in Belton), four national fast-food restaurants, ten locally owned eating places, over 30 retail businesses, five banks, and countless service industry establishments dot the one-mile radius that marks Belton's city limits. The 2000 census recorded 4,463 persons living within the city, and over 8,000 addresses bear the 29627 zip code.

Belton is also a stop on the South Carolina Heritage Corridor. With two events (the Standpipe Festival and the Wachovia/Palmetto Junior Tennis Championships) that draw in thousands of visitors/tourists each year and a civic pride matched only by an enthusiasm to see the city preserve its past and grow to meet the challenges of the future, Belton is a city worth documenting in pictures.

Pictures have been gathered from the Belton Area Museum, picture-sharing days held at the Belton Center for the Arts, and personal collections that span the earliest recorded images to those of 2003. Those people who have shared their pictures, identified people in the photographs, told stories, or given information are noted in the acknowledgments.

If you find any mistakes, incongruities, or misidentified people, please contact me. It is my greatest aspiration to make this document as historically accurate as possible. I wish I could have included every picture that was submitted, but time constraints and space limitations prohibited the use of all of the images.

It has been a tremendous honor to gather the materials, talk with longtime Belton residents, record their memories, and organize this book. I hope you'll be satisfied with the result.

Happy 150th Birthday, Belton!

AAD
memoryln@innova.net

One
A Child of the Railroad

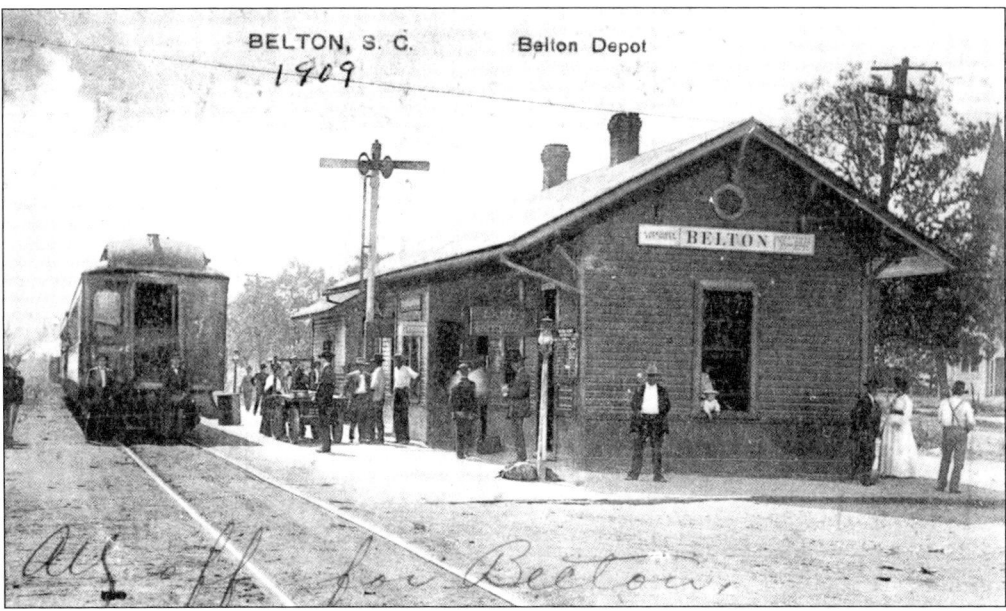

All Off for Belton! Piedmont farmers and businessmen had long dreamed of a reliable railway service to transport the vast agricultural bounty of the upstate to the port at Charleston. In 1845, the Columbia and Greenville Railroad Company was formed and shares were sold for $1. The first depot, shown here as it appeared at the turn of the century, was completed by 1852 at the present roadbed where Anderson Street meets Main Street. The building measured 40 feet long by 20 feet wide. The first train arrived at the depot in May 1853 and a huge celebration was held to commemorate the completion of the rails. Over 3,000 people from neighboring towns attended the gala. F.W. Selleck, editor of the *Abbeville Banner*, remarked that the "mountains of ham, loaves of bread, pies, cakes, and custards" were a testament to the town's "hospitality and kindness." Dignitaries Dr. F.G. Thomas of Abbeville and J.P. Reed and James L. Orr of Anderson made speeches that historic day.

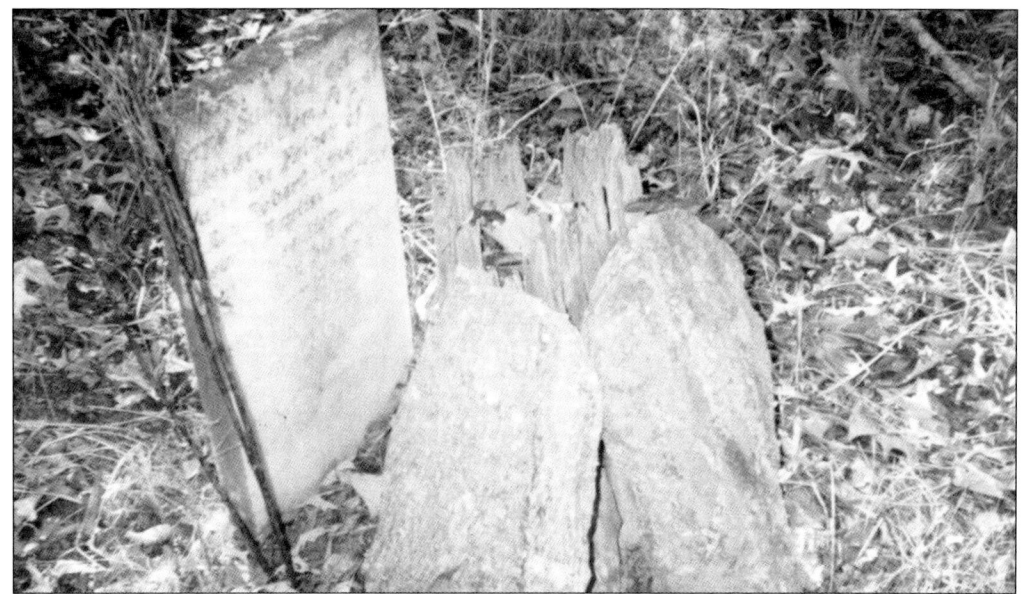

AMONG THE FIRST SETTLERS. After arriving at Baltimore, the King family left Maryland, drove down the Western Trail, and built a log cabin at the present crossroads of Cherokee Road and West Road. Family tradition holds that Robert King arrived in the Belton area around 1772, bought an English league of land, made a pact with the Cherokee Indians, and began raising livestock and crops. Leaving 23 children behind to populate the county, Robert King died on December 13, 1826. Here, the patriarch's gravestone (field rock with just the initials and date of death) is accompanied by the stone erected by his grandson J. Mack King in 1929.

BELTON'S FOUNDER. Dr. George Reece Brown (born 1800 and died 1881) is shown here with his second wife, Maria Louisa Horton, whom he married in 1844. Brown grew up in the Calhoun Community (present-day Shady Grove area), worked for Maj. Aaron Broyles in his store, earned enough money to obtain his medical degree at Transylvania University in Lexington, Kentucky, and returned to marry his childhood sweetheart Edney Broyles in 1824. In 1830, he purchased a 374-acre tract that would eventually become the city of Belton. He sat in the legislature from 1852 to 1856 and, in addition to his extensive medical practice, took on apprentices who read medicine under him. Most of all, he enjoyed overseeing the land that he cultivated. When talk of the railroad project broke out, Brown had his brother-in-law John Horton survey the land for a town, setting aside lots for a school and church. His daughter Josephine had the privilege of naming the town. She chose Belton in honor of the president and promoter of the Columbia & Greenville Railroad, Judge John Belton O'Neall.

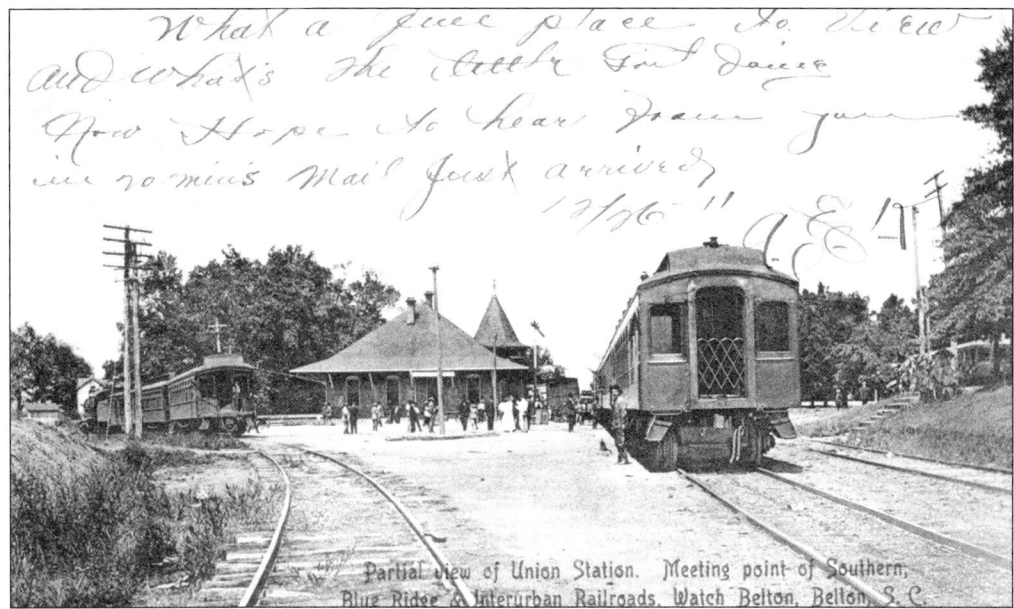

THE SOUTHERN DEPOT, C. 1911. Built next door to the site of the original frame structure around 1910, the new brick building, called Union Passenger Station, housed separate waiting areas for passengers of different races. In 1894, the Columbia and Greenville Railway changed its name to the Southern Railway. By 1914, there were an estimated 85 trains or trolleys of the Southern Railway, the Piedmont and Northern Line, or the Blue Ridge arriving or departing Belton each day. In 1932, one could travel the Southern on a round trip excursion from Belton to Charleston for $2. The last passenger train left Belton on its final 110-mile run to Columbia on February 19, 1961. Today, one freight train passes through Belton in the morning and returns in the afternoon.

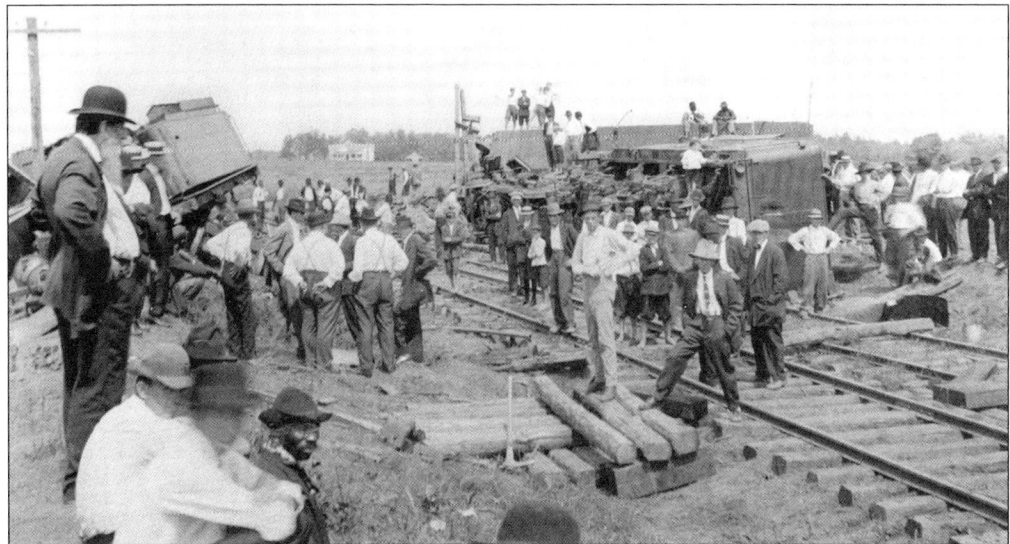

TRAGEDY. On September 14, 1912, a train bound for Greenville and running through the Cheddar Community north of Belton ran off the tracks, killing some people and wounding others. A special crane was sent for to hoist the trains back on the tracks so the railway line could continue.

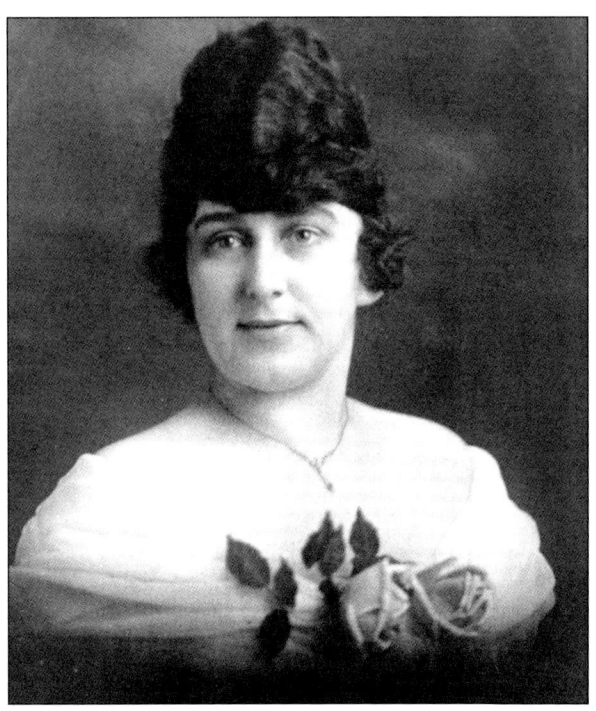

MARY JANE ROGERS, 1883–1966. Mary Jane Rogers served as the telegraph operator and ticket seller for the Southern Railway for over 43 years.

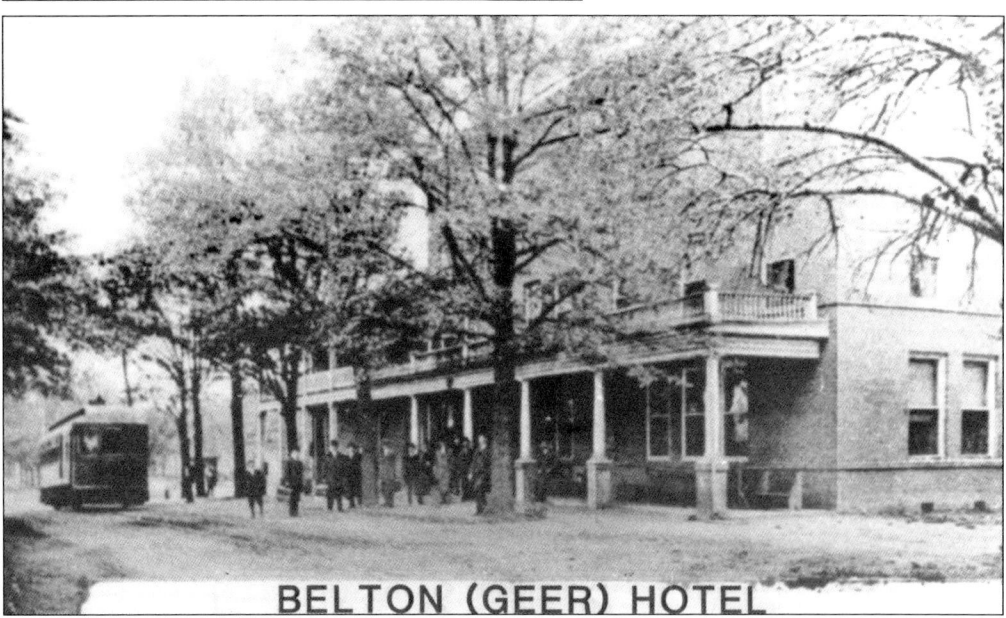

THE INTERURBAN LINE. George E. Coughlan and James P. Wilson were granted a franchise in June 1902 to operate an electric interurban car with one terminal at or near Greenville and the other within the city of Anderson. The Belton Town Council granted permission to use such streets as necessary to operate the line efficiently, including Main Street, and Belton gained access to another railway system. The electric trolleys inexpensively carried passengers on the 11-mile run from the porch of the Belton Hotel to Anderson. In fact, around 1905, many an Andersonian and his family took the Interurban to Belton after church on Sunday, ate a fine meal at the hotel, and returned home on the trolley, all for around $2.80.

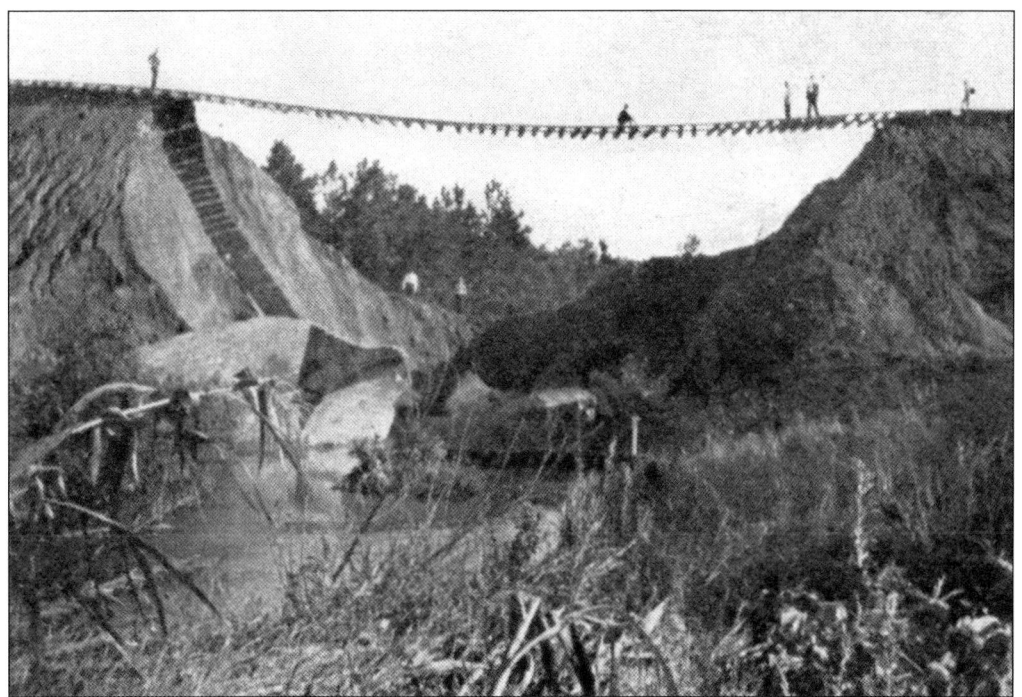

FRESHET DESTROYS LINE. On August 25, 1908, 11 inches of rain fell during one day, leaving the creeks and rivers swollen nearly 10 feet from the freshet. This bridge serving the interurban line from Belton to Anderson collapsed, leaving passengers stranded and business halted.

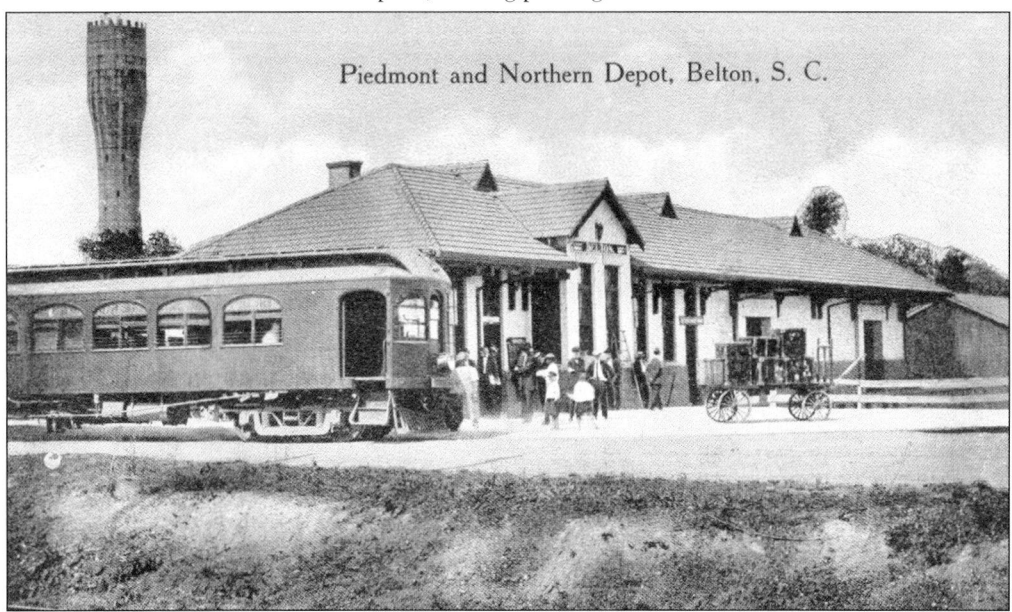

THE PIEDMONT AND NORTHERN DEPOT, C. 1914. The Greenville, Spartanburg, and Anderson Railway, predecessor of the P&N, completed its main line from Greenwood to Belton terminal by 1912. By 1914, the section between Greenville and Spartanburg was constructed, and final consolidation of the railway system occurred in June of that year. The railway was renamed the Piedmont and Northern. This depot was torn down in the 1980s.

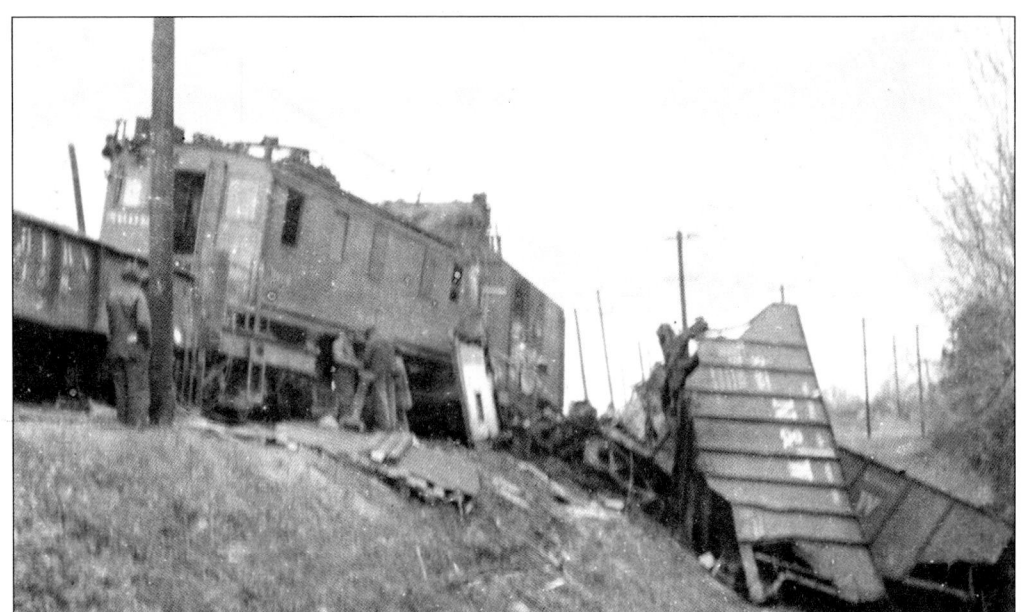

FROM PASSENGERS TO FREIGHT. With industrial growth came the need for more freight trains, so the P&N has focused solely on freight transfer from 1951 to the present. Unfortunately, even freight trains wreck, and in 1944 one P&N locomotive rear-ended another train behind the present-day Belton Plaza Shopping Center. There was one fatality. The engineer of the second train got trapped in the wreckage. When the train caught fire and efforts to free him failed, he died in the ensuing blaze.

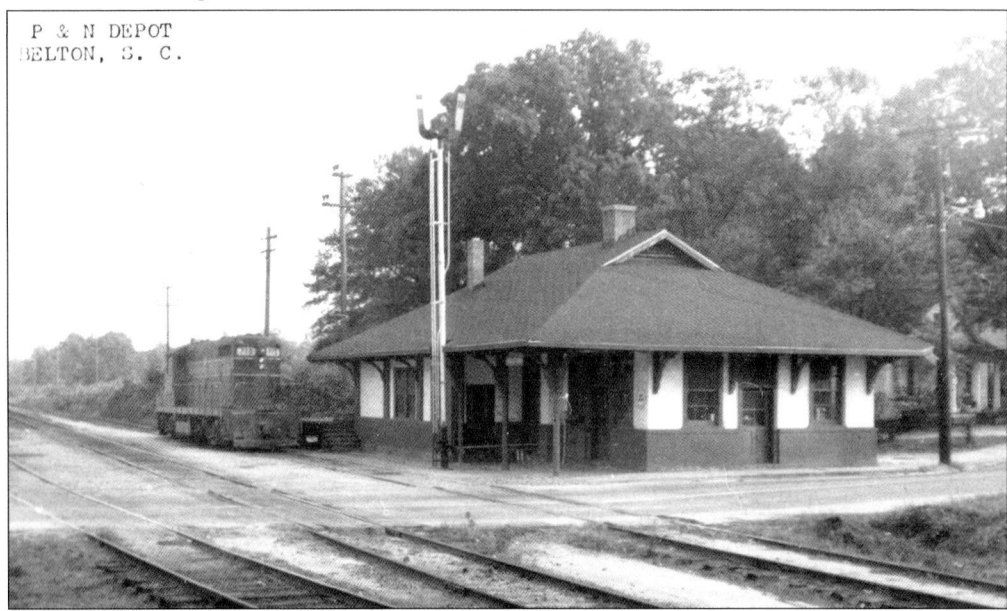

THE POOR AND NEEDY. The P&N was given this nickname by Belton students riding the line to Furman University. The P&N station was located a few blocks east of the square and held waiting rooms for passengers. When passenger service was discontinued in 1951, the station served primarily as an office for the P&N agent. In 1960, the Belton agent was O.K. Horton. The building was torn down in the mid-1970s.

Two
BUSINESS PURSUITS

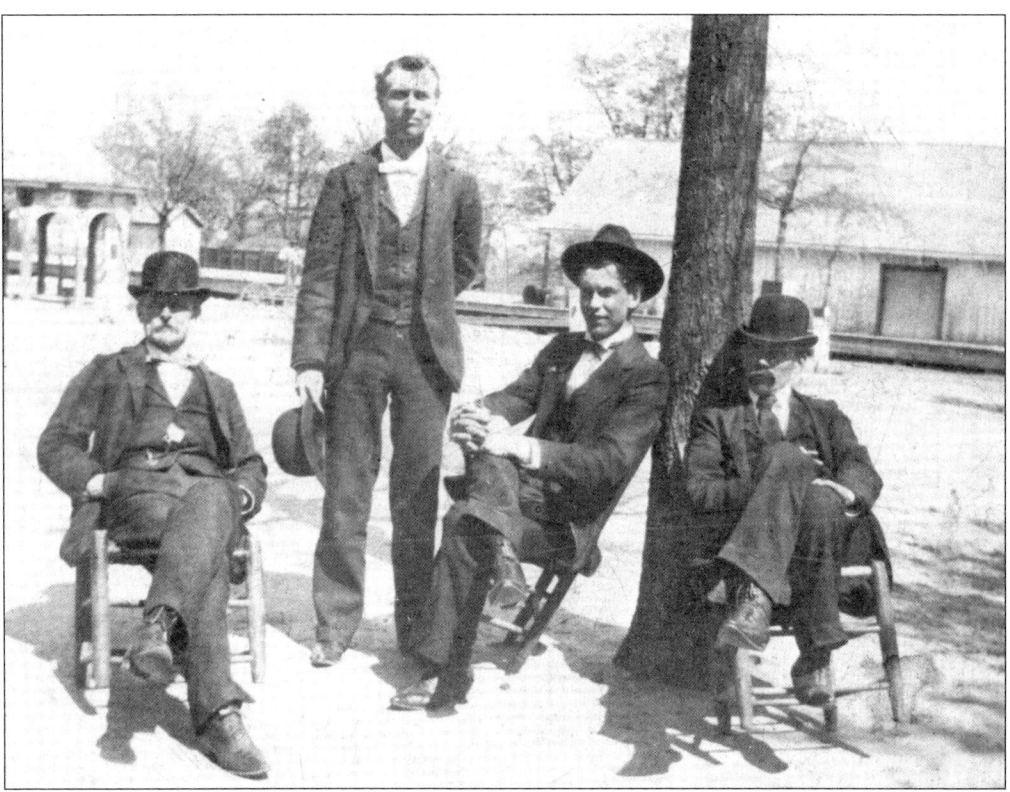

THE LIVING'S EASY, 1898. These gentlemen—W.J. Moorehead, John Horton, George Tate, and Reid Campbell—await customers and pass the day in the company of their peers. Since the pace was slower in those days, a cool breeze, a cane-bottomed chair, and good conversation made for a pleasurable and comfortable living. But these were no slackards. Moorehead spearheaded the campaign to build the Standpipe; Horton was one of the organizers of the Farmer's Bank; Tate was a successful businessman; and Campbell, owner of the general merchandise firm of F.W. Campbell and Company, served as longtime city clerk and treasurer. The picture is taken in front of the Rice block of buildings on North Main Street, and the city well and railroad warehouses are in the background.

A DOCTOR OF GREAT REPUTE (1829–1884). Dr. William Carroll Brown, nephew of founder Dr. George Brown, was schooled at Williamston under the famed Prof. Wesley Leverette and settled in Belton around 1850 when he began working as the schoolmaster at the Belton Academy. After graduating from Jefferson College in Philadelphia in 1854, he returned to Belton to practice medicine in partnership with his uncle. In 1857, George Brown decided to quit his medical practice and move to a farm near Dalton, Georgia, so W.C. bought out his interest. At the outbreak of the War Between the States, W.C. Brown volunteered for service in the Confederate Army. A petition from the citizens of Belton was presented, proclaiming that the townspeople's needs far outweighed the army's, so he was relieved of his duties to service the town. A small one-room house with a large fireplace was built on the corner of Brown Avenue and Carroll Lane and served as "The Doctor's Shop."

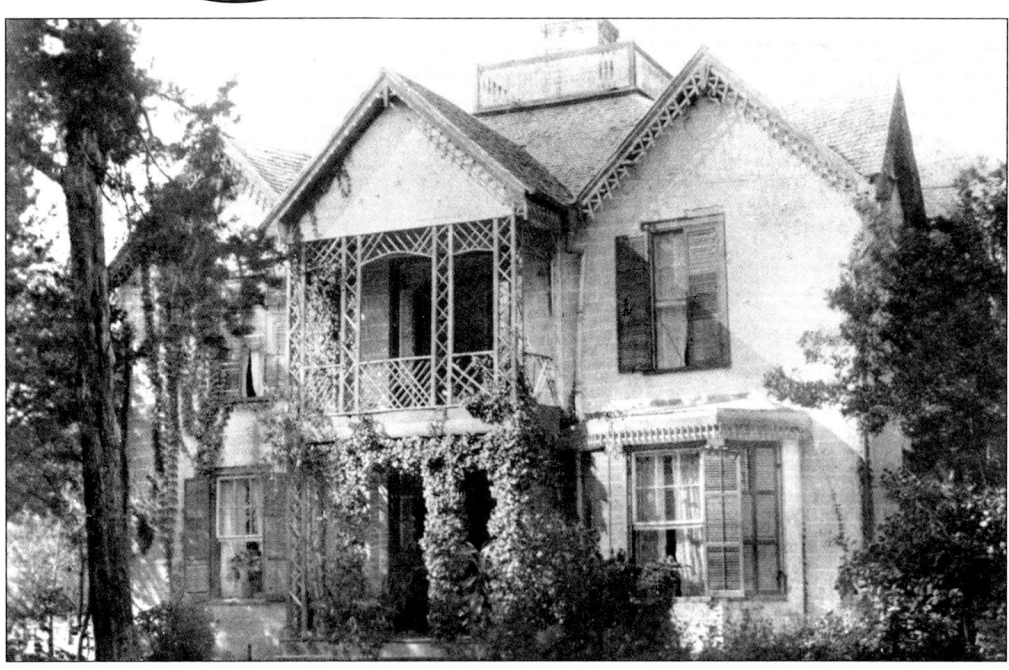

THE SHADOWS, C. 1900. Dr. W.C. Brown built this beautiful mansion on the site where Dr. George Brown had lived. The mansion's 16-inch walls were made with bricks constructed in a kiln located near Cynthia White Springs on Crayton Street (present-day Brown Avenue). W.C.'s wife, Anna Dean Brown, a distant cousin whom he married in 1856, was a gracious hostess. The family recounts that two or three extra place settings were put on the table at each meal just in case a relative, a friend, or a patient might be visiting at dinnertime. The house was torn down in 1987.

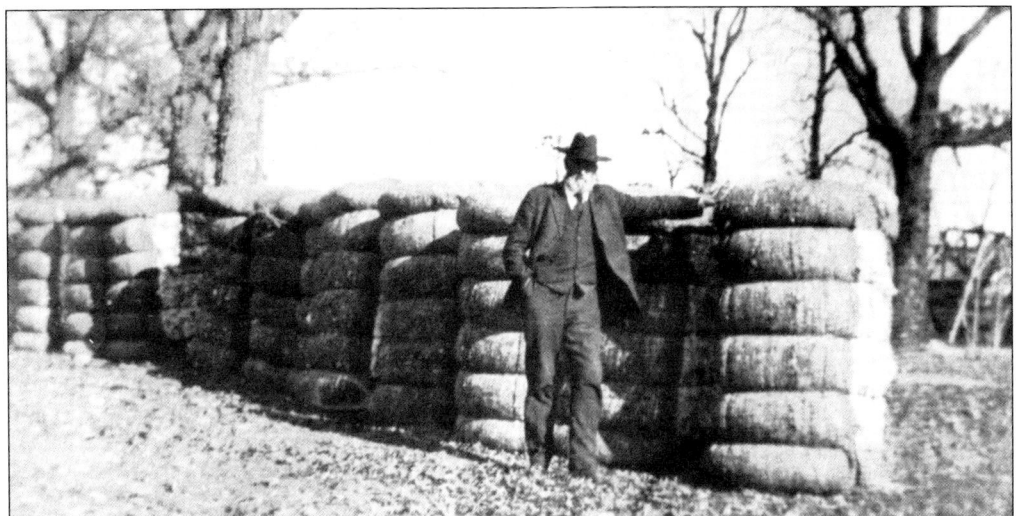

WHEN COTTON WAS KING. The fertile fields surrounding the fledgling town of Belton grew the finest short staple cotton around. For the 1894–1895 season, 6,325 bales of cotton were marketed in the town by area farmers, circulating at least $200,000 through the community. Over 8,000 bales were purchased by Belton cotton factors in 1897. Secondary markets prospered also due to the cultivation of cotton: 1,500 tons of fertilizer were purchased during that same year. Here, T.C. "Lum" Poore poses with his cotton yield in 1918.

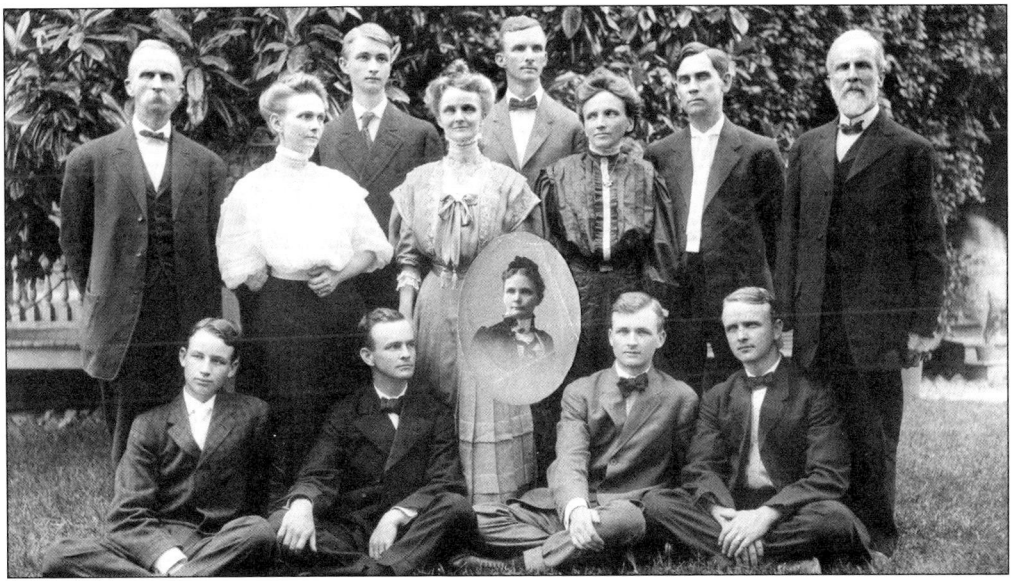

THE JOEL TOWERS RICE FAMILY, C. 1912. J.T. Rice was a savvy businessman who, along with his brother E.B. Rice, pursued many ventures. The brothers started their business pursuits with a traveling cotton gin, finally constructing a row of buildings on North Main Street to house the gin and their growing trade as cottonseed oil producers. For several years, J.T. served as intendent of Belton at the turn of the 19th century, chaired the school board, managed a brick mill, and bankrolled business ventures such as the Belton Mill. Here he poses with his family, who are shown from left to right as follows: (first row) Max, Blair, Rex, and Leon; (second row) J.T. Rice, Rena, Idell, and Daisy; (third row) George, Clarence, Ben Geer, and brother Enoch; (inset) Sadie McGee Rice, who died in 1907.

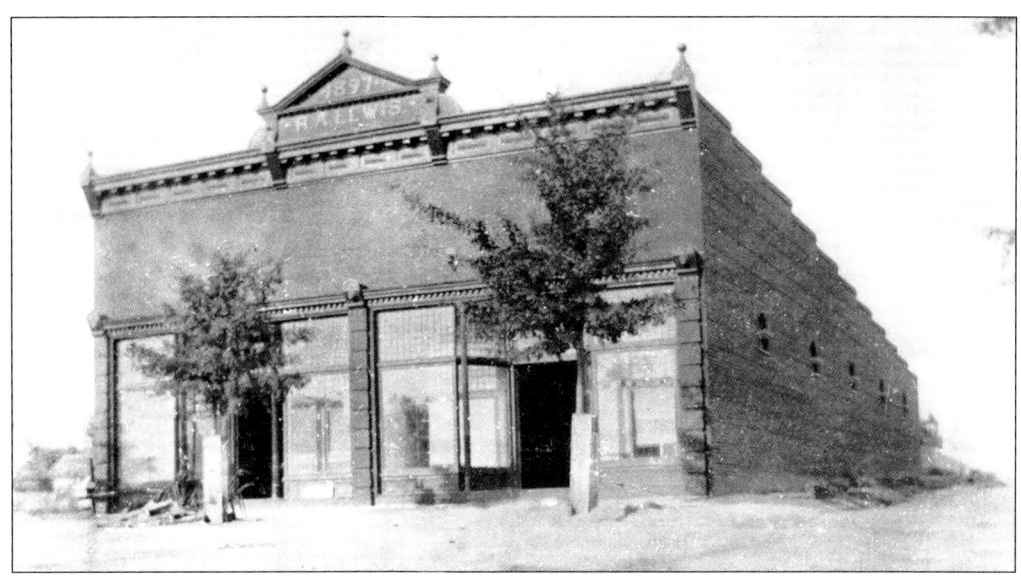

A MERCANTILE MAGNATE. Robert A. Lewis began his career as a salesman for the A.J. Stringer Company in 1873. In 1882, he ventured out on his own with the firm R.A. Lewis and Company. His store carried a large line of general merchandise, fertilizer, buggies, mules, and wagons. In 1895, his sales amounted to $200,000, including cotton receipts. Concerned with the progress of the city, he tirelessly worked to raise interest and capital for the Belton Mill, the Belton Power Company, and the Belton Bank. Lewis built this towering structure on the northeast portion of the square in 1897. He also had ventures in Pelzer and Darlington. The Belton Center for the Arts and Kutz on the Square now occupy this building.

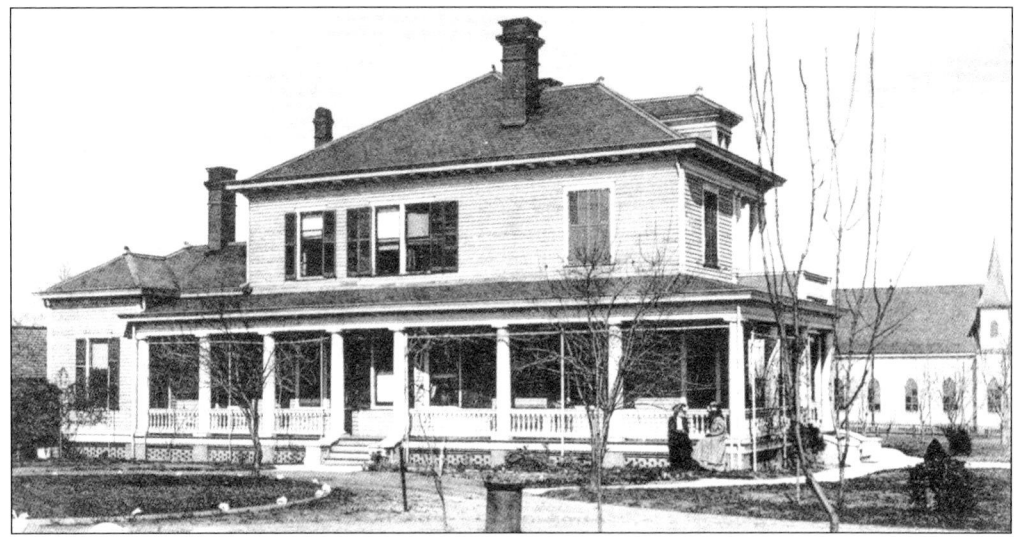

SUNNYVIEW, C. 1905. The R.A. Lewis home was situated on River Street at the present site of Fred's. A beautiful structure, it was enhanced by the green thumb of the merchant's wife, Jessie Breazeale, whom he married in 1882. In a 1938 article entitled "Strolling About Belton," the author comments on the honorary president of the Civic League's yard: "Her grounds are so large that there is nothing crowded or cramped about her planting. Mrs. Lewis is a real flower lover, and has a bit of everything, all of which she shares with her friends." Latimer Memorial Methodist can be seen in the background.

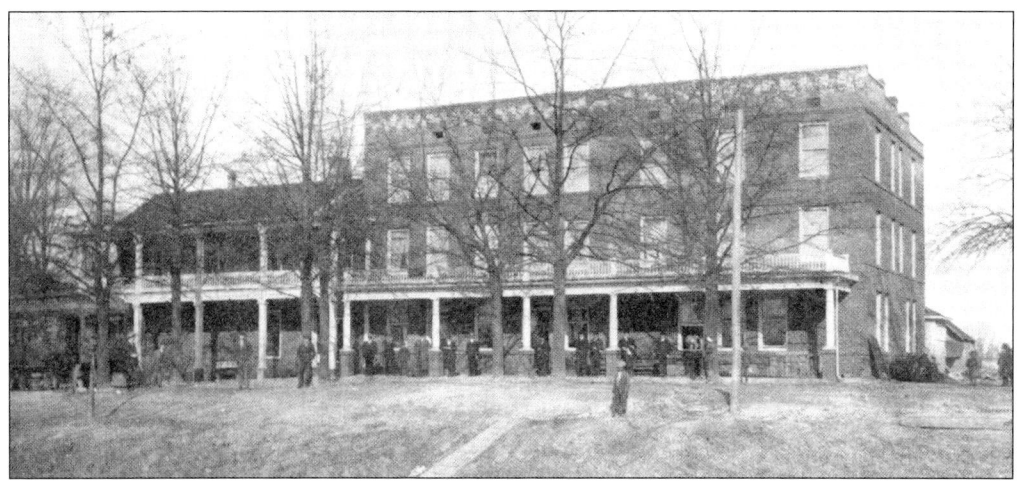

THE OLD LADY. When the town of Belton was just beginning in 1853, Dr. George Brown and his son-in-law A.R. "Wit" Broyles built a two-story hotel with overhanging porches on the south end block of the Square. In a few years, it was sold to G.W. "Wash" McGee and became known as the McGee Hotel. It was managed by a member of the McGee family until H.M. Geer bought the place in 1907. Traveling salesmen, or drummers as they were called, would leave the depot or get off from the Interurban in front of the hotel, enjoy a leisurely visit on the porch, eat a scrumptious meal, and take a hot or cold shower. The three-story brick addition was converted to apartments for Belton Mill employees in the 1940s but was eventually torn down in July 1965. The original structure still remains as the home of Horton's Pharmacy.

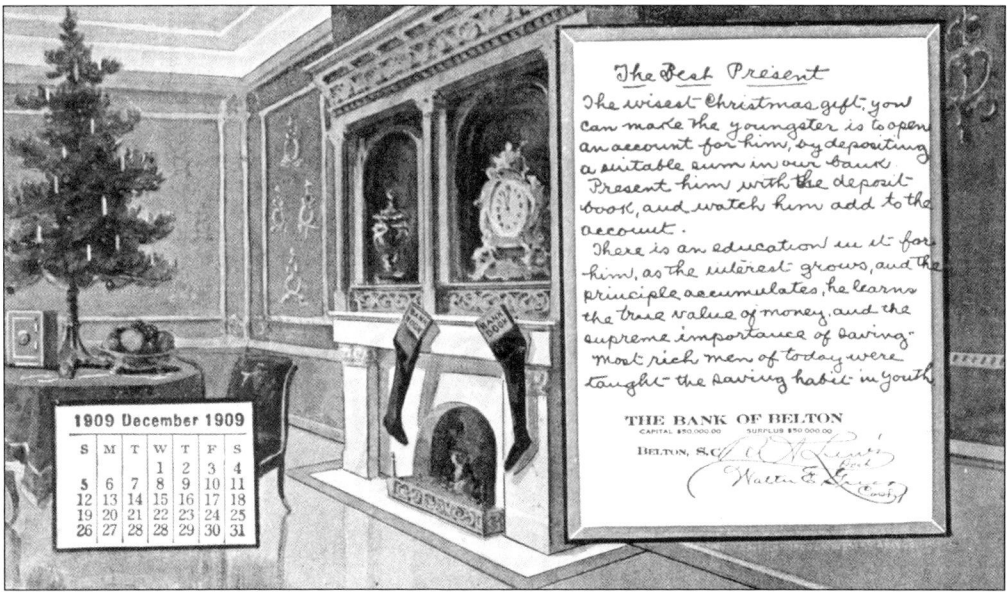

RECOMMENDED SAVINGS. Since R.A. Lewis engaged in the buying of cotton, during the cotton season his cashier would weigh the cotton and give a price voucher to the farmer, tally up the amount needed to cover receipts that day, telephone the old Bank of Anderson for the needed cash, and await the arrival of the train to meet the ticket sales for that day. Seeing the need for a local enterprise, R.A. Lewis decided to establish a bank in town, so the Bank of Belton was born in September 1899 with capital stock of $50,000. In this 1909 calendar postcard, customers are encouraged to consider opening savings accounts to give as Christmas presents.

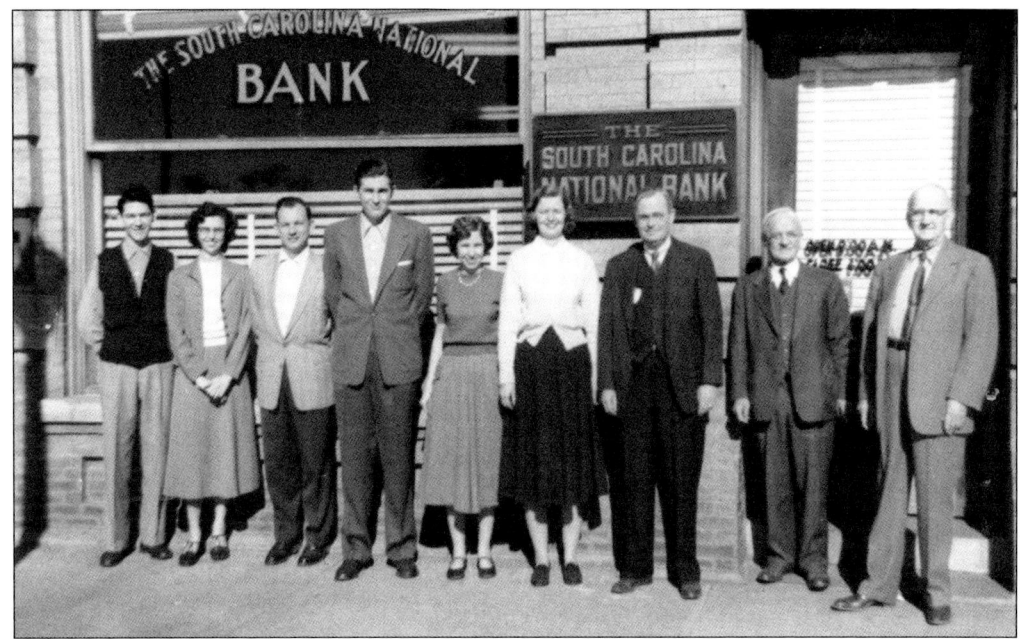

SCN EMPLOYEES, 1955. In 1935, the Bank of Belton became a branch of the S.C. National Bank, which is now Wachovia. SCN had its beginnings in the Bank of Charleston. Employees shown here are, from left to right, Charles Saylors, Ellenna Morgan, Earle C. Williams, Ray Mattison, Mae M. King, Annie Lou Russell, B. Fred Greer, H.R. Campbell, and Walter E. Greer.

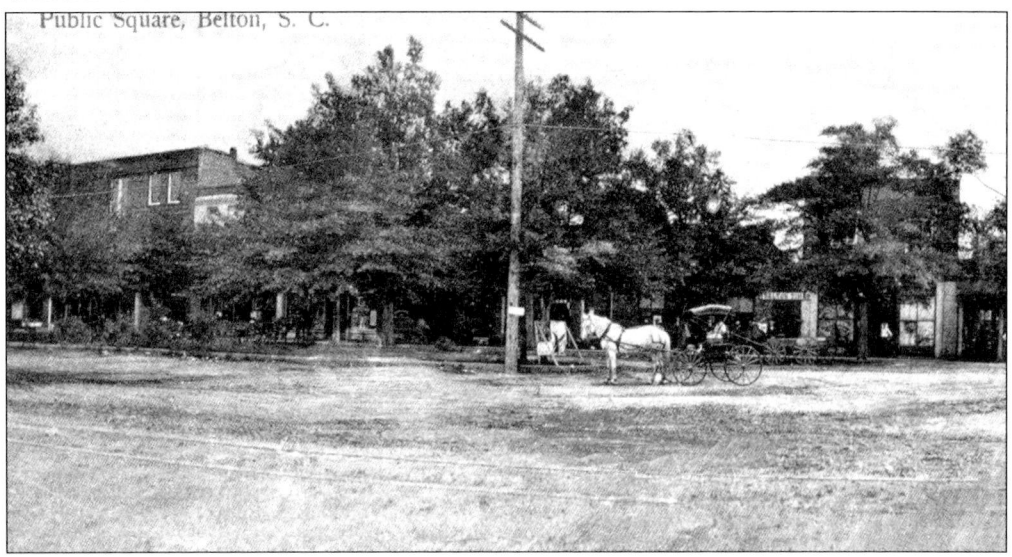

BELTON SQUARE, C. 1900. Belton began replacing its wooden structures from the last half of the 19th century with brick structures. Brick was obtained from the kilns established on Crayton Street by both the Brown and Rice families. Even though the Stringer building to the left looms three stories high, this picture shows that many of the other east block buildings are not yet two-storied. The signs for the *Belton Times* building and Fair's Pharmacy are shown behind the carriage drawn by the beautiful white horse. The *Belton Times*, the local newspaper first published in 1903, was followed by the *Belton Journal*, published from 1914 to 1924.

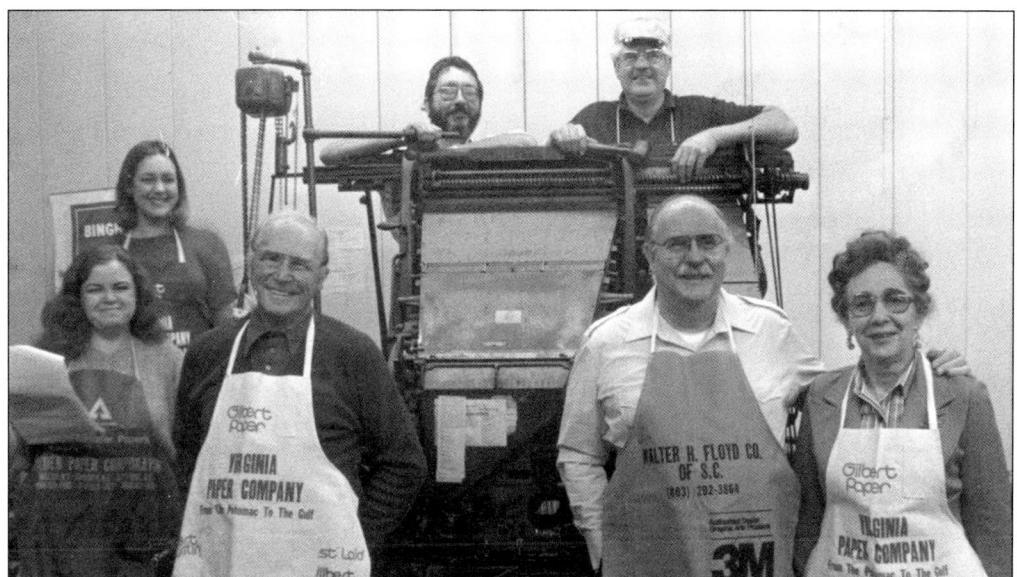

ALL THAT'S NEWS IS IN *THE NEWS*. In 1925, Nathan Coward moved to Belton and bought the *Journal*, renaming it the *Belton News*. He was later joined by his younger brother, Glenn Coward, in 1930, and the two Coward boys reported and printed the news of the day. Nathan's son Joe remembers his first job at the newspaper: sweeping floors all day on Saturday for just 10¢. After serving in the Air Force, Joe came back to work with his uncle and became president of the paper in 1962. He sold it to Elaine Ellison Rider, the current publisher of the paper, in 1994. Shown here in 1986 are, from left to right, (front row) Elaine Ellison Rider, Glenn Coward, Max Williams, and Sara Sharpe; (back row) Jan Lasera, Harry Culpepper, and Joe Coward.

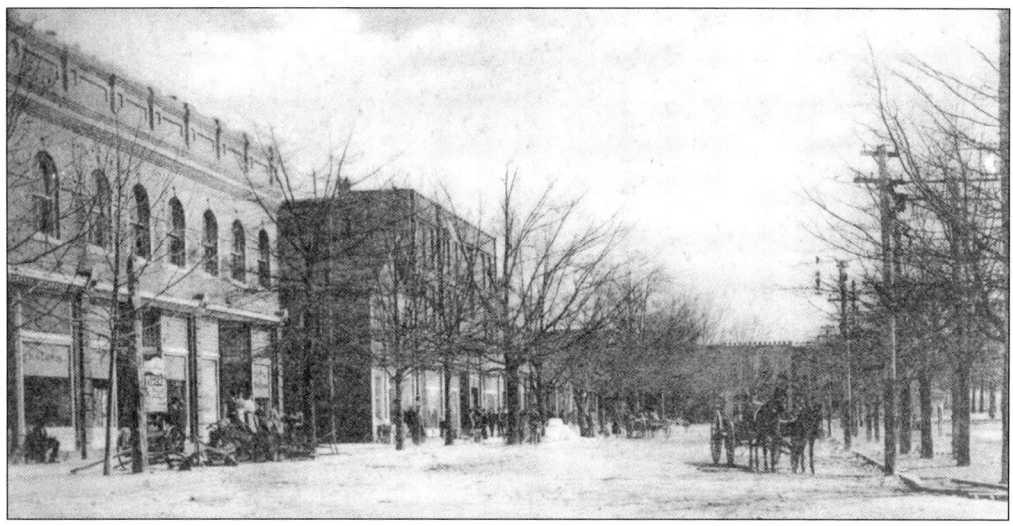

THE EAST BLOCK OF SQUARE LOOKING SOUTH, C. 1900. Belton's downtown grew from wooden structures housing two mercantile stores, a post office, and a hotel to brick rows of buildings arranged around the depot on the north, east, and south. Pictured here is the R.A. Lewis store, later the Geer-Mattison store, and in the center is the Stringer Building, the first brick structure built in 1877. The top two stories of this building were used as an opera house and many performances were put on there by the Belton Dramatic Club.

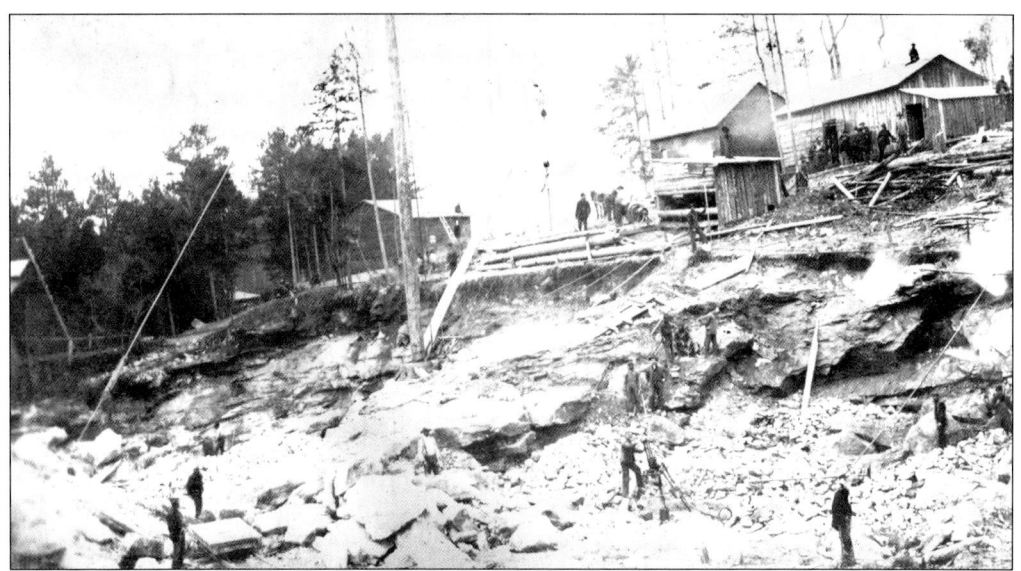

HYDRO-ELECTRIC PLANT CONSTRUCTION, 1904. With the growing need for power came the desire by Belton leaders to procure a hydro-electric plant. J.B. Adger and A.T. Smythe of Charleston, E.A. Smyth of Pelzer, J.P. Gossett of Williamston, and R.A. Lewis, J.T. Rice, and W.K Stringer of Belton applied to the state commission in July 1904 to install an electric plant on the Saluda River at Holliday's Dam. These seven men took all of the $100,000 capital stock. A survey of the shoals was made by J.E. Burriss of Greenville and showed that the company would be able to develop 4,500 to 6,000 horsepower under normal conditions. Here, work on the dam is progressing. W.H. Cobb Sr. operated a commissary at the site.

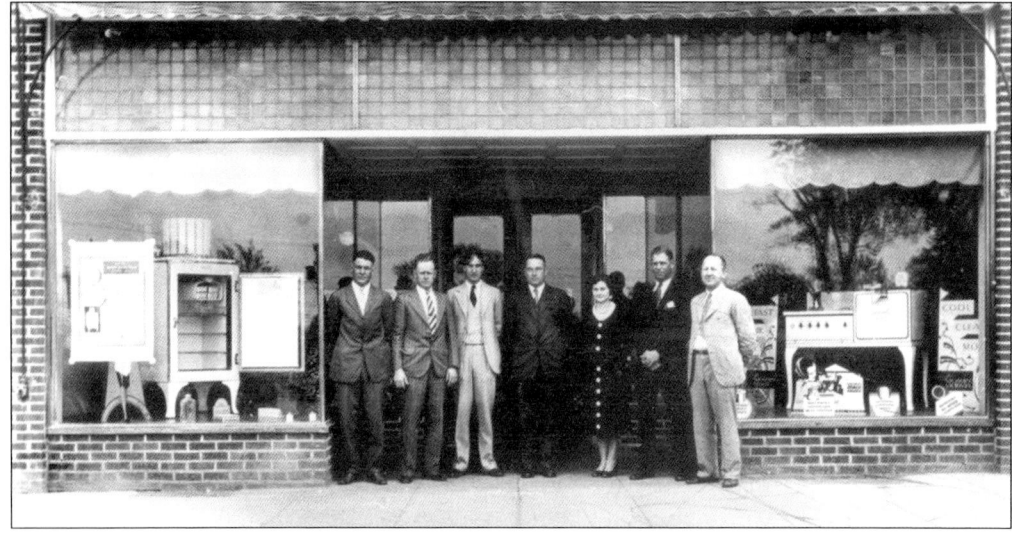

AND LET THERE BE LIGHT. When work was completed on the dam project in 1905, service began immediately with 15 customers in Belton and Williamston, including mills in both towns. The original company was sold to Belton Light and Power Company in 1925, with Louis Seel as president. By the 1930s, the latest in kitchen appliances was offered at the company, including an electric range and ice box with three-year guarantees. From left to right, Alvin Greer, Furman Browning, Julius Blake, Louis Seel, Miss Nell Hogg, Roscoe Willingham, and Julian Walton pose for a picture outside their office.

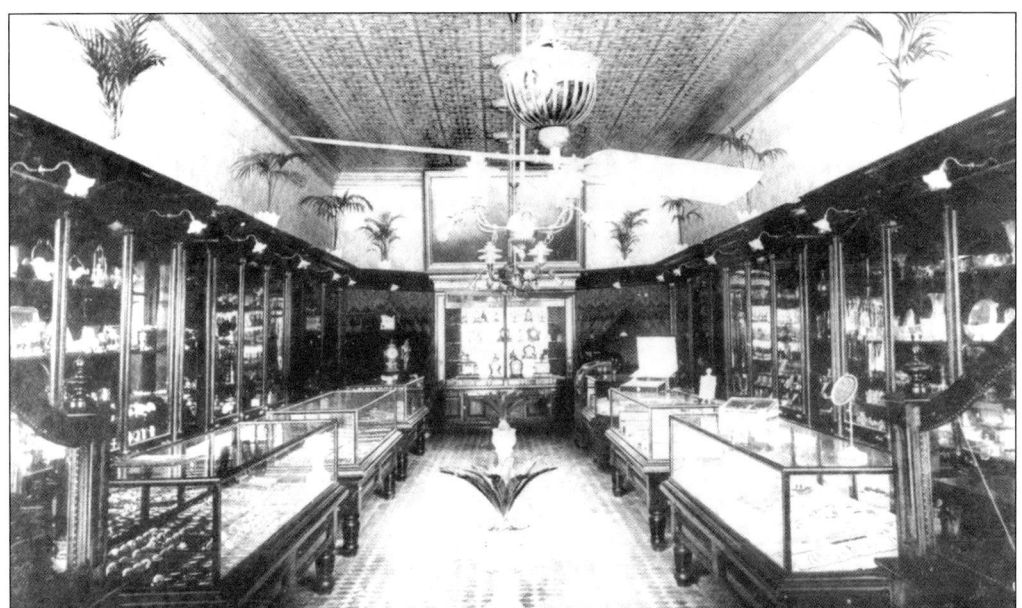

A LITTLE BIT OF LUXURY IN BELTON, C. 1910. These display cases brim with clocks, watches, china, silver, rings, and baubles to make any patron proud. Brothers W.N. (Bob) Hanks and W.G. (Guy) Hanks opened the store together. In a 1912 advertisement, the brothers adopted their slogan, "Selling honest goods to honest people at honest prices."

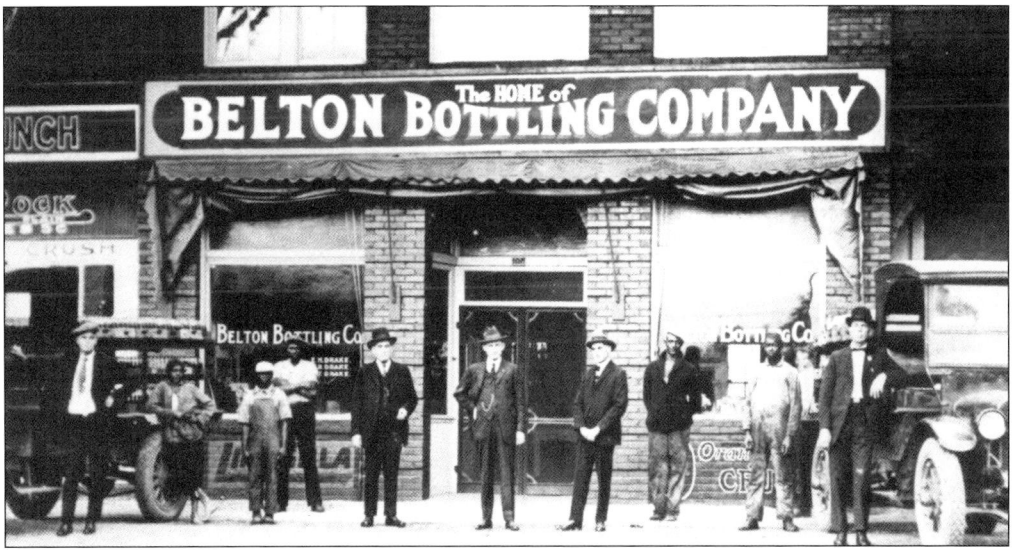

LOADED UP WITH COCA COLA, C. 1915. The Belton Bottling Company was formed in 1903 by E.H. Drake and was originally located in the Rice Block of buildings on the north side of the Square. The first franchised bottler in the state, Drake obtained the rights to bottle Coca Cola, Old Colony, Pepsi Cola, Nu Grape, Mt. Dew, Budwine, B1, Cheerwine, Nesbet's, Pinder Punch, Buffalo Rock Ginger Ale, and Orange Crush. By the 1930s, Belton Bottling Company was selling 100,000 cases annually. A 1937 newspaper advertisement promotes bottled Orange Crush for 3¢ a piece. Johnny Anderson, Ed Kay, Juke Blake, and Squat Mattison purchased the company from the Drakes in the 1940s. Anderson's son Sam remembers working at the plant when he was 12 washing bottles six days a week, from 7 a.m. to 7 p.m. for $20 pay.

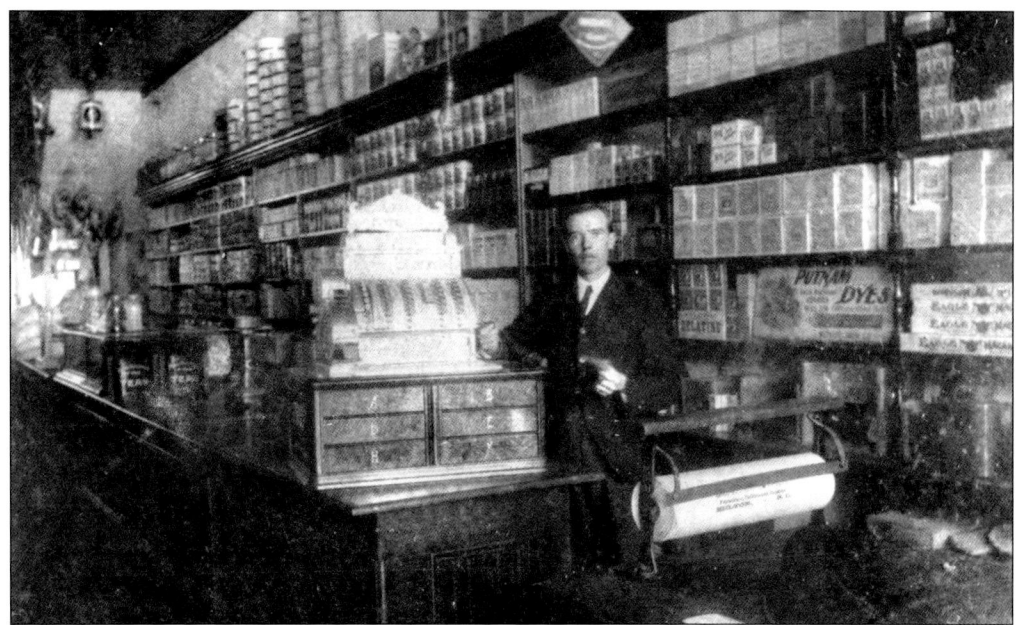

AWAITING CUSTOMERS, 1908. This handsome gentleman is Joel C. Kay, working at Horton and Gambrell's store. Later, the establishment became Gambrell and Kay. Hoop cheese, imported teas, canned goods, candies, gelatin, dyes, and macaroons line the shelves. The butcher paper on the counter advertises furniture, cotton, and caskets.

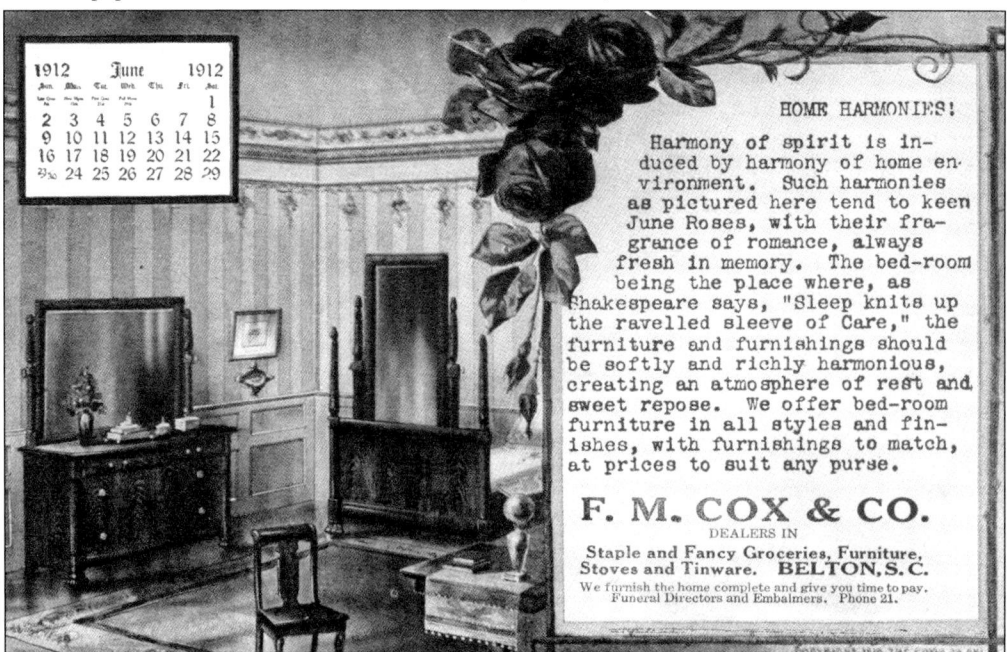

FROM FUNERALS TO FURNITURE. Preparing for the barrage of June brides, Cox Furniture Company sent out these calendar postcards in 1912 suggesting that bedroom furniture should provide an atmosphere of "rest and sweet repose." Charles Cox recalls that in the 1940s, a newly married couple could buy bedroom furniture, living room furniture, and dining room furniture to outfit a three-room house for around $200.

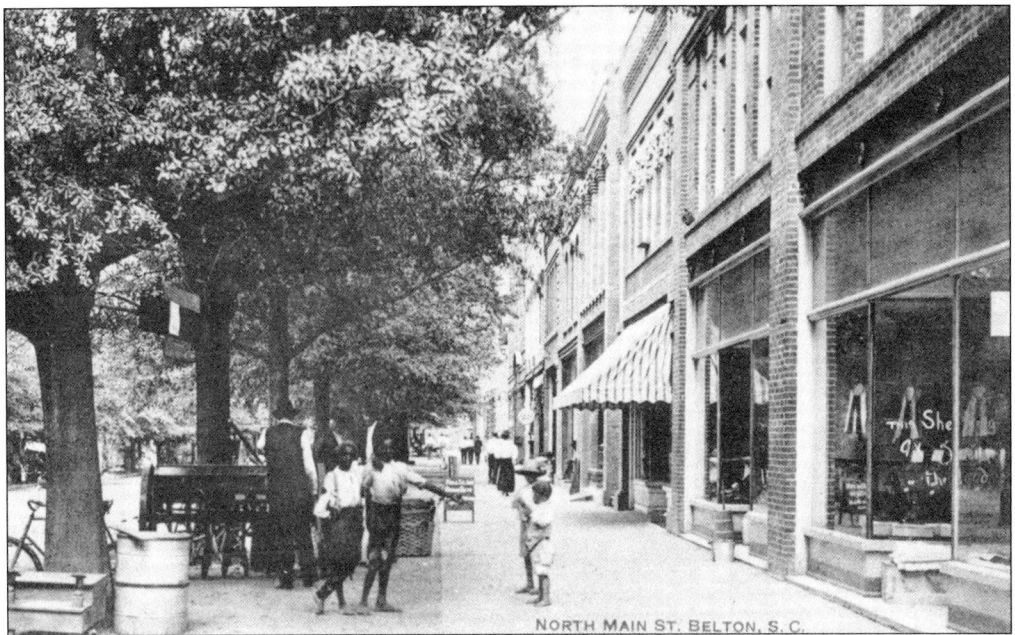

VIEW LOOKING NORTH, C. 1910. While their parents shop on the square, these children make friends with a pair of brothers. As was the custom, boys were not allowed to wear full-length pants until they reached the age of 16, so these three all wear knickers. A clothing store, general merchandise store, and a pharmacy are located in the buildings to the right of the children.

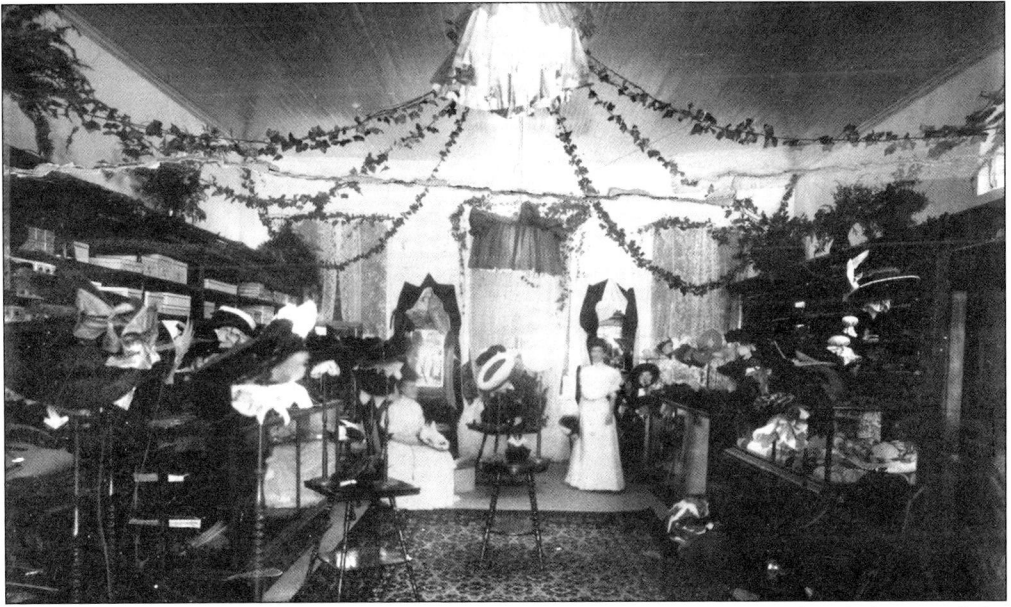

A FANCY HAT SHOP, C. 1910. Millinery departments were common in the clothing and dry goods stores at the turn of the 19th century in Belton. In fact, R.A. Lewis attributed the millinery department of his store with increasing his wealth significantly. By 1911, however, the popularity of hats increased to such an extent that two haberdasheries had opened on the Square. Ethel Broome Johnson, Maude Kay Cox, and Mollie Cunningham were noted creators of women's hats in Belton.

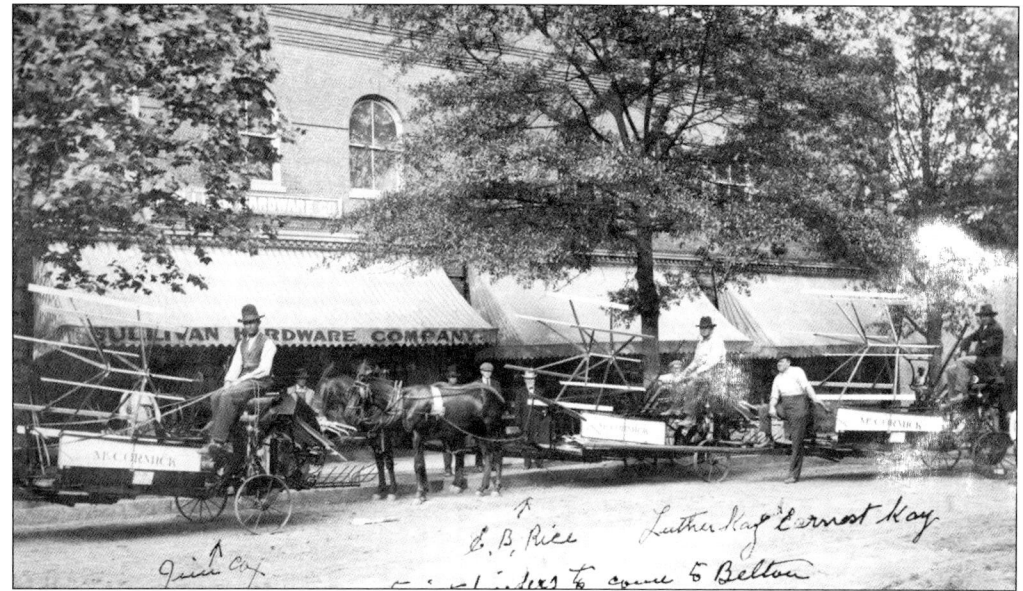

FARMING WAS BOOMING, 1913. Jim Cox, Luther Kay, and Ernest Kay had purchased the first binders to come to Belton and are pictured here in front of Sullivan Hardware Company. Drawn by horses, a binder could cut and tie sheaves of wheat. A farmer in Illinois commented in 1905 that his hired girl using a binder could do the work of 10 men laboring by hand. After a trip to Washington's famed museum in the 1960s, J.D. Major approached curators of the Smithsonian Institute and asked if they would like to have a binder for their display. "Of course," replied curator Edward C. Kendall, so the binder was shipped by rail and is in the collection of the Division of Agriculture and Forest Products at the Institute.

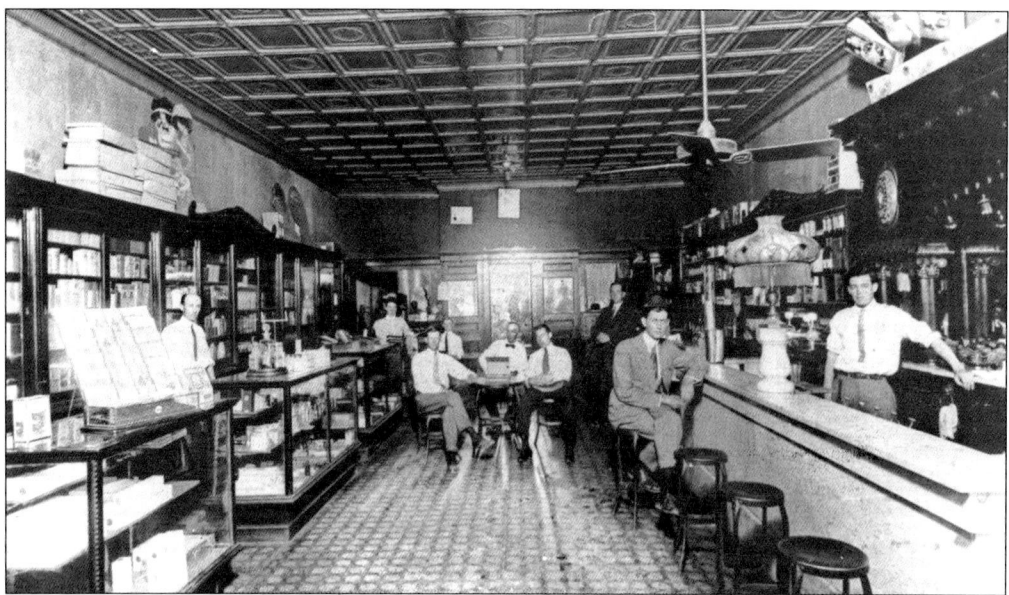

HOPPER'S DRUG STORE, 1914. Grange Cuthbert, Gilbert Campbell, Ross Mitchell, Hulon Campbell, E.T. Breazeale, Louis Seel, Charlie Brown, and Lewis Cox are among the patrons and workers at the drug store. Coke advertisements line the fountain shelves, a Tiffany lamp lights the counter, and in the forefront, postcards featuring scenes of Belton are on sale.

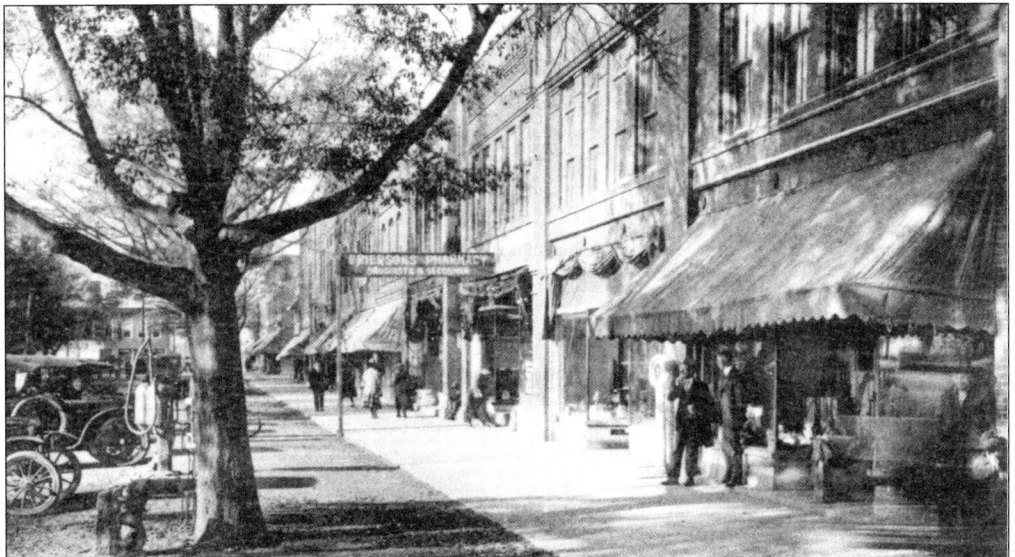

BUSTLING DOWNTOWN, C. 1922. Reid Campbell, with coat over his arm, and J.W. Payne stand outside the Belton Mercantile and chat during the making of this postcard picture. Frierson's, the drugstore located two doors down, started business in September of 1909 and boasted a full line of drugs, patent medicines, seeds, sporting goods, tobacco products, Guth's fine candies, and an up-to-date soda fountain complete with an electric ice cream freezer. The second floor was fitted up as physicians' offices.

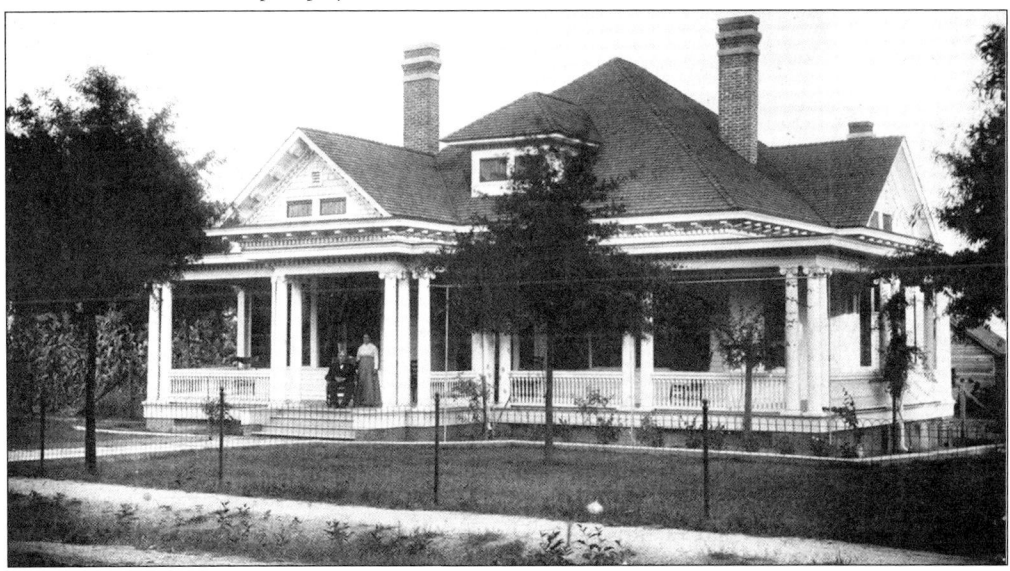

TURN-OF-THE-CENTURY HOME SERVES AS BUSINESS OPERATION. J.T. Cox, a skilled cabinet maker, turned to crafting coffins and sold them at his family's business, FM Cox and Company. Along with brothers Floyd and Charlie, he provided funeral and embalming services in addition to furniture sales. In 1921, when J.T.'s son Charles finished Furman University, Charles and his brother Walter bought out the funeral part of the business from their uncles and established Cox Funeral Home. It has been operated exclusively by Charles Cox Jr. since 1980. This picture shows the house around 1910. On the porch are J.O. (Pope) and Dorrie (Parry) Cox. The house has served as headquarters for the funeral home since 1939.

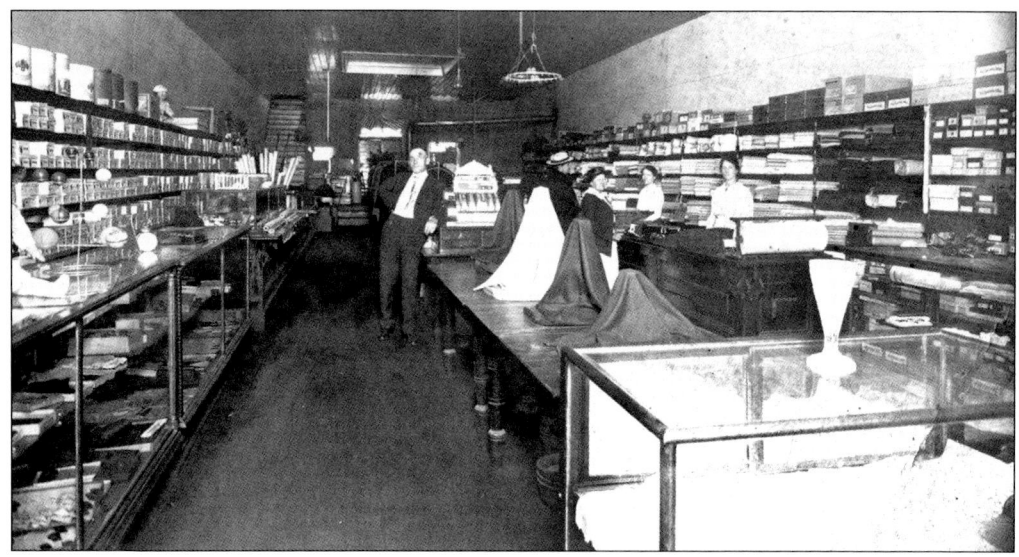

FASHION AT THE BEST OF PRICES, 1916. A 1912 advertisement boasts that the IW Cox store makes "a specialty of selling the very best of everything we keep in stock of dry goods, notions, shoes, hats, and in fact everything kept by a first class Ladies' and Gents' furnishing store is here for you at the very rock bottom prices." Since there were no dressing rooms, patrons were required to go to the Stringer House (present site of Sullivan Hardware Company) behind the Square to try on clothing. I.W. Cox appears beside the cash register and the lady to his left behind the sales counter is Zuella Wright. Zuella, along with her sister Bertie, opened Wright's Quality Shop in 1933.

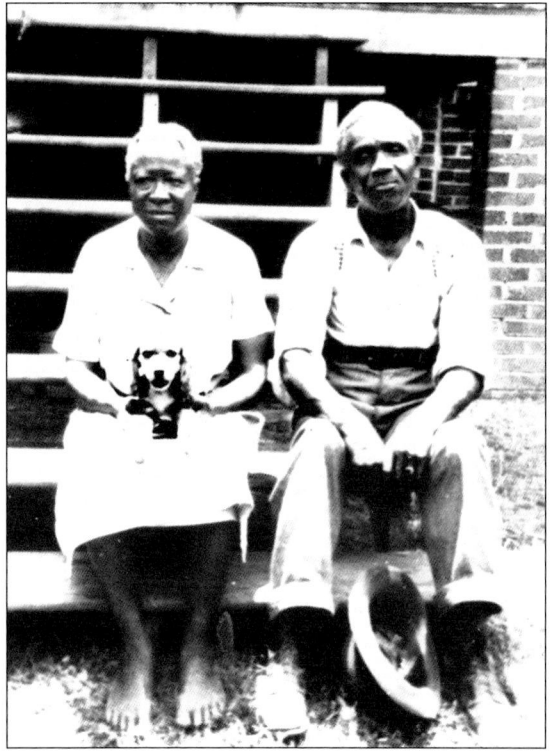

TENDER LOVING CARE. Mittie and Gib Green, shown here, took care of the Marshall Family for over four decades. When Brooks Marshall was hired as the superintendent of schools, he and his family convinced the Greens to move from Greenwood to Belton with them in 1929. A little house was built on Campbell Street for their use. Expanded by their son Gilbert, it is the present home of their daughter-in-law Hattie Green. Mittie cooked and cleaned and Gib did the milking, tended the chickens, and gardened. Hundreds of domestics ran the homes of many of Belton's citizens, of all income levels, until the late 1960s.

THE HORSELESS BUGGY NEEDS REPAIRS. The advent of the automobile made it necessary for new businesses to spring up to serve the cars' needs. After Henry Tollison retired from the railroad in 1908 at the age of 40, he opened a grocery store, farmed a bit, dabbled in real estate, and then started a garage on North Main Street in the 1920s with the help of his son Hugh. He sold gasoline, Fisk Tires, and auto supplies and serviced the townspeople's wave of new cars. The Tollisons were great musicians and would gather at Henry's large house next door to this business to play and sing.

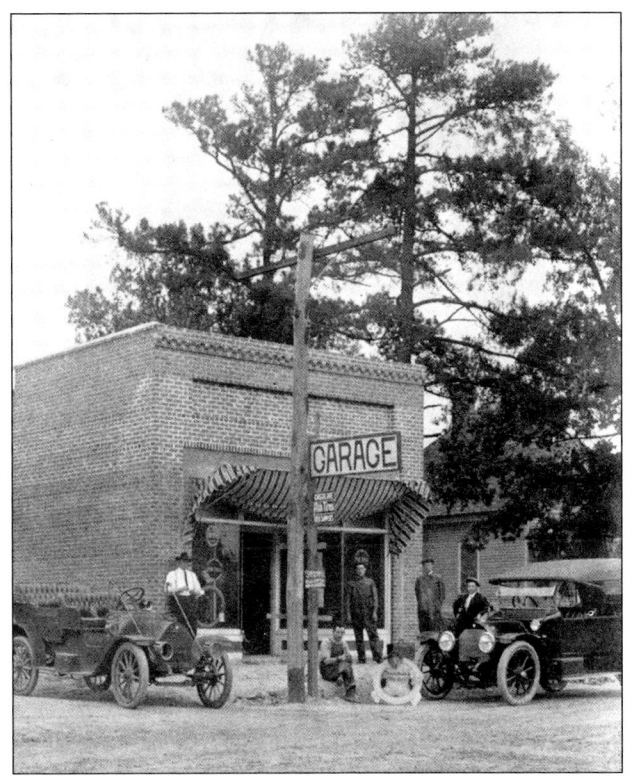

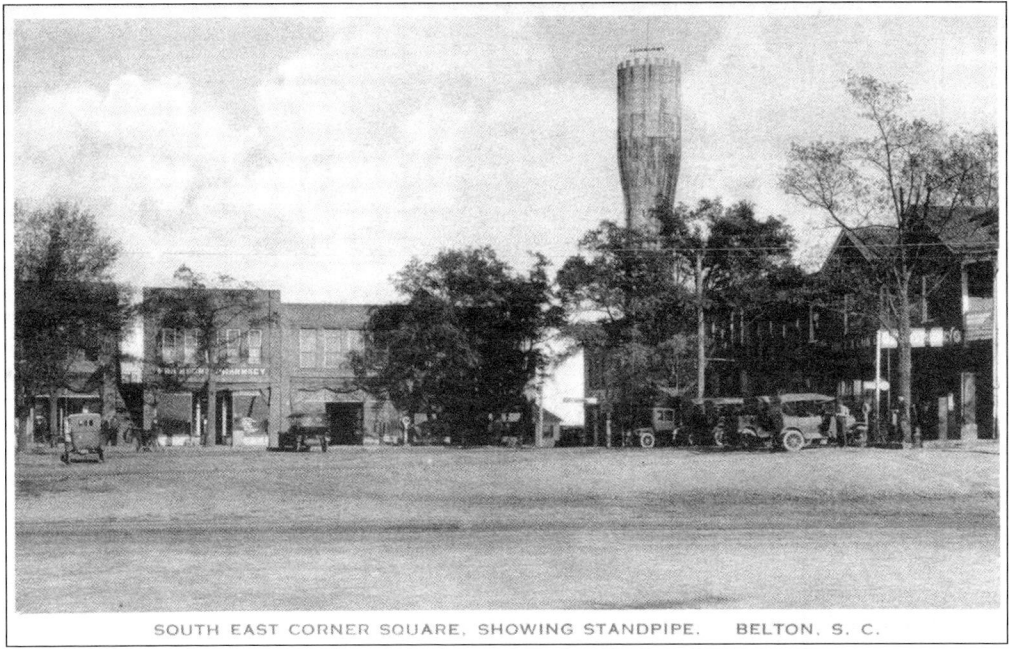

SOUTHEAST CORNER OF THE SQUARE, C. 1922. At this time, the south row of buildings contained Horton's Pharmacy (established 1914), a barbershop, the Farmer's Bank (established 1903), the telephone exchange, the Masonic temple, a restaurant, and the post office. The dirt Square gave way to paved streets in 1924.

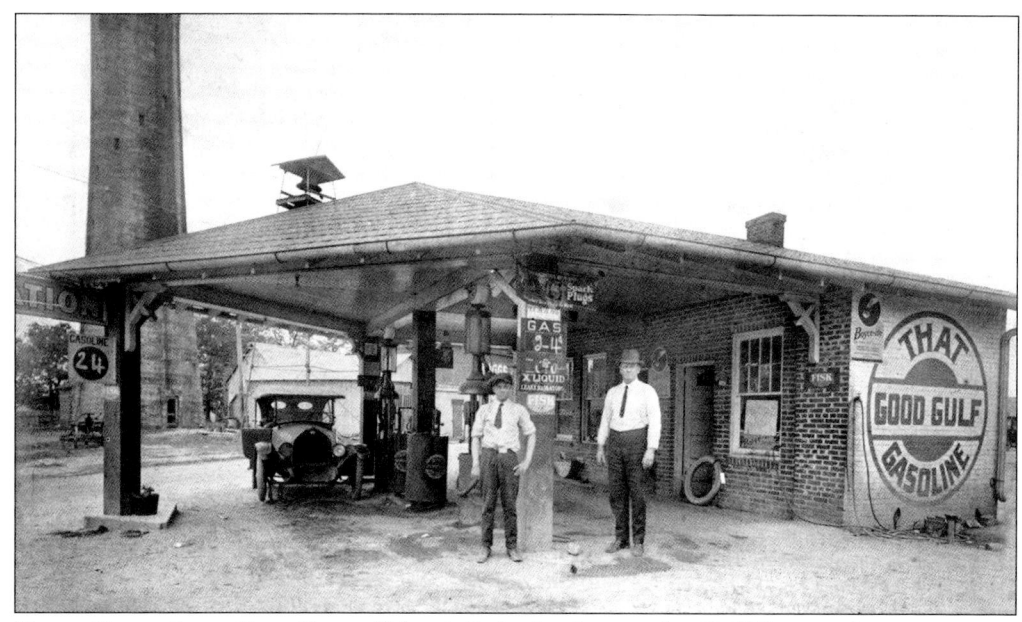

THAT GOOD GULF GAS. Henry "Moot" Sutherland opened a Gulf Service Station prior to 1922 on the corner of O'Neal and Campbell Streets. Gas was 24¢ a gallon. In the 1940s, a Mr. Sinclair owned the site until Jimmy Guthrie put a laundromat in the building. The building was torn down in the 1950s. In 1958, bricklayers Gus Mahaffey and Bennett Chapman working for David Haynie used the brick of this demolished building to build a fireplace in Sara Sharpe's Ridgecrest home. The Standpipe and the fire department's bell tower appear in the background.

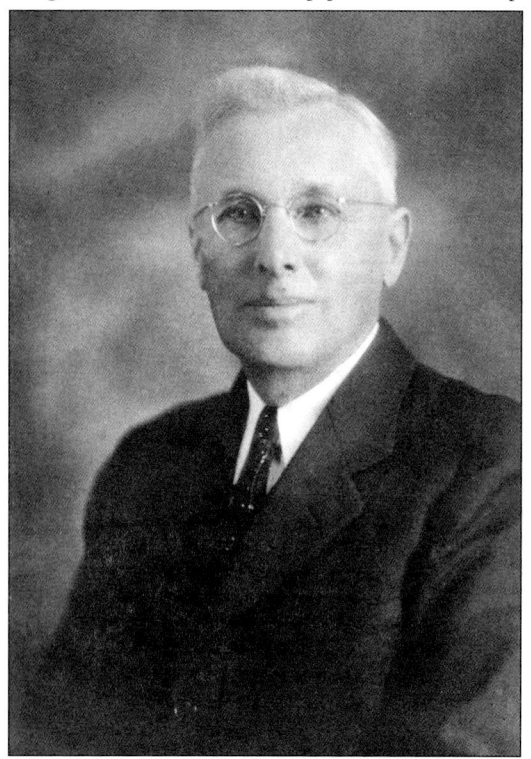

THE GOOD DOCTOR. Dr. William Haynie served the people of Belton for over 50 years, tending to the sick, birthing babies, and offering congratulations and condolences. A story was told that he wouldn't allow new fathers to pay for the delivery of their children, saying that helping to deliver babies was a privilege to him. However, if a father insisted and pushed some bills into the good doctor's hands, that same father might find weeks later the same amount or more in his coat pocket. Dr. Haynie died March 6, 1950.

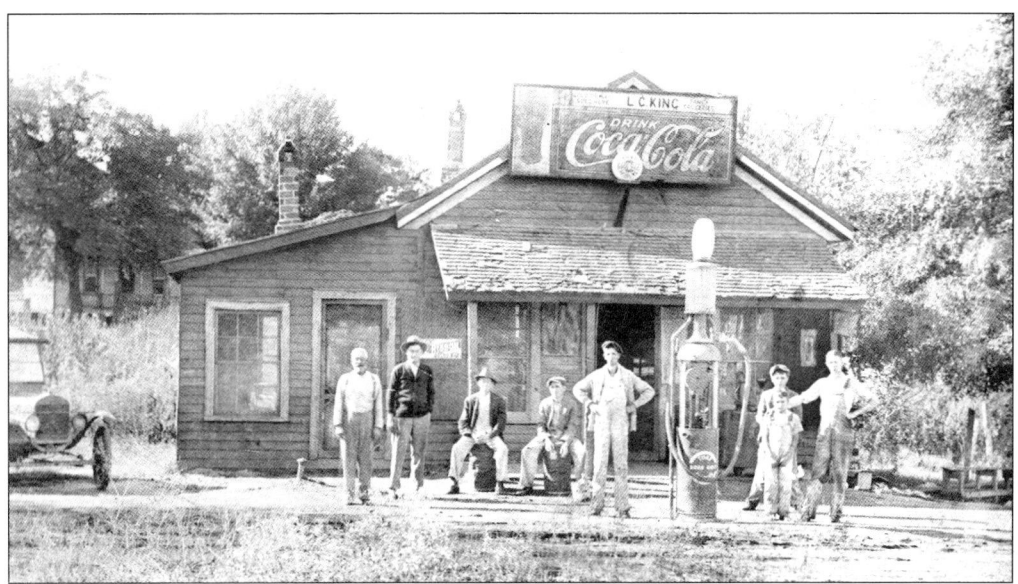

COME SIT A SPELL, 1935. On the corner of Poplar Avenue and Breazeale Street stood an establishment operated by Cornelius Levi King. From 8:30 a.m. until 9:00 p.m., the store was open for anyone who wanted fancy groceries, candy, cold drinks, cigars, or gasoline. Patrons would gather around the pot-bellied stove, trade stories, play music, and boil eggs or cook wieners. In the side yard, a checker table awaits a game to be played. From left to right are C.L. King, unidentified, Jim Cox, John Mattison King, "Fiddlin' " Bob Thompson, two unidentified, and Paul Cox.

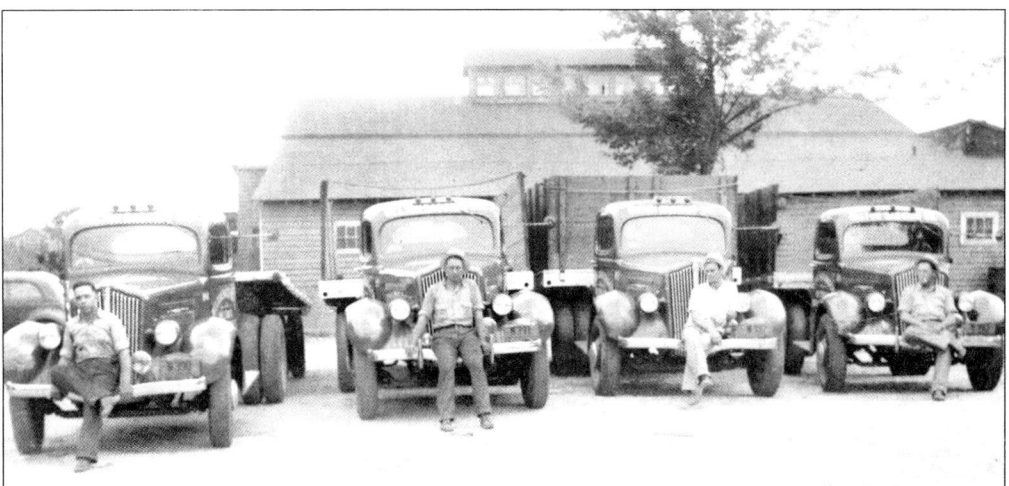

BELTON BAGGING COMPANY DRIVERS, 1938. Drivers Bill Cooley, Henry Mathis, Marvin Byrd, and Luther Morrison pose before taking off on their routes to deliver jute bagging to area cotton farmers. When the jute made in India reached the mill, workers would shred it, spin it into yarn, and weave it into bagging material. The bagging was cut in three-yard pieces, two of which made what was known as the "pattern." One pattern of bagging and six cotton bale ties were required for wrapping a bale of cotton. W.C. Brown Sr. founded the company in 1916. Soon after the business was begun, it was changed to a partnership with J.T. West Sr. and became known as Brown and West. In 1927 it was incorporated into the Belton Bagging Company. It is known as Belton Industries today.

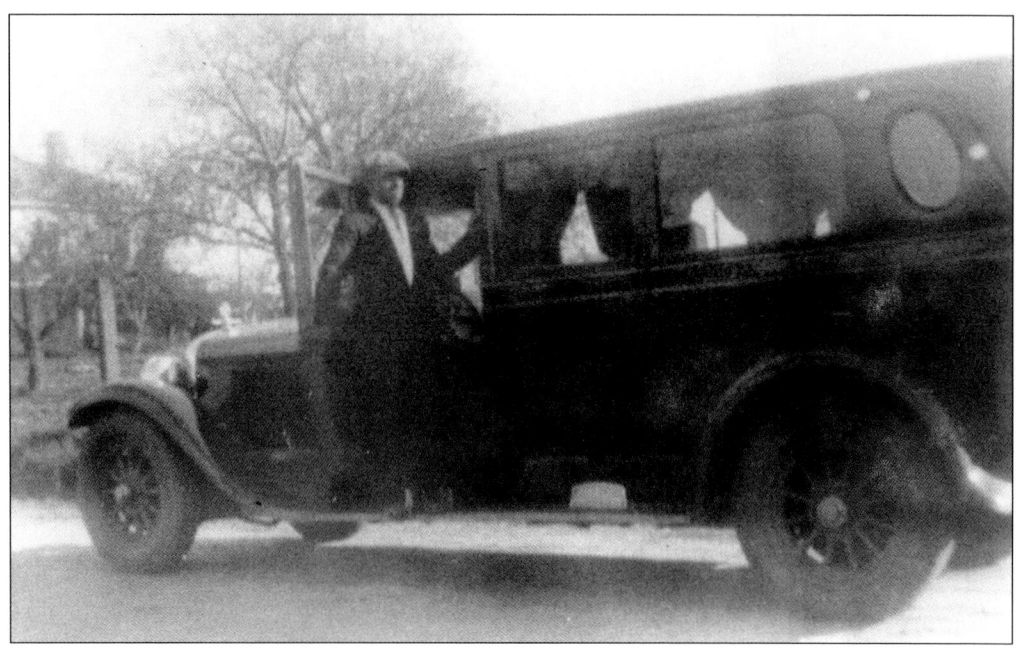

THE BEGINNING OF A FAMILY TRADITION. Clifton C. Clement established the first funeral services for blacks on Green Street in Belton in the 1930s. His son-in-law, Luther Holloway, carried on the enterprise in the name of Holloway's Funeral Home. The third generation, consisting of Horace and Harold Holloway, are operating the business today.

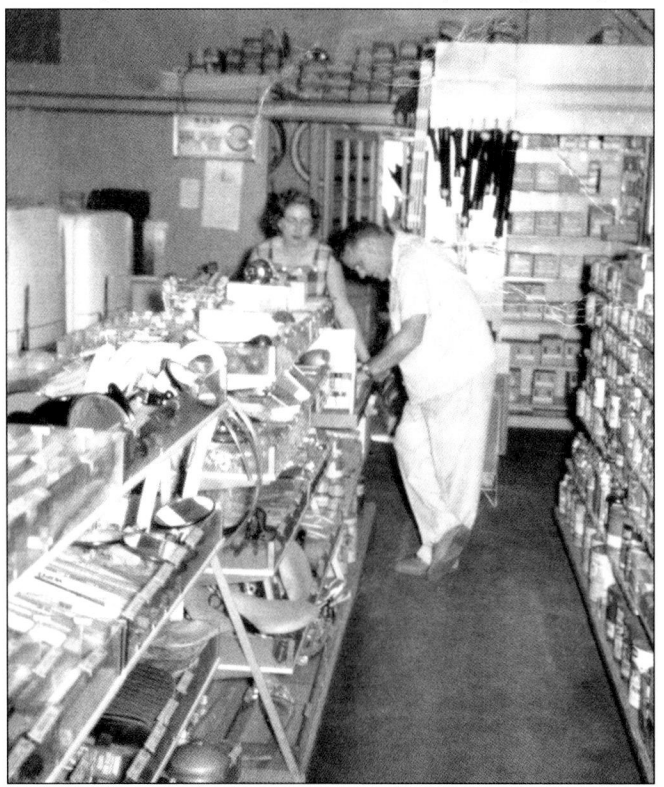

WESTERN AUTO, C. 1945. The Western Auto Store was opened on the Square in 1938 by Robert Allen Ferguson, and his brother Andrew Ferguson opened a franchise in Honea Path at the same time. Their uncle, Rob Ferguson of Abbeville, helped establish both nephews in business. Here, Robert and Mary Ellen Ferguson restock the well-appointed shelves with merchandise. Western Auto is now run by Harold and Gayle McDowell at their location on Anderson Street.

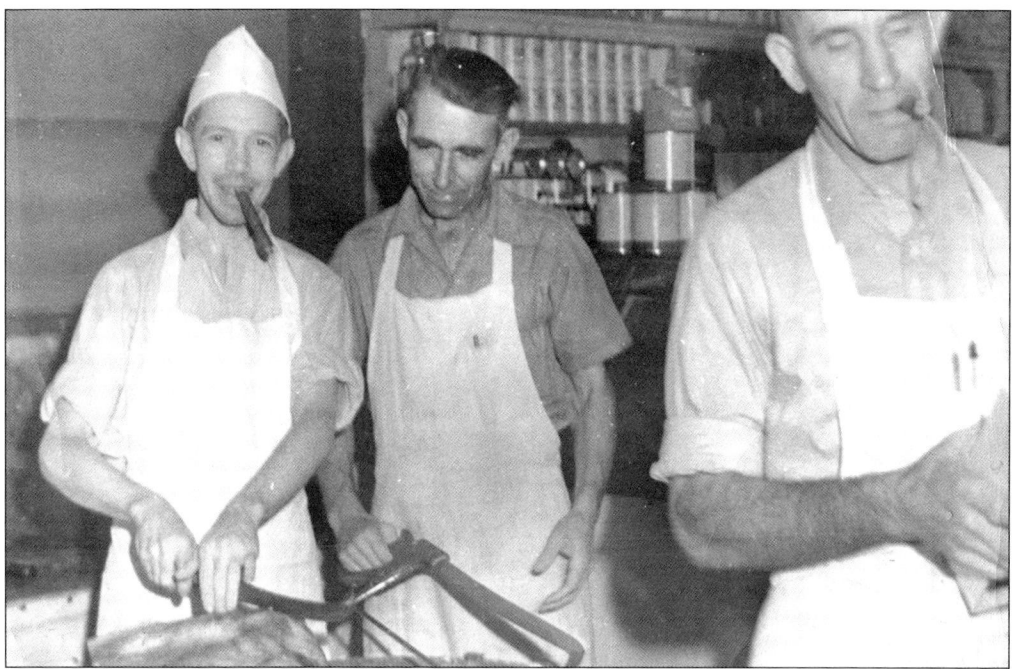

A BIG CIGAR AND A BIGGER SENSE OF HUMOR. Kay's Grocery opened in the second building from O'Neal Street on the eastern block of the Square in the 1930s. The proprietor, Bud Kay, shown cutting meat, is assisted by John King and Roy Kay. Rumor has it that Bud was a real kidder and practical joker, so anyone who entered the store in a foul mood usually left with a smile on his face. Jill's Carpet and Wallpaper is located in this building today.

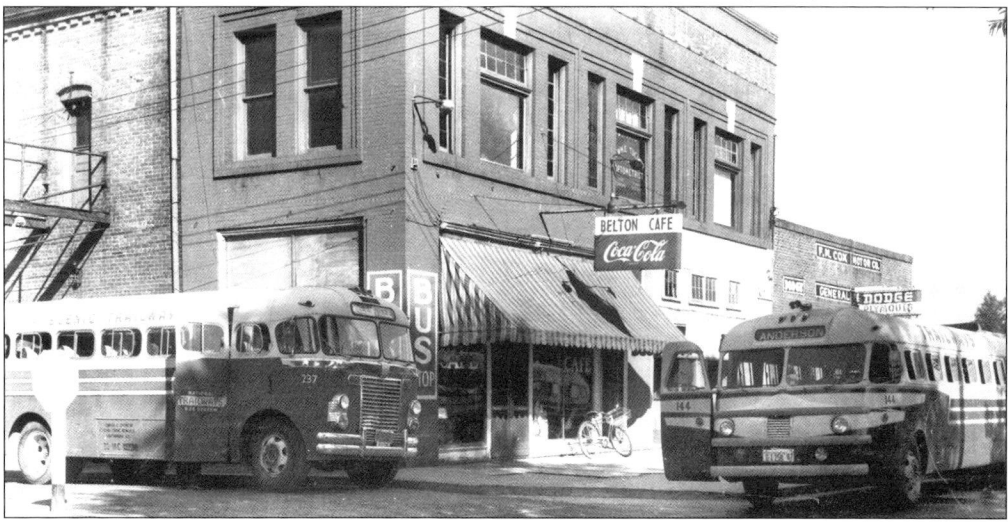

NOW A PARKING LOT FOR BB&T. The Wertz Building, as it was called, contained the Belton Café, run by Curly Gambrell; the Virginia Theater, owned by Adger Gray; apartments for the hotel; an optometrist's office; and the F.M. Cox Motor Company. Carolina Scenic Trailways Bus tickets were purchased at the café, and daily service ran to Greenwood, Greenville, and Anderson, replacing the defunct Interurban. Bud Hiott remembers going to see the premiere of *Gone with the Wind* when it appeared at the Virginia in Belton. The line to get into the movie was so long, it reached around the corner of the south block of the Square.

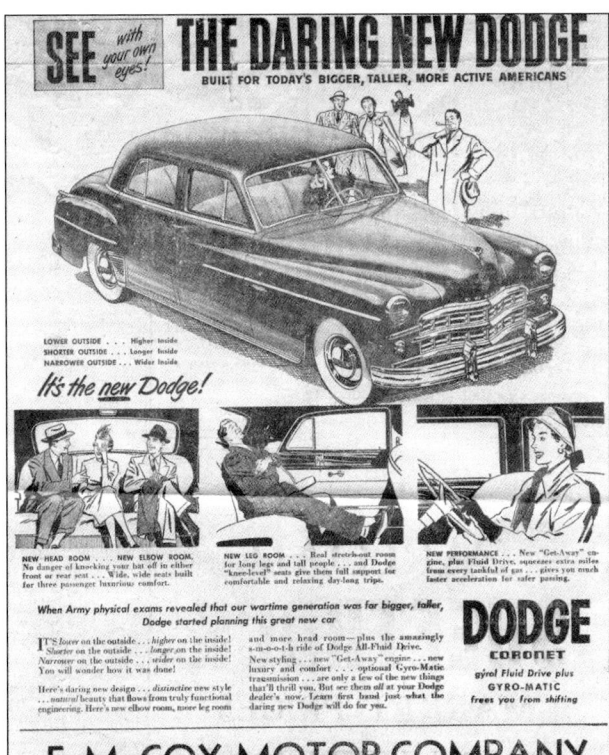

BIGGER, TALLER, MORE ACTIVE. Right after World War II, when production was getting back into swing, dealerships were encouraged by the Big Three to provide cars first to veterans and teachers when they received the new cars from the Detroit lines. Everyone else had to wait. This advertisement from 1949 shows that Dodge remade its Coronet to reflect the bigger and taller Americans who would purchase them. F.M. Cox Plymouth and Dodge dealership was in operation until the mid-1950s.

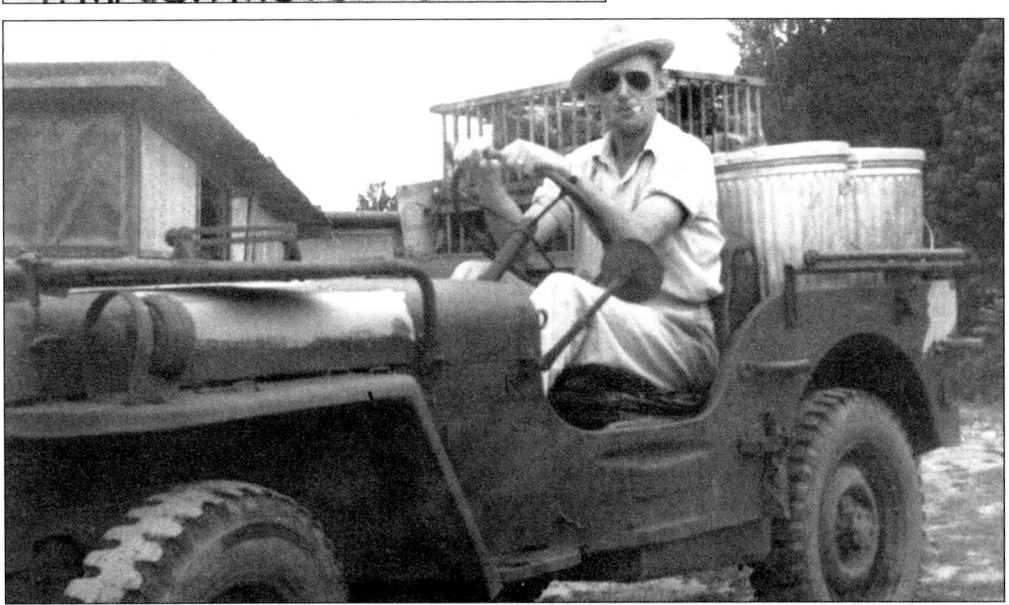

THE BEST DRESSED CHICKEN IN TOWN. Brothers Stan Marshall and "Buck" Marshall started Marshall Farms right after World War II with two small chicken houses. The next season their buyers wanted the broilers already processed, so the brothers built a dressing plant. As business grew, more chicken houses, sub-contractors, and production plants were added. Their other brother, "Hap" Marshall, joined them as the expansion continued. Here, Buck Marshall drives the war-battered jeep to deliver chickens to their retailers in 1947.

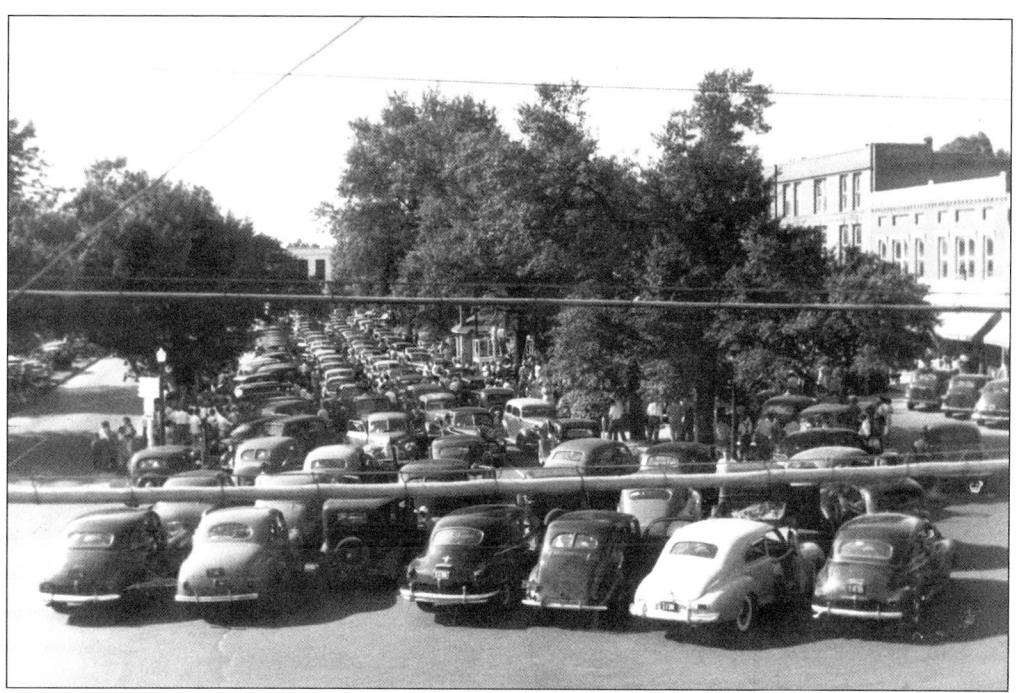

WHY SO MANY CARS ON THE SQUARE? In the 1940s and 1950s, Belton merchants raffled off special items every Saturday. For every dollar purchased, the buyer would receive a raffle ticket and prizes would be awarded. The stores stayed open until 10:00 p.m., and everyone came to town to shop, socialize, and share news.

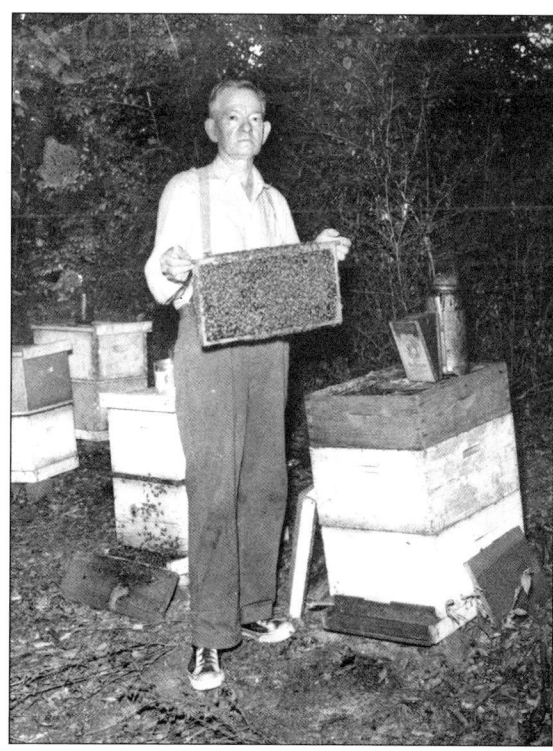

HONEYBEE ELLISON, 1957. An avid beekeeper, C.G. Ellison placed about 200 hives on people's farms along the perimeter of town. People from miles around came to get his frames of honey and honeycombs. Each frame cost about 50¢.

OUR TOWNS

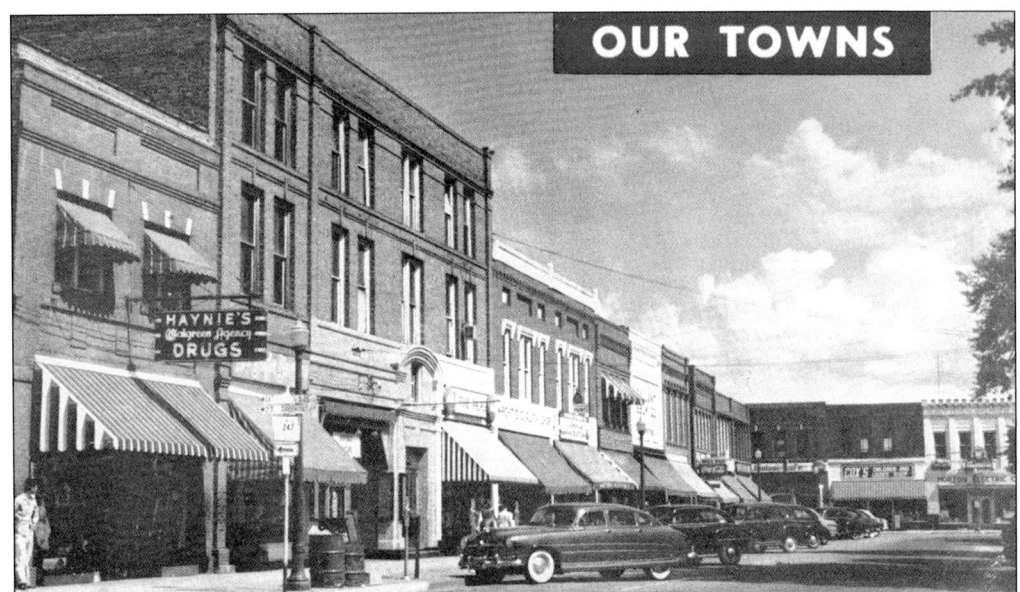

TOWNSCAPE IN 1953, EAST ROW LOOKING SOUTH. Business establishments in the 1950s included Haynie's Drug Store (established 1930), the Belton Theater (established 1910 as the Pastime Theater), the Food Palace, Wright's Quality Shop, Gallant Belk, Wilson's (established 1927), Harper's 5 & 10, Cox's Family Shop, and Horton Electric Company. Haynie's was run by Dr. Moffatt Haynie, who was also a builder.

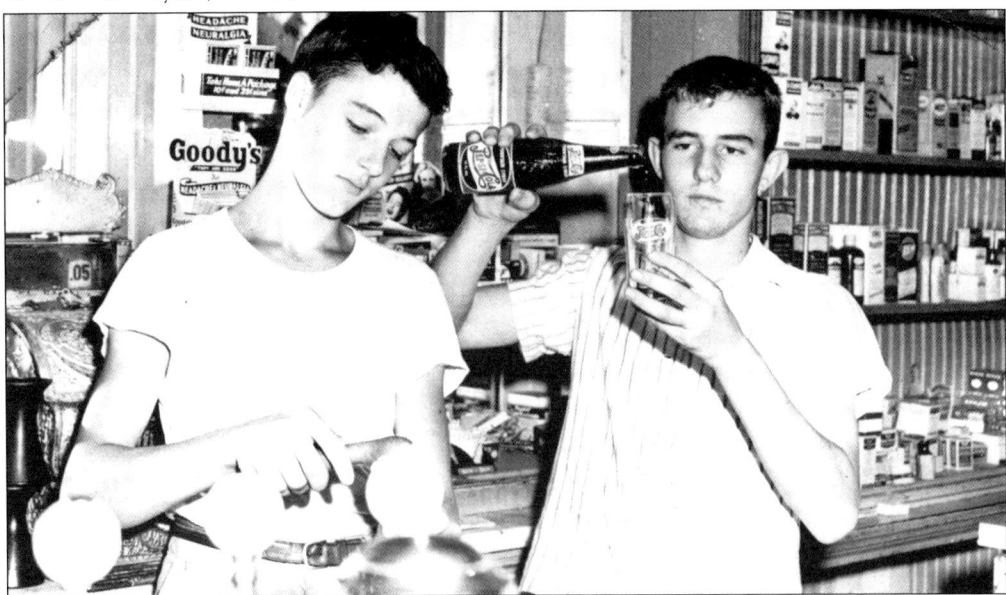

THE BEST COKE FLOAT AROUND, C. 1943. Max Williams and Larry Fullbright mix up a float for customers. Every day after school, teenagers would hang out at Horton's Pharmacy's soda fountain. Cokes, milkshakes, sandwiches, soups, and hotdogs were available for moderate prices. Mrs. Ray Clinkscales would make the chili daily in her kitchen and send it up to the pharmacy. Millard Horton established Horton's in 1914. Henry Clinkscales is now the proprietor of Horton's, and Hank, his son, owns and operates Clinkscales Pharmacy on Anderson Street.

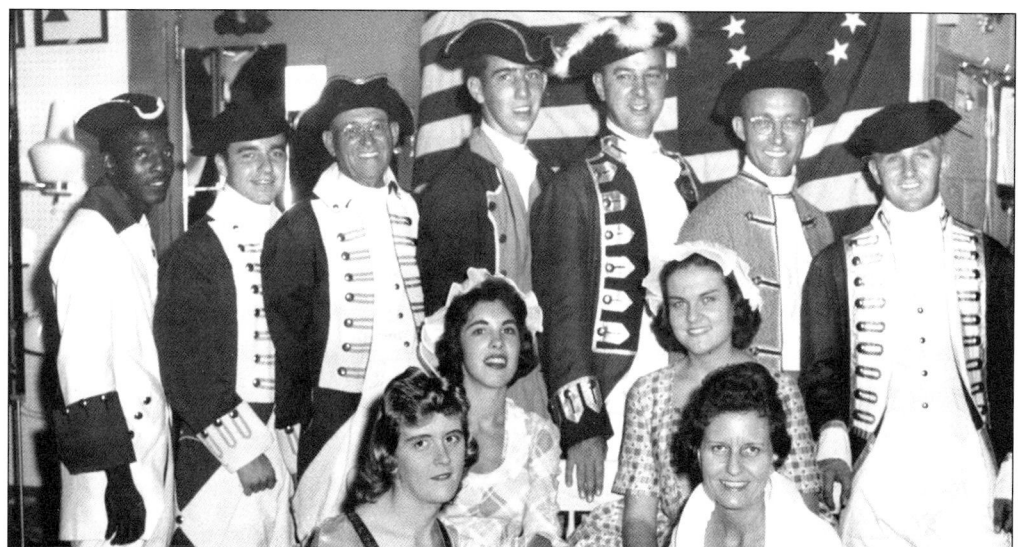

THE COLONIAL SHOP, 1961. Maynard's Colonial Shop opened in the summer of 1961. Pictured here in their colonial garb are employees along with owner Al Maynard, in the back row with the three-pointed fur trimmed hat. A marketing genius, Maynard began his furniture company in 1947 in a two-story building on the north row of the Square. Within five years the company had grown substantially, so Maynard built a structure on Anderson Street and named it Maynard's Wayside Furniture, serving customers within a 100-mile radius. This building has been enlarged and renovated several times, and a grand reopening was orchestrated in 2003. Maynard's sons Rex and Skipper and grandson Alderman run the business today.

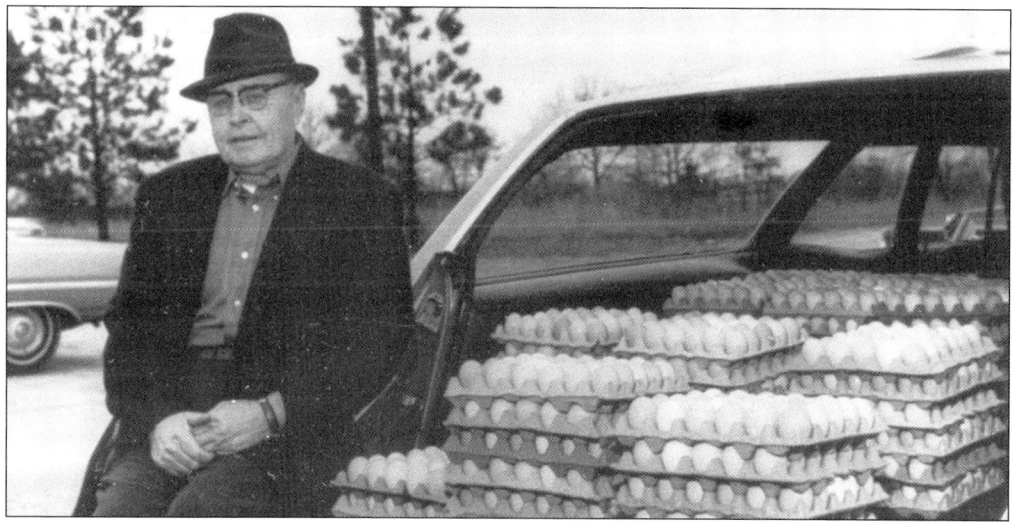

TOP NOTCH EGGS. Charles Meeks and his cousin George Graham started the C & G Egg Ranch in 1965 with 40,000 laying hens. During the late 1960s, after he had retired from his position as supervisor of city streets, Waymon Meeks, Charles's father, would load up the old green station wagon with eggs on Fridays and run the route he had developed to fill his retirement hours. His biggest stop was at Rice Mills, where employees who were leaving the plant for the weekend would pick up five to ten dozen eggs each to take home for their use. The company has evolved into Top Notch Inc., which buys and sells eggs wholesale for distribution in the upstate area.

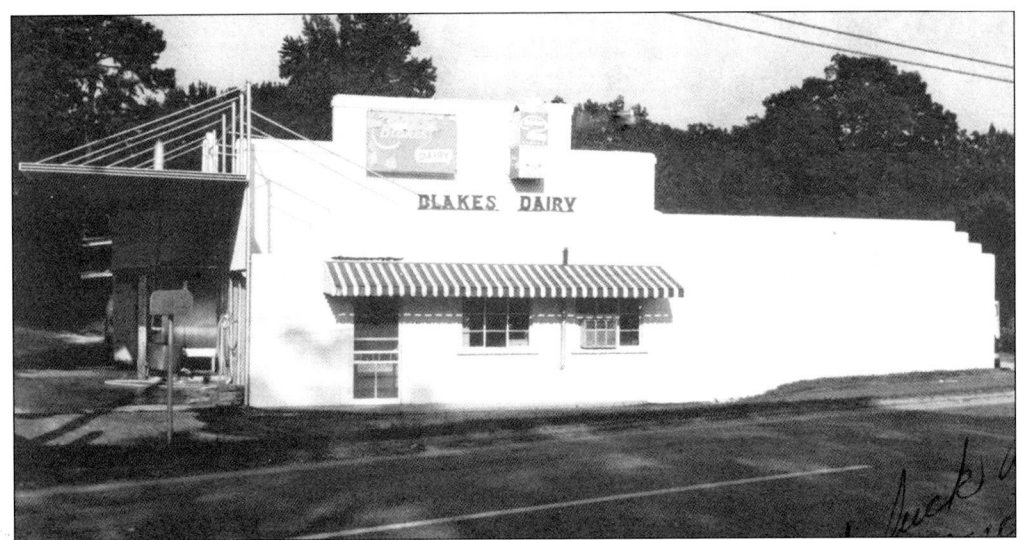

THE BEST HEALTH INSURANCE: BLAKE'S PURE JERSEY MILK. "Baby and Invalid Thrive on Blake's Milk," asserted an advertisement in 1937. Established by Smyth Blake, Blake's Dairy was in operation from 1928 until 1964, when the operation was sold to the Pet Milk Company. After Lewis Blake finished Clemson College with a major in dairy science, he joined his brother's operation. The dairy produced sweet milk, buttermilk, chocolate milk, cream, orange juice, and butter. At the height of its success in 1953, the dairy delivered milk to 12 schools, 15,000 houses, and 125 stores and canteens.

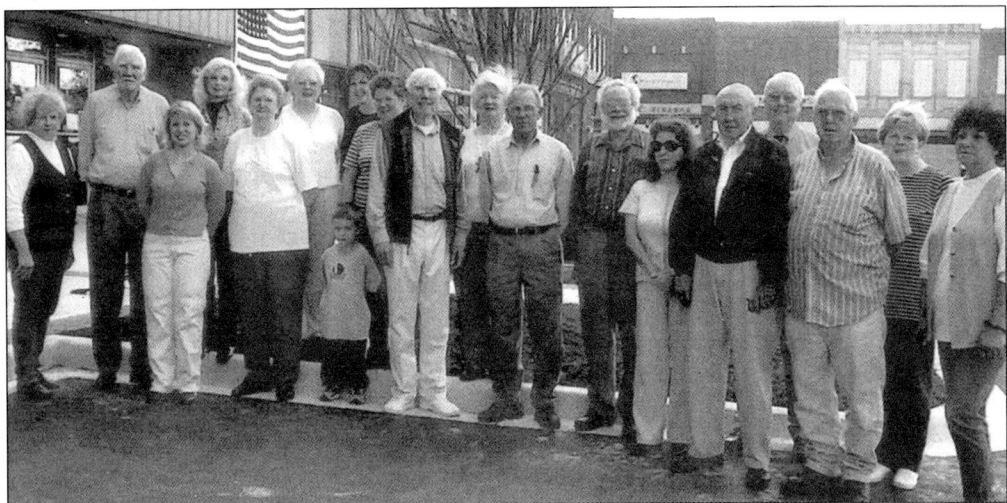

THUMBS UP TO PHASE I. After the first phase of renovations was completed on the Square in 2001, the merchants gathered for this photograph, which was sent to the construction company who contracted the work. They are, from left to right, (front row) Jean Martin, The Jean Shoppe; Tracy Woods, Kutz on the Square; Mertie Kelly, Mertie's Jewelry; Thomas Holliday; Charles Martin, Wilson's; Homer Booth, Gemini Style Shop; James B. Mattison, Mattison Hardware; Milton Myers, Page's Shoe Store; and Eunice Fields, The Jean Shoppe; (back row) Redus Martin, Wilson's; Pam Cooley, Community Finance; Peggy Culpepper, Shear Perfection Hair Salon; Barbara Finley, Shear Perfection Hair Salon; JoAnne Owens, Taylor's; Clifton Hunter, Wright's Quality Shop; Connie Hunter, Wright's Quality Shop; Henry Clinkscales, Horton's Pharmacy; and Lou Bolton, Mary Cox Frame Shop.

Three
BELTONIANS AT WAR

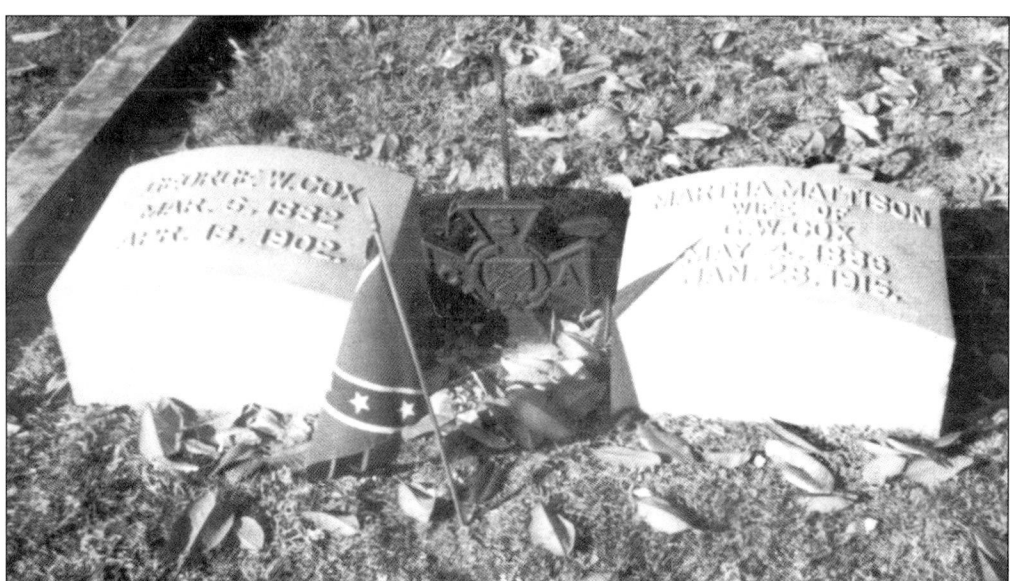

A CONFEDERATE HONORED. G.W. Cox organized a group of Belton men and marched to Anderson to join Orr's Rifles, part of Hampton's Legion. In a battle in North Carolina, the soldier was wounded in the leg. His attending servant found him among the fallen and brought him to the rear triage. The surgeon wanted to amputate G.W.'s leg, but the stricken soldier forbid him to cut it off. He healed and returned from the war but always walked with a limp. An iron cross, the result of a movement by the United Daughters of the Confederacy, is placed on his grave to mark his participation in the war.

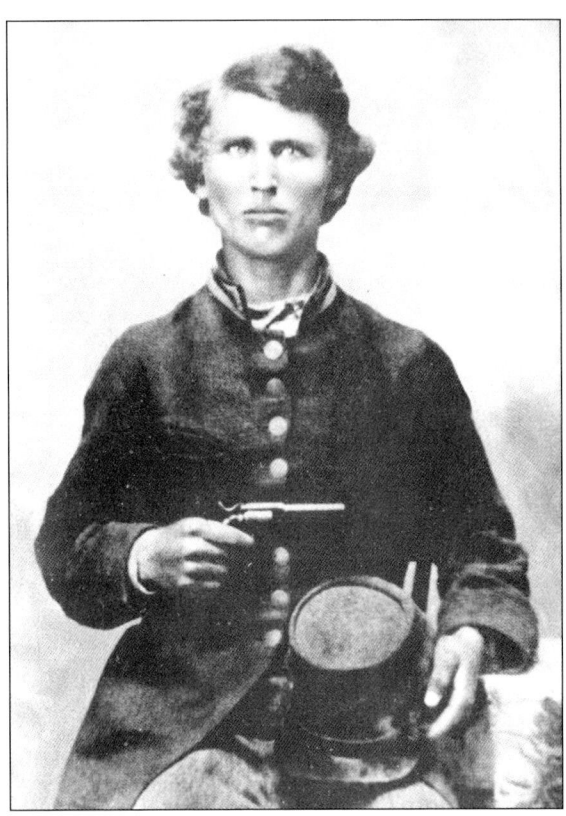

PRIVATE E.T. TOLLISON (BORN AUGUST 18, 1845 AND DIED MARCH 7, 1939). Tollison volunteered for service on August 16, 1863, two days shy of his 18th birthday. He was placed in Co. E, Hampton's Legion, Gary Calvary Brigade, CSA. He was engaged in battles and skirmishes in Georgia, Tennessee, and Virginia.

TOO LITTLE, TOO LATE. Pvt. A.O. Brown, son of Belton founder George Reece Brown, was given furlough to visit his family in January 1865. This is the note he carried. The Browns had rented a farm near Belton after refugeeing from Georgia. When Albert arrived, he was much weakened. A few days after returning home, he died of overexposure and malnourishment. He is buried at Shady Grove Baptist Church cemetery.

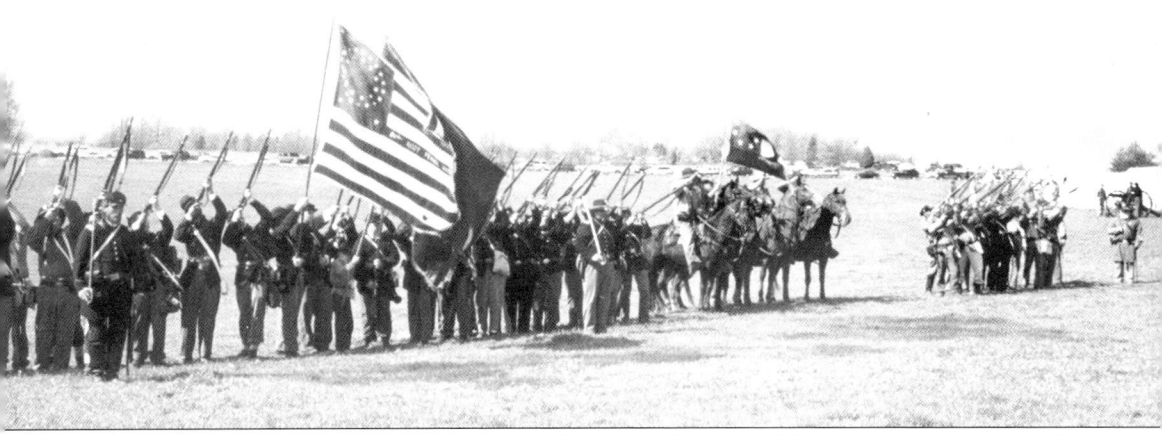

SALUTING IN BLUE AND GRAY. Members of the John Thomas Ashley Camp of the Sons of Confederate Veterans and Civil War re-enactors pay tribute to the fallen soldiers on both sides of the conflict. Held near Belton in March of 2003, the reenactment recalled the events of the last battle on South Carolina soil.

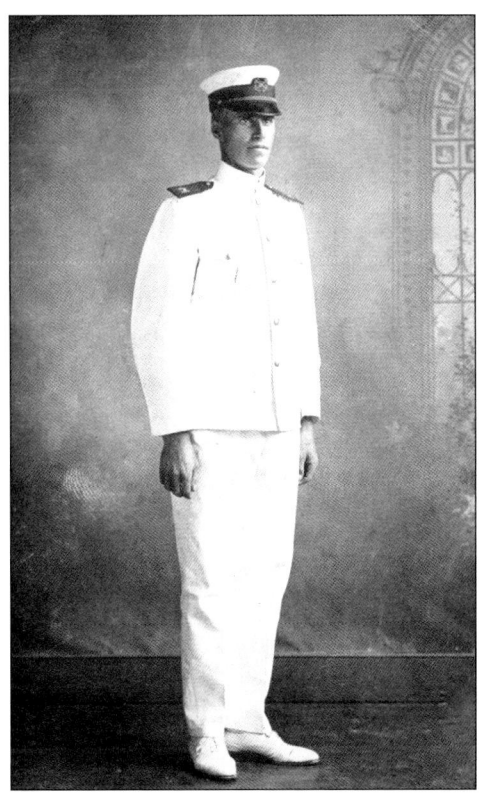

NAVY DRESS WHITES. During World War I, Nathan Coward, the famed *Belton News* owner and editor, served as the warrant officer of a commandeered yacht used to patrol the waters off the coast of South Carolina. He served until the war ended. In January 1925, he began printing the *Belton News* and increased circulation to over 900 papers weekly. A civic-minded person who was a member of several organizations, Coward also served in the South Carolina legislature from 1932 to 1936.

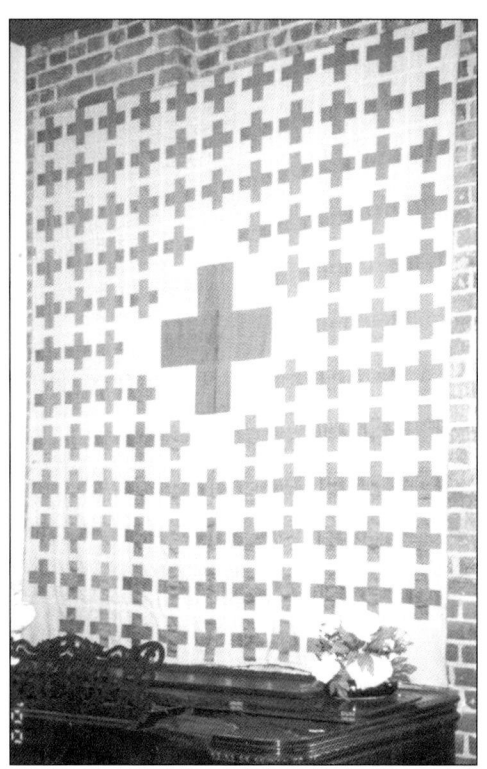

FUNDRAISER, 1918. Members of the Red Cross Society painstakingly stitched this quilt and sold patches to local people to raise money for the soldiers overseas during World War I. Names appearing on the quilt include J.L Chapman, Max Greer, Mr. and Mrs. F.M. Cox, Mr. and Mrs. J.R. Cox, E.P. Gambrell, Mr. and Mrs. Julian Walton, Mr. and Mrs. Reid Sherard, Mr. and Mrs. A.S. Fant, Thos. Pennell Jr., J.A. Cason, and Mr. and Mrs. Max W. Grubbs. Belton sent a total of 316 (238 white and 78 black) soldiers to the Great War. Ten did not return.

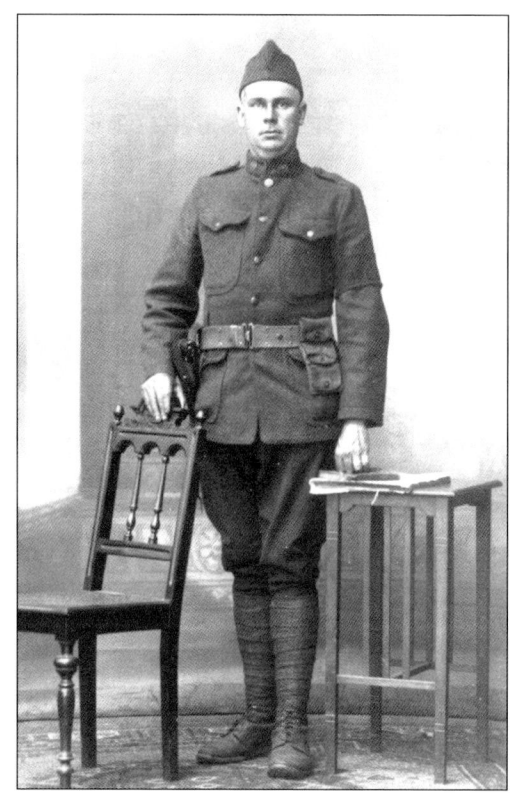

THE EUROPEAN THEATER. Charlie Whitner Mitchell (1886–1944) served in France during World War I. He returned to Belton and became a constable for the police force.

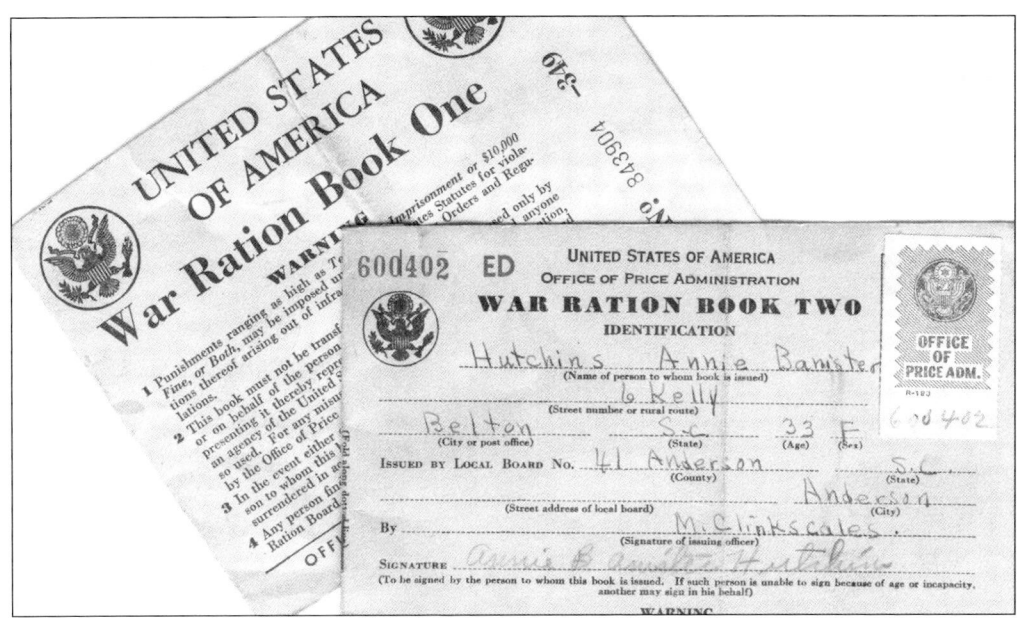

RATIONING RECORDS. During World War II, staples and supplies were limited because everything was being sent overseas for the support of the troops. War ration cards were issued to accommodate the lack of supplies, ensuring that everyone had an equal access to necessary items. Even though books could not be exchanged, whenever a person didn't need an item that was being issued to her, she would take the item and barter with her neighbor for something her family needed.

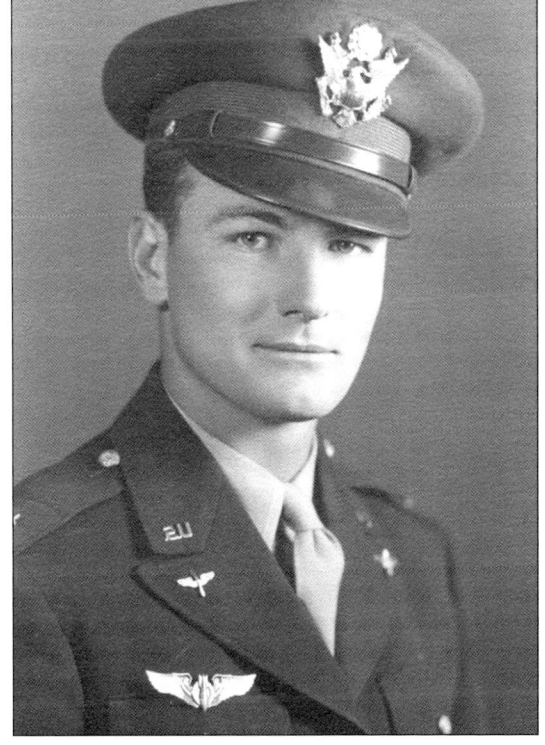

MISSING IN ACTION. Rex Alderman Rice (born June 7, 1917, MIA September 1943), a graduate of Riverside Military Academy and the University of North Carolina, volunteered for service as a lieutenant in the army. He was a bombardier in a B-17 that was lost over the British Channel after a bombing raid over Germany.

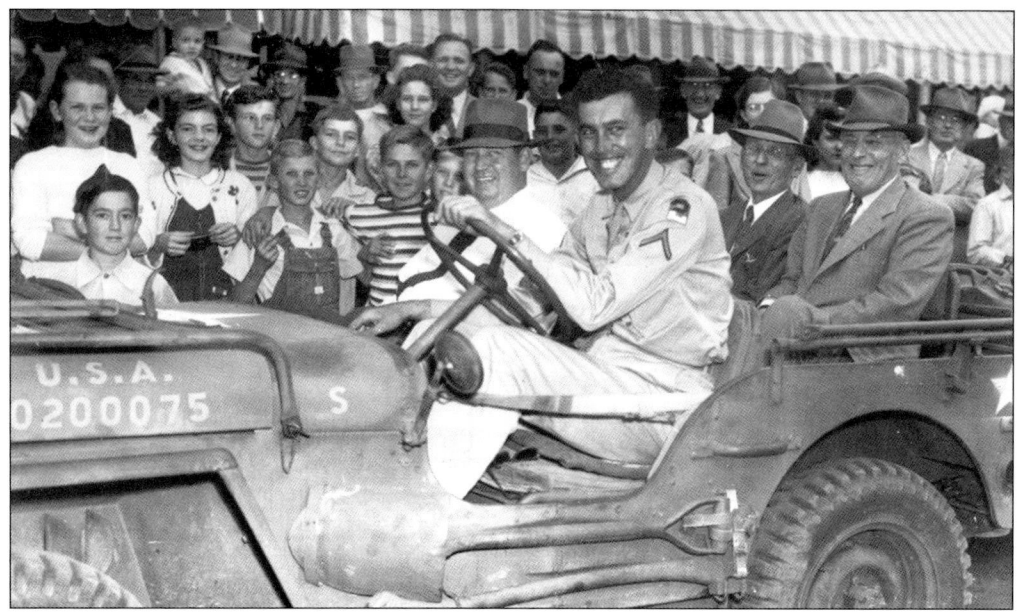

MILITARY PROMOTION. This unknown army sergeant traveled to Belton to promote the purchase of war bonds. Dr. W.L. McIlwain is sitting beside the driver and in the back are Will Clinkscales and Dr. W.R. Haynie with townspeople gathered behind them. People sold scrap metal to buy the bonds that would help fund the military action and supplies needed to win the war. Jukie Blake was so caught up in the patriotic furor that he sold his pony to buy a war bond.

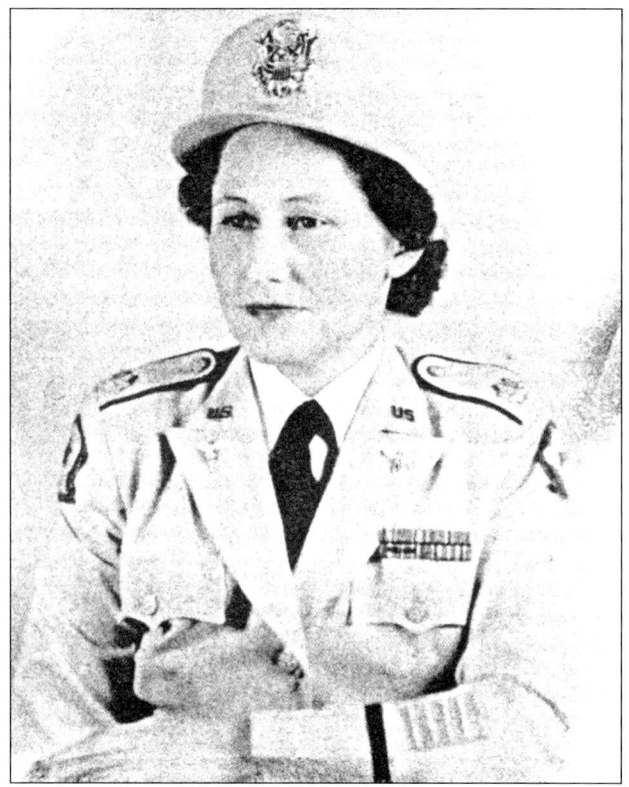

DECORATED "MISS BESSIE." Bessie V. Fullbright became a nurse and joined the Army Nurse Corps in 1941. She served for over 20 years, becoming one of the highest ranking and most decorated women in World War II. She served in the European operation until VE Day and then moved to the Pacific theater until the Japanese surrendered. She died in 1998 while a resident at the Richard Campbell Veterans Nursing Home.

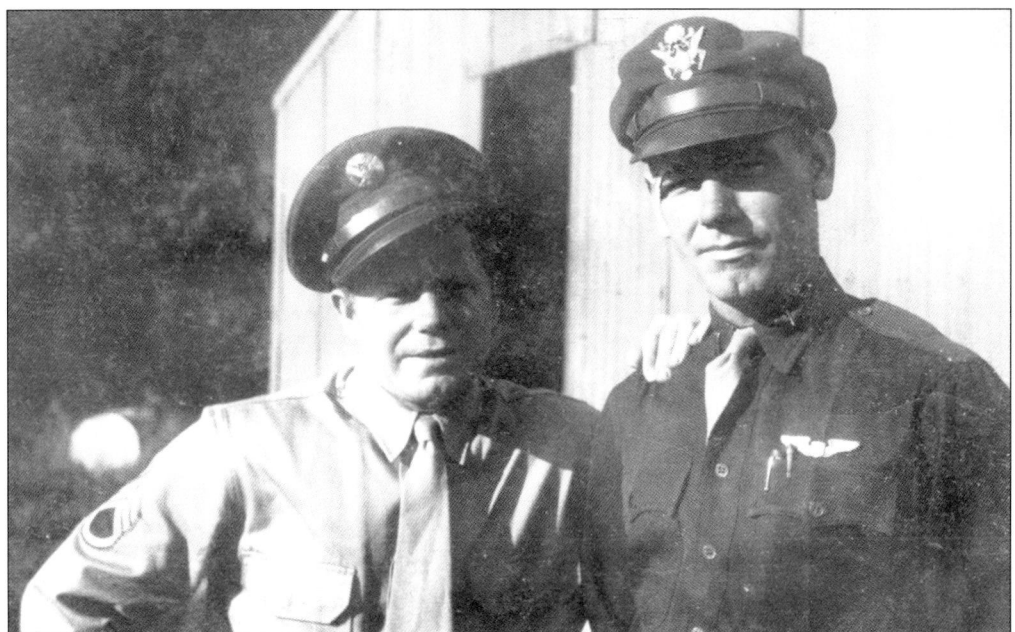

BROTHERLY SACRIFICE. Both G.F. "Scoop" and Joe M. Acker volunteered the day after Pearl Harbor was rocked by Japanese kamikazes. G.F. became a staff sergeant and, after fighting in the Battle of the Bulge, was made a lieutenant. Joe went to flight school at Randolph Field in San Antonio, Texas, and became a lieutenant in the U.S. Army Air Corps. They were stationed at different bases in England, but they got permission to take a furlough to meet up in August 1943, when this picture was taken. Three days later while piloting a B-17 during a bombing raid, Joe was shot down over Gelsenkirchen, Germany, and was later declared dead.

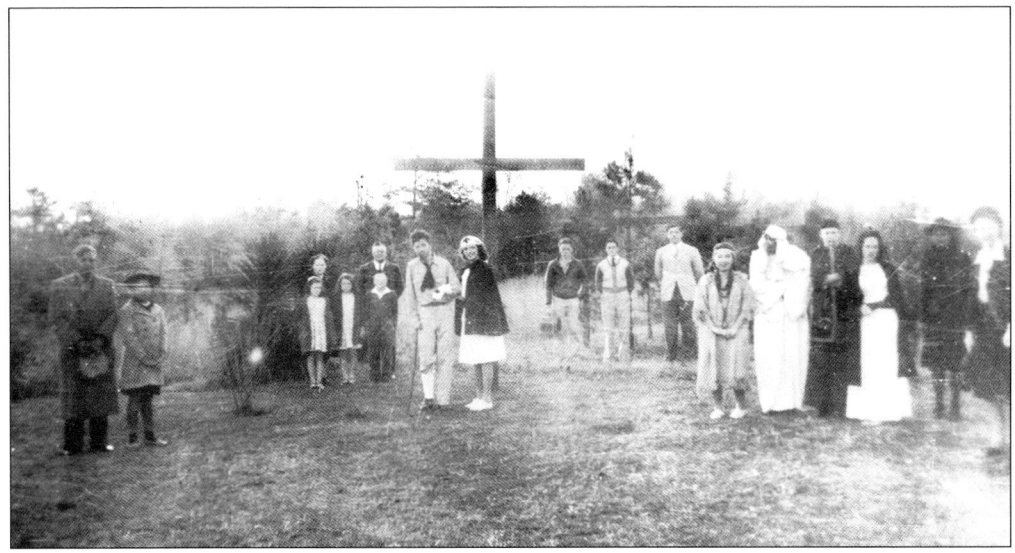

HOLIDAY TRADITIONS AFFECTED BY WAR. Even a traditional Easter Sunrise Service during World War II was embued with a wartime theme. Entitled "Room at the Cross" and written and conducted by Grace P. Durham, the play juxtaposed Biblical scenes with military ones. Here, an army nurse escorts a wounded soldier to the foot of the cross in this service held at George White's Anderson Street home.

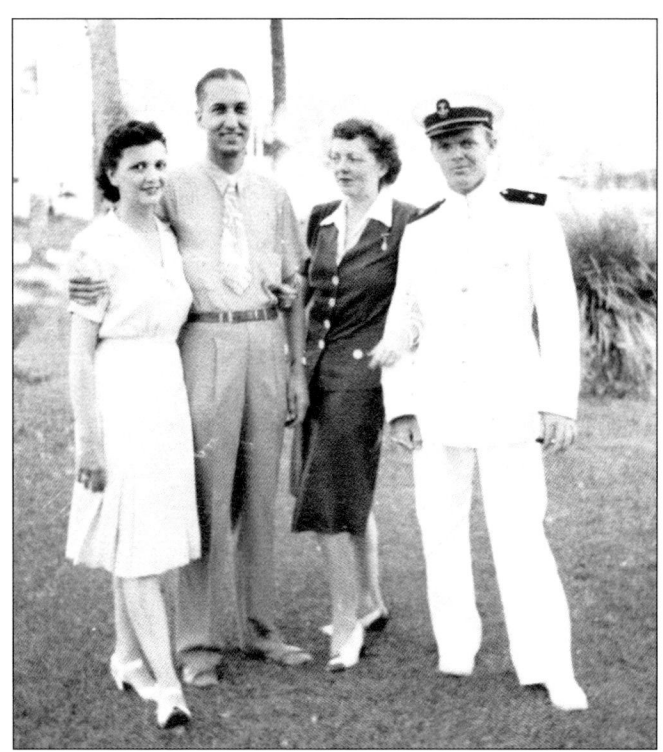

THE PANAMA CONNECTION. Throughout the duration of the war, Harold "Hack" Clinkscales served in Panama in the VI Bomber Command. He is seen here with his sister Kat, her husband Juke Blake, and Hack's aunt Varina Eaddy when they visited while he was on furlough. He served as a PBY-5 Catalina seaplane pilot searching for enemy submarines trying to endanger the Canal, a necessary connection to get American naval ships from the Atlantic to the Pacific.

PROUD SAILOR. At the age of 17, Matthew Crayton volunteered for service and joined the U.S. Navy during World War II. He worked at bases in San Francisco, California, and Honolulu, Hawaii. After attending college on the GI Bill and receiving a degree from Benedict College, he took a job teaching and coaching, first at Honea Path and then at Geer-Gantt High School. He eventually became assistant principal and then principal of the all-black school. After consolidation and integration of Belton-Honea Path High School, Crayton moved to become the assistant principal in charge of discipline. His motto, "Treat people fairly, firmly, and consistently," endeared him to students and teachers alike. He retired after 32 years of service to the district.

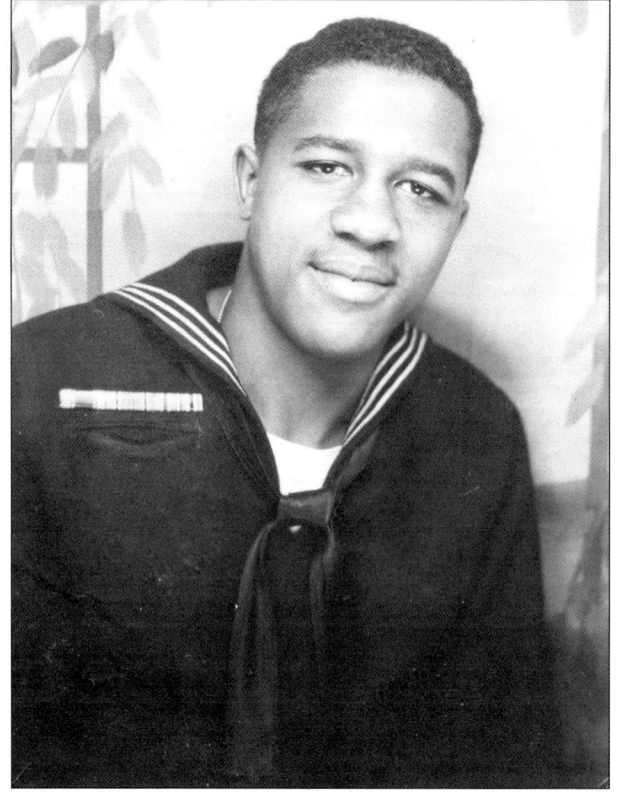

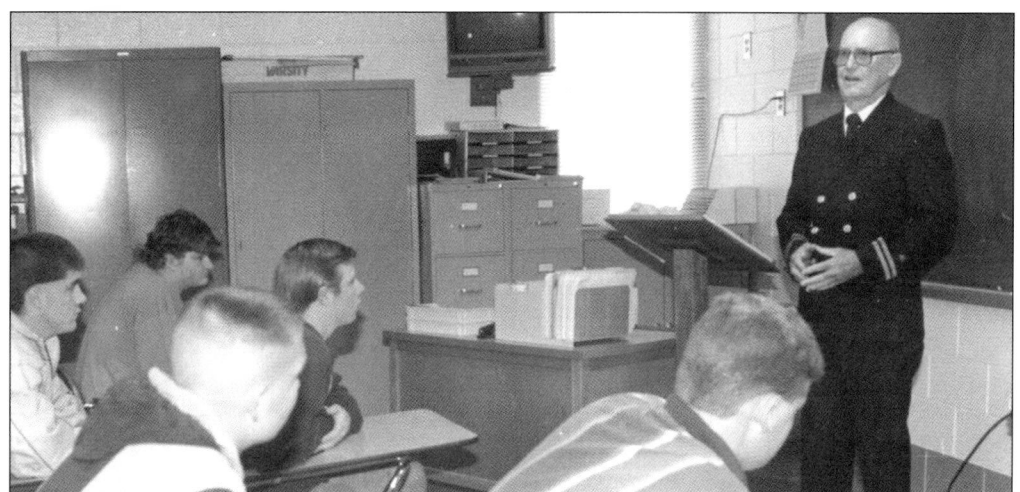

PT BOAT COMMANDER. Still able to fit into his uniform after 40 years, Stan Marshall recounts his military experiences to students at Belton-Honea Path High School. Marshall was a PT boat commander in the Pacific. After receiving a coconut with the inscription "Trust these men to lead you to us. One burned, one badly hurt" from some native islanders, he set in motion the rescue of the future President, John F. Kennedy, and his men who had been torpedoed aboard PT 109. When Kennedy recovered, he hounded Marshall for the coconut, to which Marshall quipped, "This is an official communiqué and it must remain in the files." Of course, Marshall gave it back to him, and it is rumored that Kennedy kept it on his desk as a reminder of his harrowing experience.

ALL-AMERICAN GIRLS PROFESSIONAL BASEBALL LEAGUE, 1945–1951. Since so many professional baseball players volunteered or were drafted to serve in World War II, a women's baseball league was founded to give those at home some entertainment. Viola Thompson Griffin was the athletic director at Mills Mill in Greenville when she was recruited to try out for the AAGPBL at Wrigley Field in Chicago. Her first year was with the newly formed Grand Rapids Chicks, coached by Baseball Hall of Famer Max Carey. She also played for the Milwaukee Chicks and the South Bend Blue Sox. The left-handed pitcher was well-known for her placement of the ball and could hit the corners consistently. She has been inducted into the SC Athletic Hall of Fame, has received the "Order of the Palmetto," and has been honored by the National Baseball Hall of Fame in Cooperstown, New York. She advised the makers of the film *A League of Their Own*. Film clips of her game days are featured in the credits of that movie.

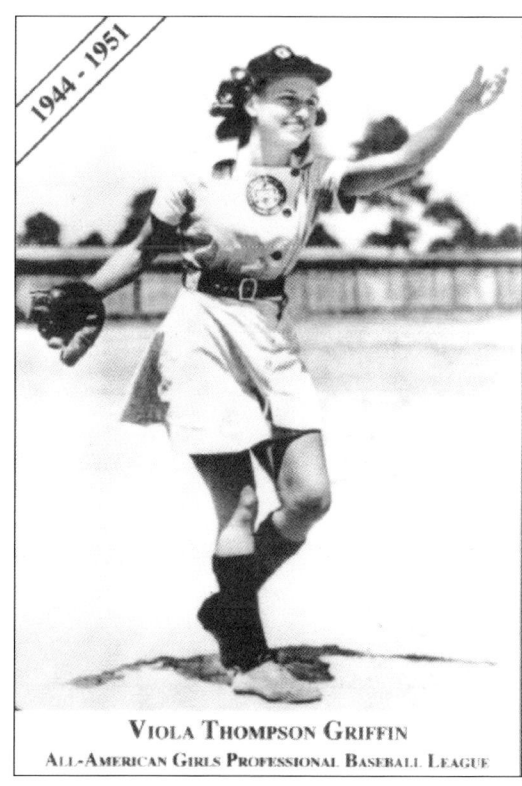

VIOLA THOMPSON GRIFFIN
ALL-AMERICAN GIRLS PROFESSIONAL BASEBALL LEAGUE

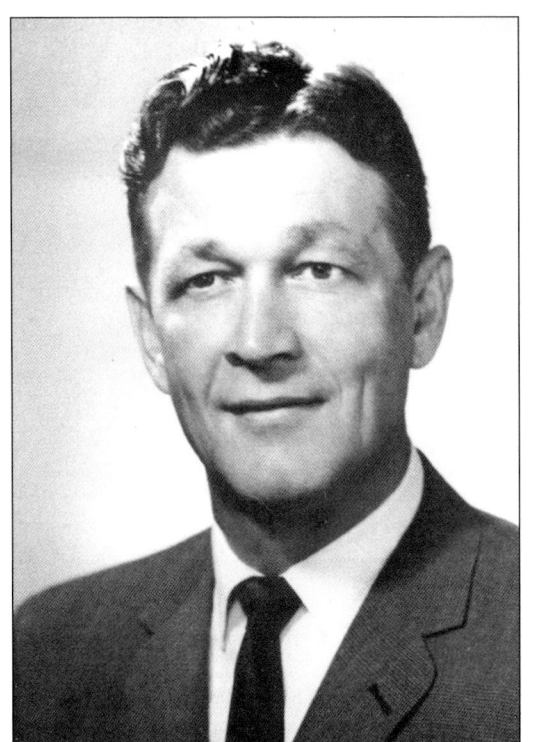

SPANNING TWO WARS. Although only 20 years old, Sgt. James Allred had already been in the thick of battle. Landing behind enemy lines in France and Holland, he was wounded three times, captured while unconscious, and escaped five times, being recaptured each time. While in a prison camp, he dropped 72 pounds. Shortly before VE Day, he was liberated from the camp by General Patton and his troops. Allred was awarded two Silver Stars and two Purple Hearts. When he returned from battle, he enrolled in Presbyterian College, excelling on the football and baseball teams, and commanded the ROTC unit there. During the Korean War, he was assigned to the 187th Parachute Combat Team under the command of General Westmoreland. Lieutenant Allred took 20 men deep into North Korean territory, completely destroyed an enemy supply point, and captured five Red Army officers, but he was wounded in the engagement. He received his third Silver Star and Purple Heart for this mission.

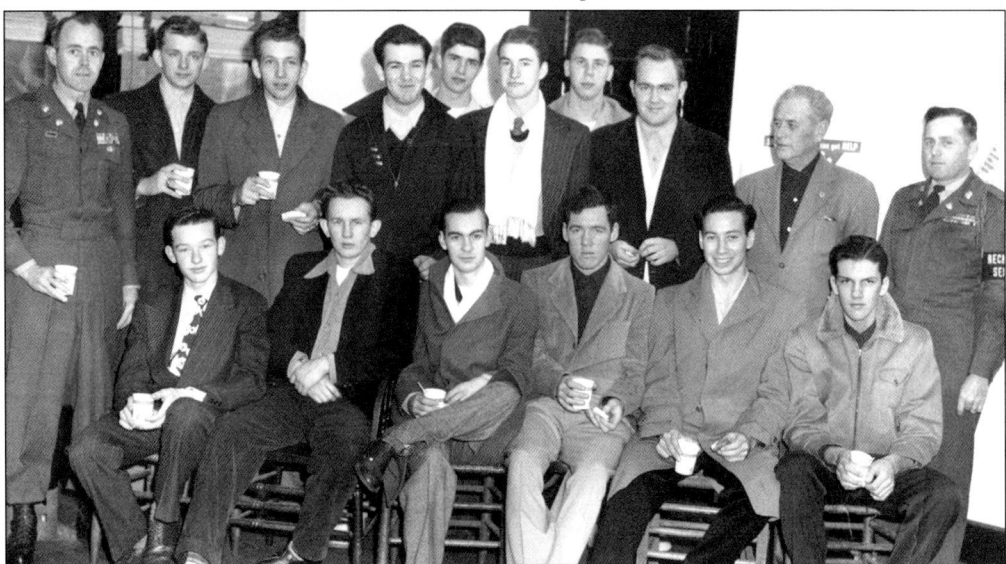

VOLUNTEERS DURING KOREAN WAR. Pictured are 13 Belton boys who volunteered for services in the U.S. Armed Forces. This group left Belton early Thursday morning, December 28, 1950. They were served a going-away breakfast by the City of Belton. Shown with the group is Mayor J.L. Guthrie, who served as master of ceremonies at the breakfast. The others are, from left to right, (front row) Jimmy F. Fullbright, Ernest D. Blackwell, John Charles Davenport, Joel E. King, Horace S. Patterson, and Dacus L. Mahaffey; (back row) Sgt. 1-C Rufus D. Arrowood, Thomas F. Shirley, Ralph E. Houston, Bobby R. Wright, Benjamin Joe Coward, Perry I. Taylor, Walter T. Daye, Thomas B. Lynch Jr., Mayor J.L. Guthrie, and M. Sgt. Vernon R. Shimanek.

BUNKER, KUMHWA VALLEY, KOREA, 1951. David Ellison entered service in January of 1951. After basic training at Fort Jackson, he headed out to Japan and then on to Korea, where he joined the 14th Infantry Regiment, 25th Division. North of the 38th parallel, he outfitted this bunker with sandbags to absorb the explosion of mortar fire upon his camp. Ellison was daunted by the absolute destruction of land and villages and deeply saddened by the sight of displaced families caused by the war.

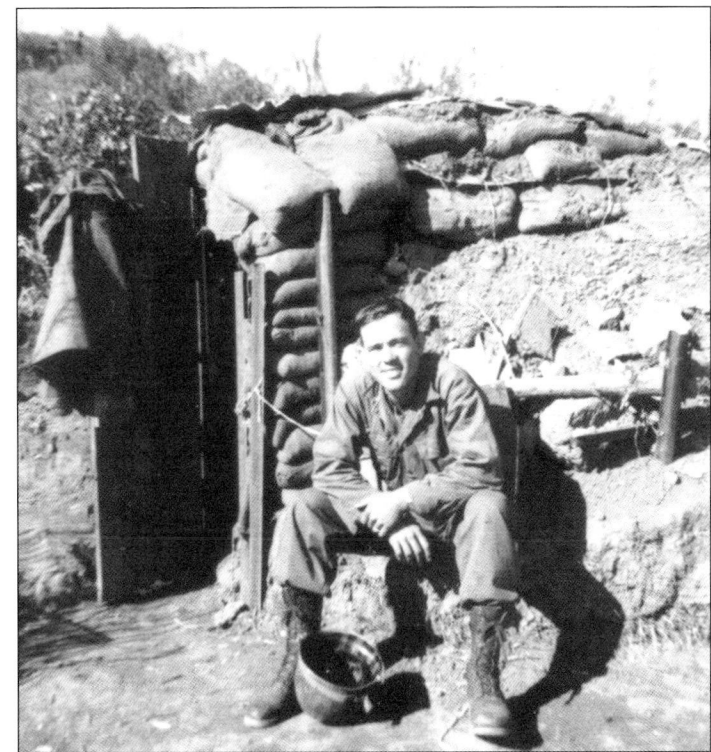

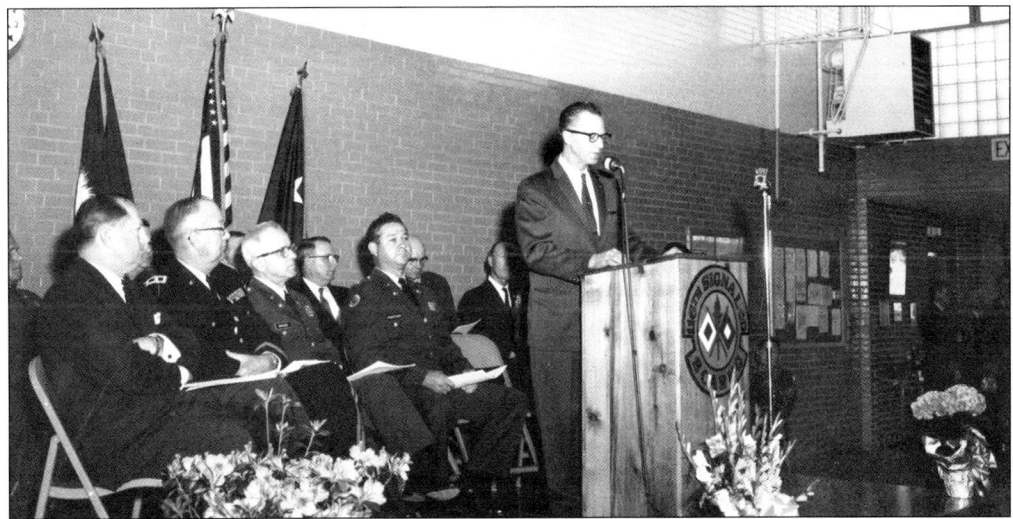

ARMORY DEDICATION. In September 1955, the National Guard in Belton was activated with two officers and 49 enlisted men under the command of 1st Lt. William F. Chapman Jr. The unit was designated as the 139th Field Artillery Battery (Searchlight) and attached to various units until it became Company B of the 151st Signal Battalion. In April of 1961, the new building was dedicated. Here, Mayor Glenn Coward speaks to the honored guests and families of the Battalion. Congressman W.J. Bryan Dorn, Maj. General Frank Pinckney (adjutant general, State of South Carolina), Colonel Wingard, and Lt. Col. Sam Robertson appear on the dais. The 151st Signal Battalion was deployed to Iraq in March 2003 to participate in Operation Iraqi Freedom.

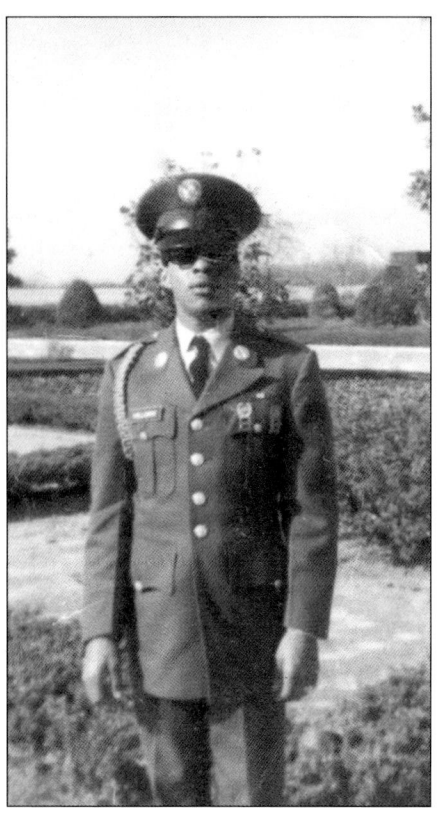

MAKING THE GRADE. Sgt. Harold Holloway reported for duty in the Vietnam Conflict in 1968 after basic training at Fort Gordon, Georgia, and Advanced Infantry Training at Fort Jackson. He was a member of the 4th Company, 39th Infantry Division stationed in the Mekong Delta and commanded a squad of 12 men. He received the Air Combat Assault Medal for logging over 30 combat drops and was a part of the Tet Offensive. Attending college on the GI Bill, he received his masters and Education Specialist degrees from Clemson and taught industrial technology for 25 years at Belton Middle School while helping to maintain the family business, Holloway's Funeral Home.

GUN POWER. This picture is of Cpl. Robert A. "Buddy" Ferguson Jr., U.S. Marine Corps, in 1969. Stationed in Quang Tri, the Republic of Vietnam, with the H & S Co., 3rd Battalion, 4th Marine Division FMF, Buddy Ferguson is shown here with his section of 106 mm recoilless anti-tank rifle and gun crew. He and his crew participated in the "Lancaster," "Maine-Craig," "Purple Martin," "Herkimer Mountain," "Arlington Canyon," "Georgia Tar," and "Idaho Canyon" operations during his two-year enlistment.

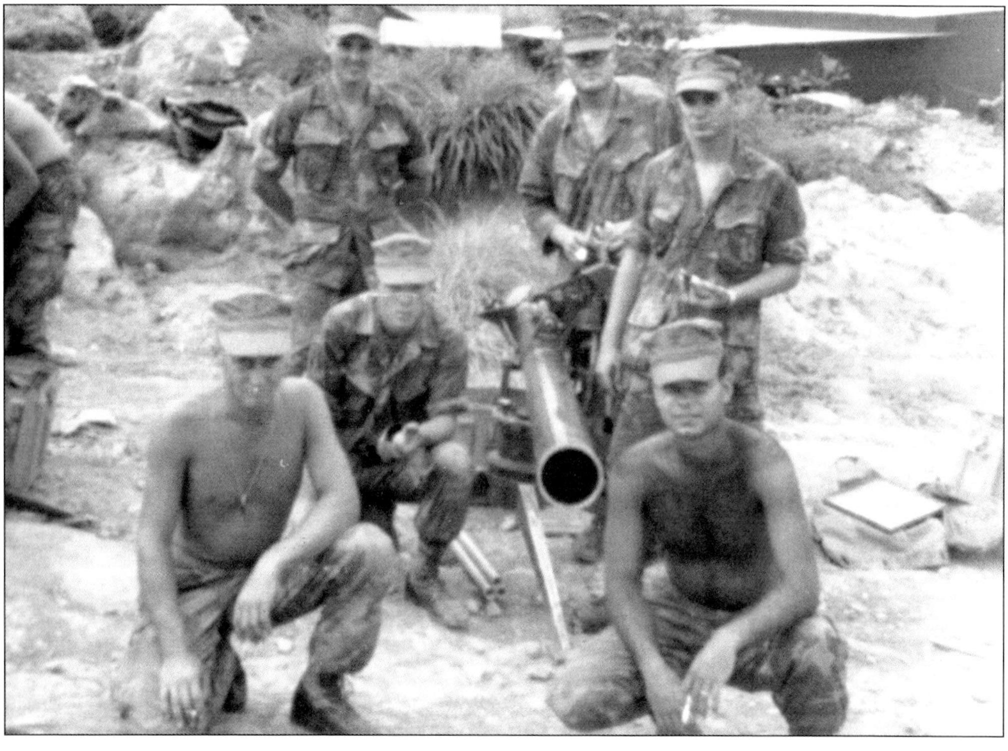

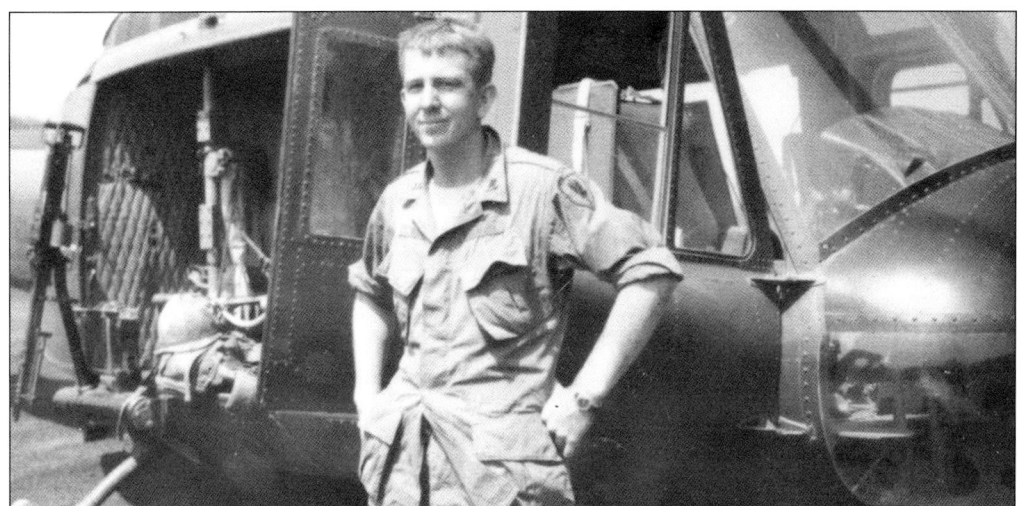

A NEAR MISS. During his year-long tour of duty in the Vietnam War, U.S. Army CWO Glenn Locke flew helicopter missions while assigned to B Troop, 3rd Squadron, 17th Air Cavalry. This picture was taken after a mission in March 1968. Following orders, Locke flew his helicopter into a hot zone, landed, and left his helicopter to report to his commander. Immediately, enemy mortar fire began barraging the landing area. In an effort to save the helicopter from damage, his co-pilot immediately started the helicopter and departed, leaving Locke stranded in a field with mortar rounds exploding all around him. He survived the downpour of shelling, sooty and grimy from the kicked up dirt and temporarily deaf from the nearby explosions. During his tour, Locke received the Distinguished Flying Cross for heroism and 20 Air Medals for combat missions flown.

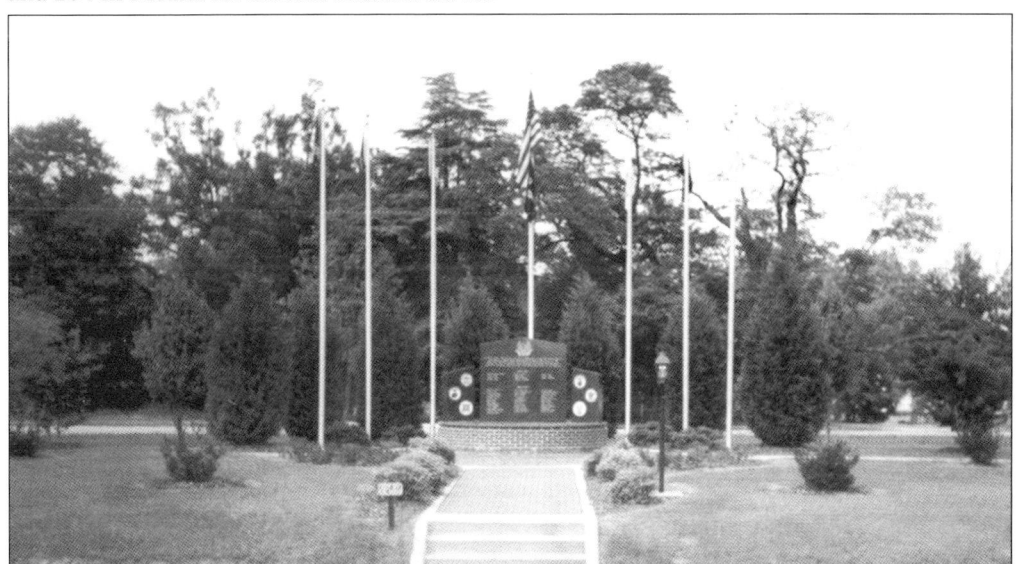

VETERANS HONORED. In May 1997, the Belton Veterans Park opened with a dedication ceremony. Designed by Michael Edwards, a Belton native and graduate of Clemson University's School of Architecture, with input from the Veterans Park board members, the monument honors each branch of service and the main marker lists Beltonians who gave their lives in service during World War I (KIA 11), World War II (KIA 40), and Vietnam (KIA 1) conflicts. Services are conducted each Memorial Day and Veterans Day to honor our fallen heroes.

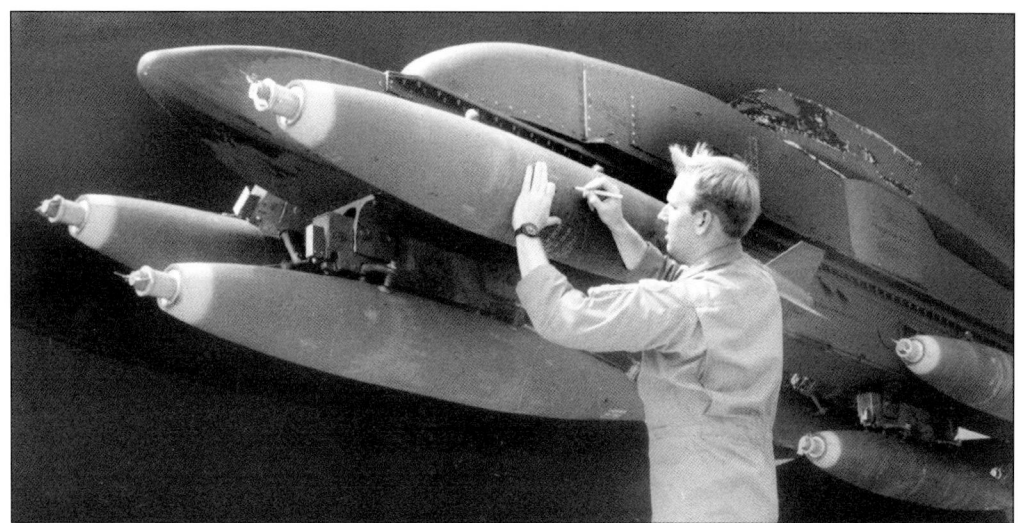

THIS ONE'S FOR BELTON. Capt. Roger Neal Anderson Jr. writes a personal message on a bomb bound for Baghdad in the Desert Storm campaign of 1991. The message reads "This One's for Belton, SC. Go Bears! 11 Feb. 91." Anderson flew seven B-52 bomber combat missions in the Persian Gulf War. Each flight averaged 16 hours and carried a standard load of 45 high explosive or cluster bomb units, each weighing 500 to 750 pounds. Many of Captain Anderson's targets were SCUD missile sites, ammunition factories, Republican Guard artillery, tank and infantry concentrations, and mine fields. He returned to home base after two months of duty in the Middle East.

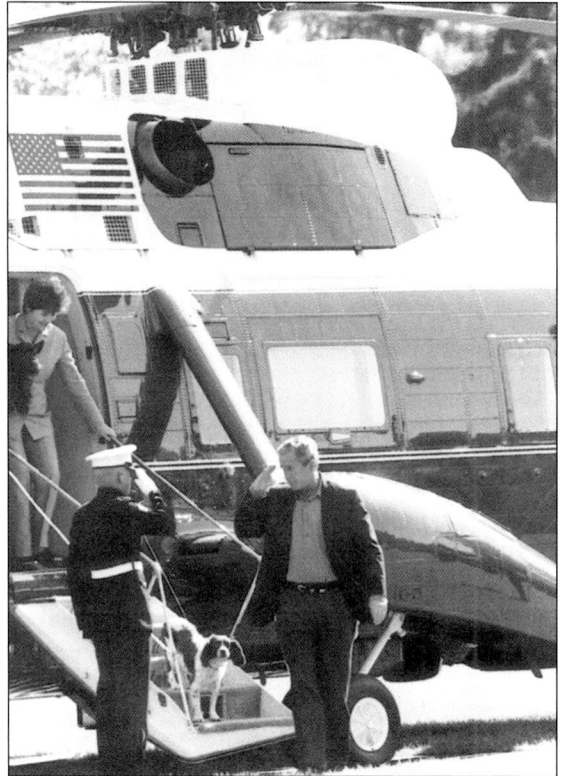

A SALUTE FROM THE CHIEF. In April of 2001, Brad Driver began a one-year stint as Marine One Crew Chief. Marine One is the official helicopter transport for the president of the United States and is seen in many a landing on the White House lawn. Donning an impeccable dress blue uniform, Driver was responsible for ensuring his aircraft was in top shape and ready for use by the President. During his tour of duty as crew chief, Driver traveled to 33 states and four foreign countries. "When the President salutes us back, that is one of the most awesome feelings in the world," Driver commented after his tour was over.

Four
School Days

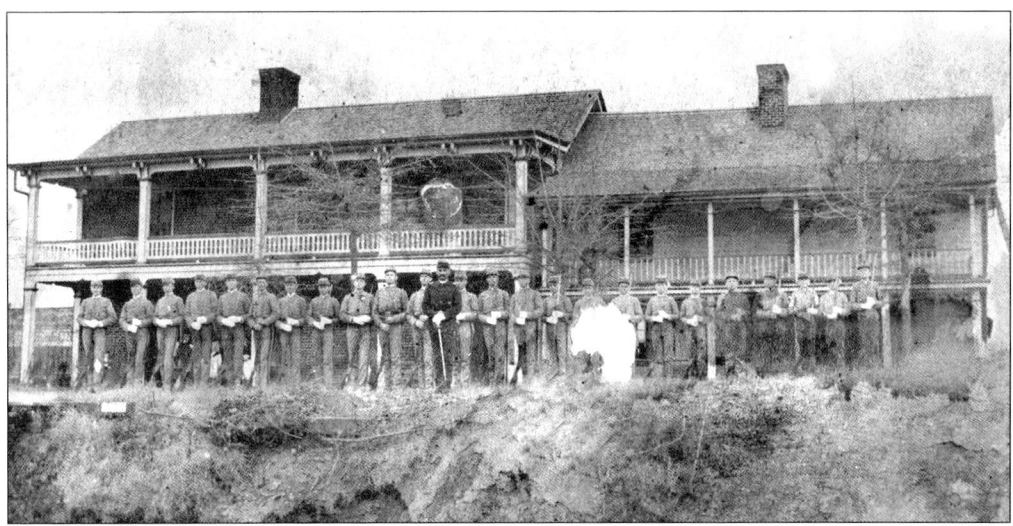

MILITARY DISCIPLINE, C. 1889. According to information submitted by Idell Grubbs Haynie, male students at the academy were submitted to strict discipline and military bearing. The commander in front is Professor Kemp. Parading must have been part of his training, for these young men are wearing full dress uniforms complete with white gloves and kepis, and they hold saber-bearing long arms. The picture was taken in front of the Belton Hotel (known as the McGee Hotel at that time), and to the left one can see that the town's first sidewalks were raised platforms.

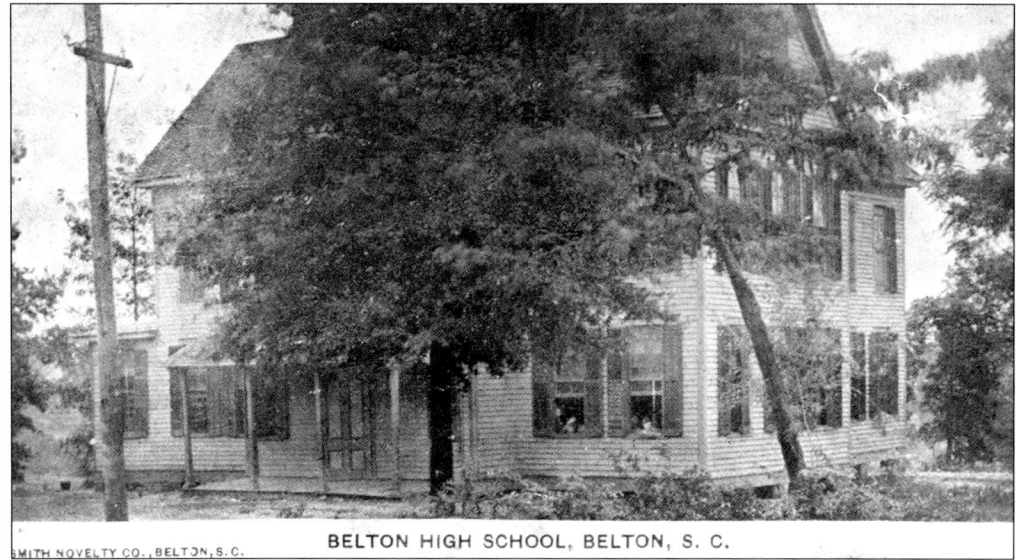

THE BELTON HIGH SCHOOL, 1893. The first school opened in 1853 on the site donated by Belton founder Dr. George R. Brown. The Belton Academy, as it was known, offered curriculum intended to prepare students for collegiate studies in medicine, law, and religion. By 1891, the Belton Academy fielded 87 pupils (100 by year's end) in a two-room building. Outraged by the overcrowded conditions, subscriptions were taken for a new school building to be built. By 1893, this commodious two-story high school was occupied

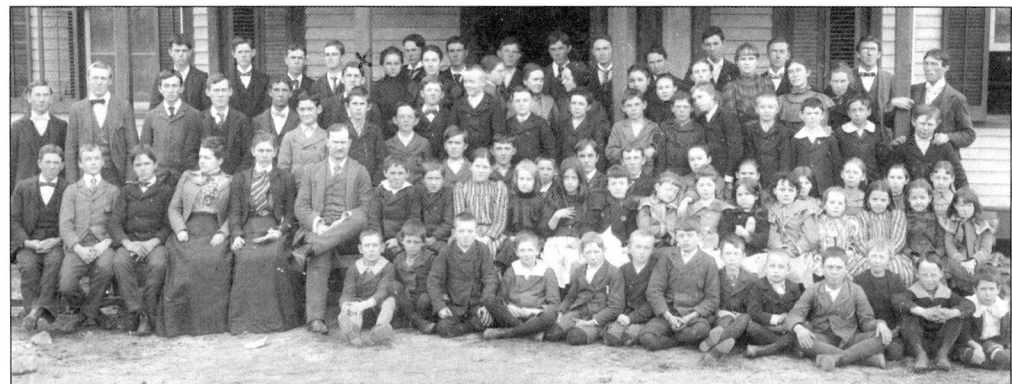

BELTON SCHOOL, 1899. Students are pictured, from left to right, as follows: (first row) three unidentified, J. Boyce, M. Rice, F. Lewis, two unidentified, S. Campbell, T. Willingham, R. Breazeale, W. Todd, and unidentified; (second row) unidentified, R. Rice, C. Clinkscales, Miss Lois Hudson, Miss Marvin Quattlebaum, W.B. West (superintendent of schools), F. Fant, unidentified, B. Boyce, F. Burch, N. Taylor, E. Todd, M. Vandiver, M. Cox, A. Stokes, D. Brown, I. Clinkscales, M. Boyce, unidentified, and N. Campbell; (third row) unidentified, C. Campbell, W. Pinson, unidentified, ? Fisher, H. Breazeale, L. Shirley, C. Brown, W. Todd, C. Taylor, S. Mattison, L. Vass, W. Fant, E. M. Green, I. Green, L. Geer, A. Shirley, A. Shirley, and A. Shirley; (fourth row) A.D. Fisher, F. McDaniel, three unidentified, L. Rice, H. Campbell, unidentified, W. Fant, M. Campbell, J.C. Griffin, G. Rice, H. Campbell, C. Brown, and G. Campbell; (fifth row) M. Green, M. Haynie, H. Wilson, B. Griffin, M. Clinkscales, M. Brown, S. Haynie, B. Green, B. Major, C. Hoffman, J. Campbell, N. Major, unidentified, and F. Tribble; (sixth row) unidentified, R. Mitchell, unidentified, R. Green, S. Griffin, J. Green, A. Fant, C. Cobb, and D. Breazeale.

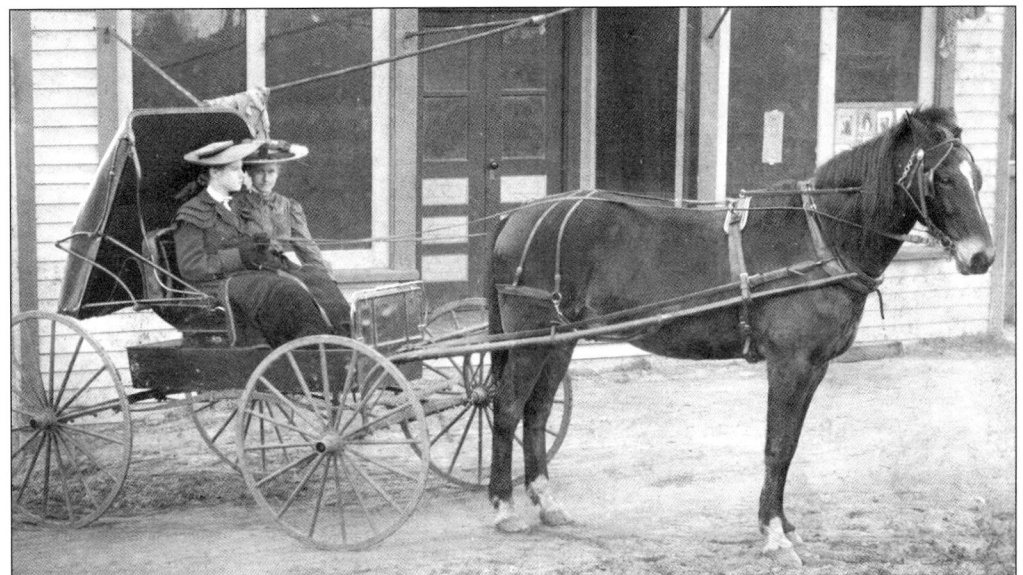

ON OUR WAY TO SCHOOL, C. 1905. Jessie Lewis (Whitmire) and Leda Poore head off to school in a buggy pulled by Old Jim. The Poore household was just two miles from town, but such was the financial situation that instead of walking, Poore could drive the distance. Poore attended Greenville Female College (which eventually merged with Furman University) and came back to Belton to teach at the Mill School.

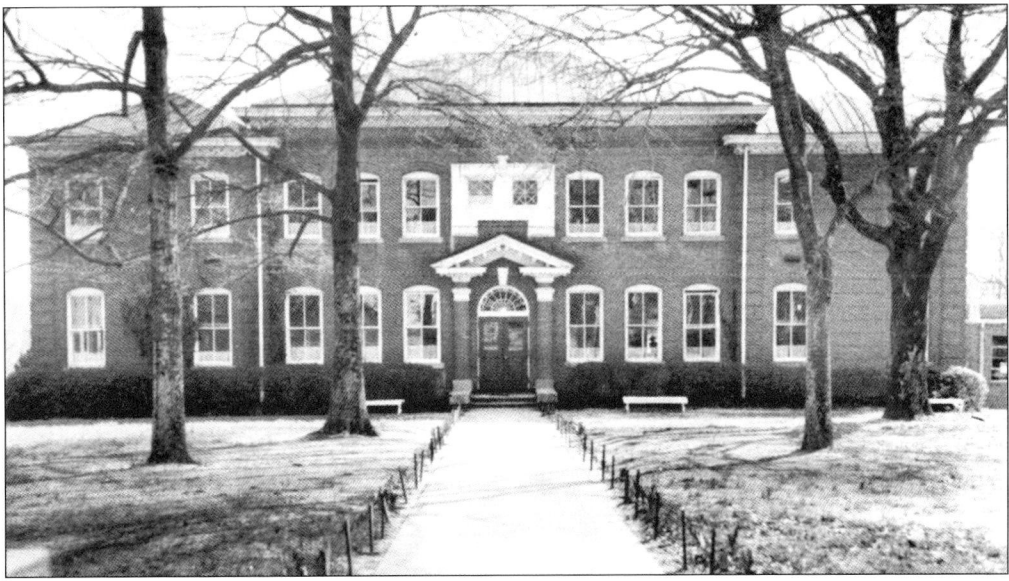

CENTRAL SCHOOL, 1951. With the influx of population due to the increased need for mill labor force, a bond issue was purchased for the erection and equipping of a new school building in 1908. The result was the Central Graded School (now the City Hall). In 1958, the school was described by a parent: "The Belton Grammar School is outstanding in many ways. Upon entering the building one is aware of a home-like atmosphere for throughout the year, the halls which are painted in shades of green, are made beautiful with seasonal flower arrangements and bulletin board displays of children's work." It originally served grades one through ten until 1922 when the new high school was built on Myrtle Avenue.

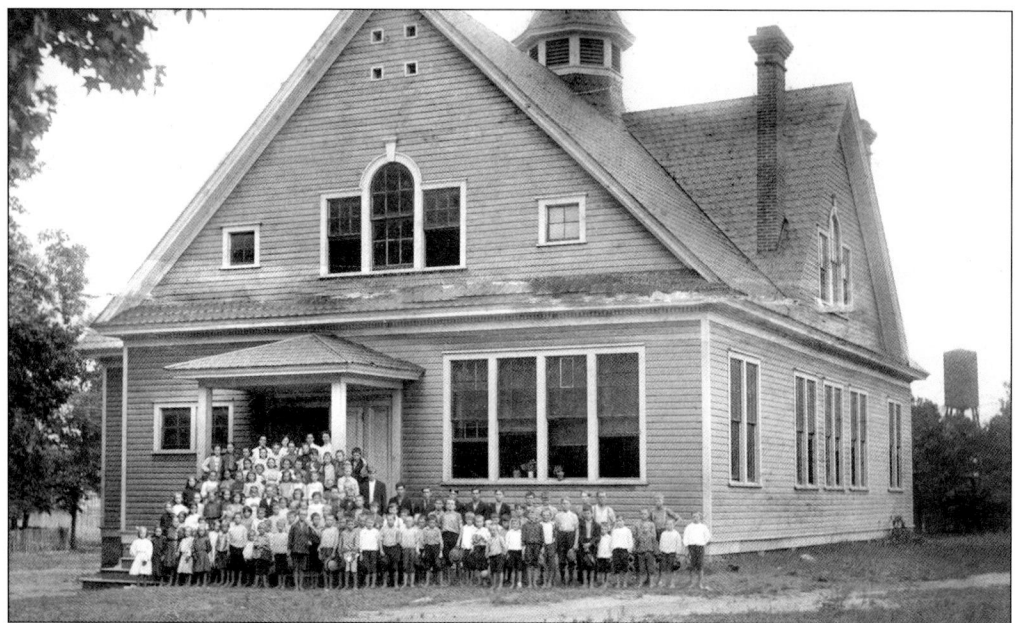

MILL SCHOOL AND STUDENTS, 1909. In 1901 a mill school was organized in the village. It held classes from grade one through grade six. The second story of the building contained a large auditorium, which was not only used by the students, but also by the community at large. The facility was destroyed by fire in December 1951. In battling the blaze during that frigidly cold day, many firefighters were frostbitten when the spray from the waterhose froze on their hair, hand, and clothes. The loss was gauged at $25,000 by Mill officials. Students were absorbed by the Central Grammar School or attended classes in a temporary facility located at 502 Brown Avenue until Marshall Primary School was built in 1954 to ease the overcrowded conditions.

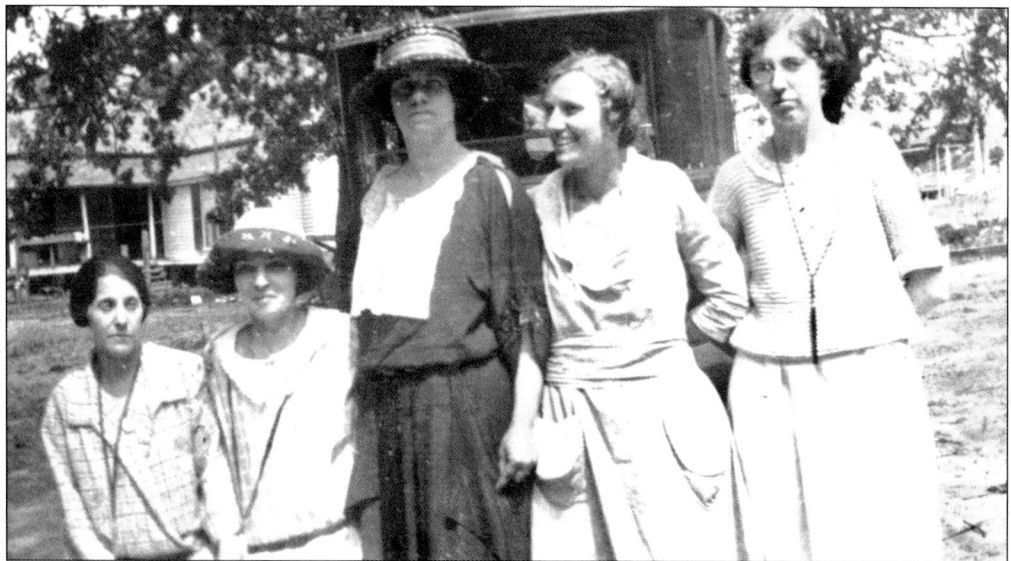

A STAFF OF THE BRIGHTEST. Oma Cox, first on left, and Leda Poore, fourth from left, pose with their fellow Belton Mill faculty members in 1923 at Poore's home on Highway 20. A consummate hostess, Poore prepared teas to mark special occasions for the faculty. These women worked tirelessly to keep the mill school academically challenging.

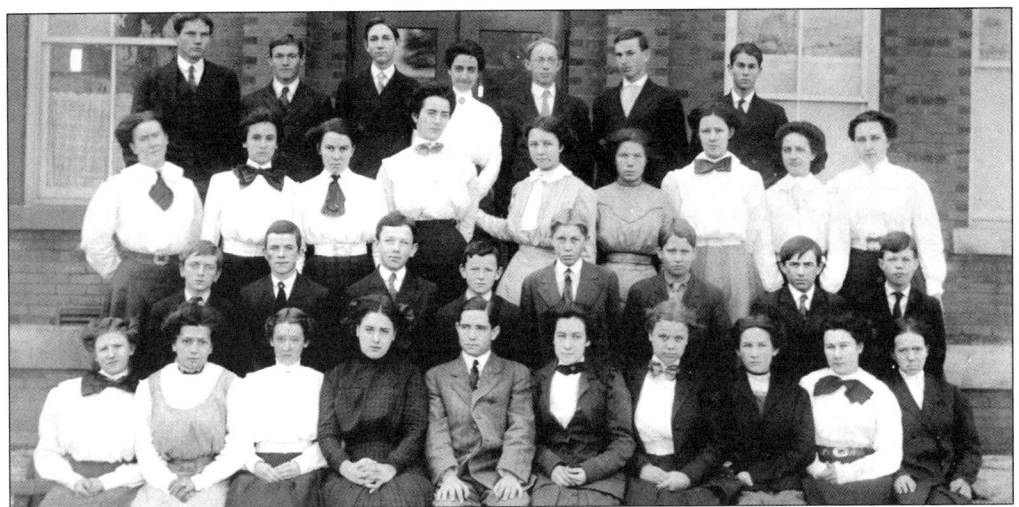

STUDENT BODY OF BELTON HIGH SCHOOL, 1909. The graduating class included, from left to right, (first row) Jessie Hunter (Murphy), Selma Gambrell (Keys), Bernice Cox, Sarah Latimer (Watson), Arthur Lee (principal), Ellen Smith (Cobb), Sadie Fant, Claire Kay (Fields), Floride Green, and Selma Hunter (Folk); (second row) Henry Clinkscales, Gary Harris, Smythe Gambrell, Gilbert Campbell, Hugh Wardlaw, Grady Brown, Eugene Geer, and George William Clement; (third row) Lola Copeland (Ellison), Oma Cox, Mae Fant (Spann), Corrie Pinson, Annie Kay (Harris), Una Shaw (Pruitt), Lorena Kay (Little), Marie Gaines, and Mildred Branyon (Beeks); (fourth row) Norris Wright, W.C. (Dock) Fields, Sloan Shirley, Fannie Crayton (teacher), Barmore Gambrell, Hugh Tollison, and Edwin Tate.

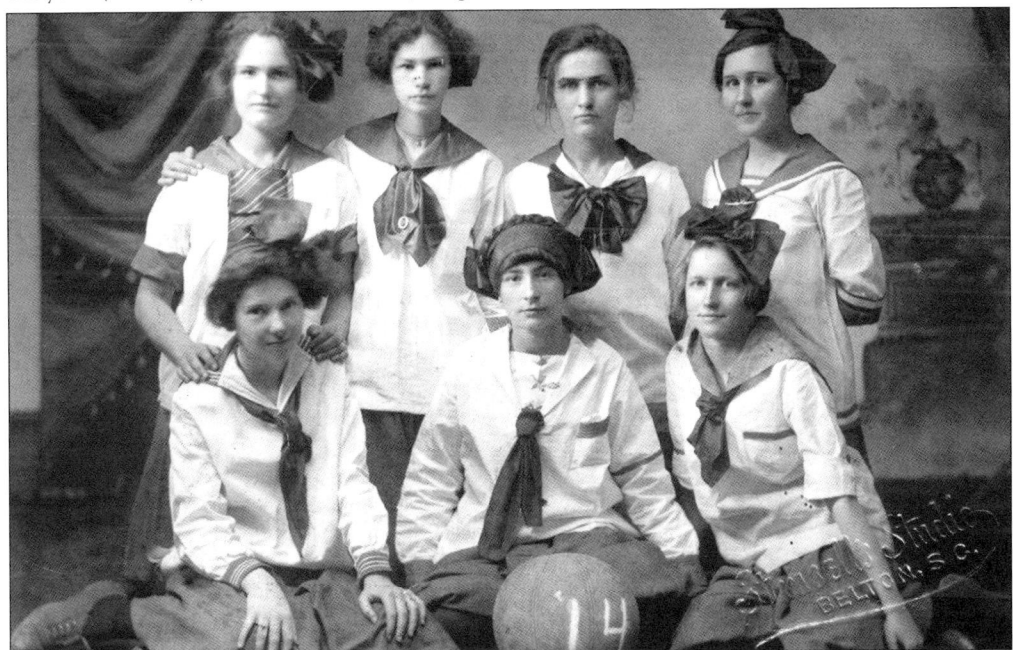

HOOP BALL. Only a few years after the invention of the sport, Belton High fielded a girls' basketball team in 1914. Games were played in cleared out classrooms. Players included, from left to right, (front row) Bessie Wilson, Georgia Fant, and Grace Campbell; (back row) Mattie McMahan, Vivian Cox, Eunice Warnock, and Etta Watkins.

57

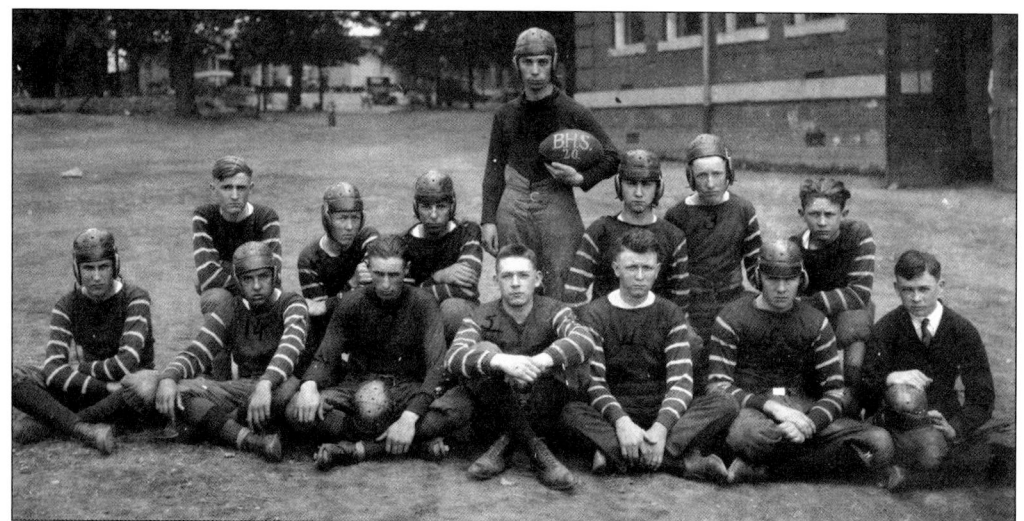

BELTON HIGH SCHOOL FOOTBALL TEAM, 1920. School athletics teams were a major force in the development of the mind and body, according to educational theorists of the time. The football team included the following, from left to right: (first row) Julius Blake (RE), Ben Mason (Sub), Paul Griffin (RG), Jim Bowen (C), Alvin Cothran (LG), Moffatt Haynie (LG), and Fred Greer (LE); (second row) Elijah Griffin (Sub), Milton Littlejohn (RHB), Paul Strickland (FB), Carroll Brown (QB), Edwin Cox (Sub End), and Paul Willingham (Sub); (third row) Prymus Strickland (LHB, Capt); Fred Butler (RG) is absent from the picture. Belton High School also sported a baseball team. An interesting note: Carroll Brown played sports even though he had only one fully-formed arm. His right arm ended at the elbow; however, he played quarterback for the football team and pitched for the baseball team.

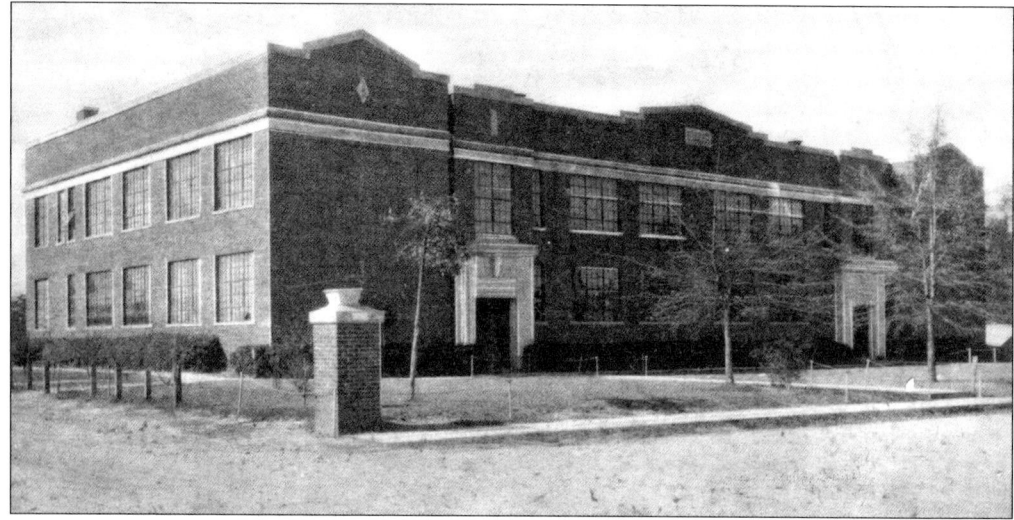

A STATELY FACILITY. Belton High School was built in 1922 with 10 classrooms, an auditorium with seating capacity of 500, a library, and the administrator's offices. An annex was built in 1949, which housed the gymnasium, cafeteria, bandroom, and two classrooms. Grades 7–12 attended this school. The original building was razed in the 1970s, and the new wing of the Belton Elementary School sits on the site. Educational facilities serving the city of Belton now include Marshall Primary School (kindergarten to second grade), Belton Elementary (grades 3–5), Belton Middle School (grades 6–8), and Belton-Honea Path High School (grades 9–12).

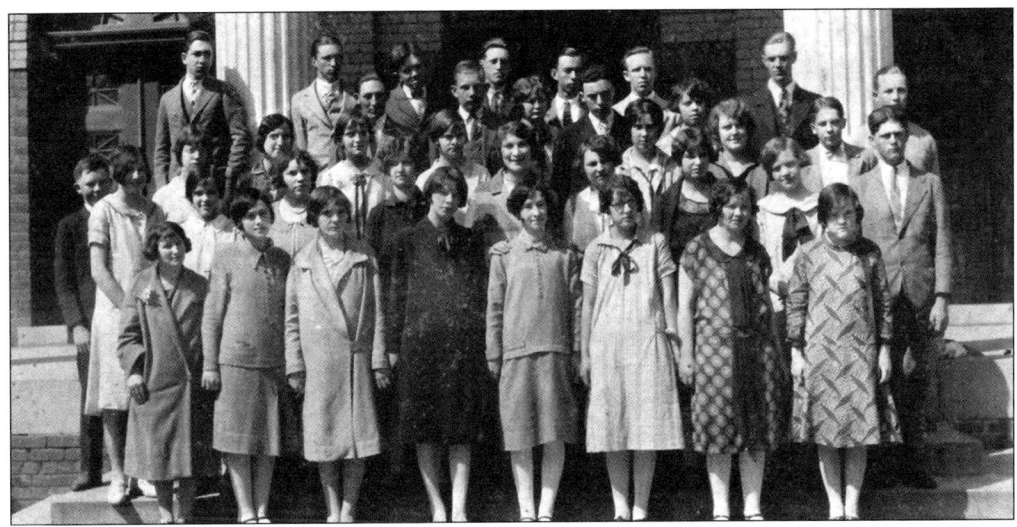

THE CLASS OF 1926, BACCALAUREATE, MAY 20, 1926. Pictured here are, from left to right, the following: (first row) Clara Deck, Hazel Weigle, Sara Ann Wood, Mae Campbell, Gladys Maddox, Selma Brooks, Dessie McConnell, and Ethel King; (second row) Lucretia Holliday, Mary Mitchell, Jessie Cox, Mary Reid, Zelma Berlin, Susie Wilson, Sue Griffin, Ellen Kay, and John Dean; (third row) Will Drake, Sadie Blake, Rachel Deanhart, Marie Poore, Myrtie Kay, Lillian Brown, Elinor Cox, William Hopper, and Jim Gassaway; (fourth row) Eitell Burgess, Bismark Acker, Martha Sutherland, Ezekial Pruitt, Elizabeth Garrett, and Matthew Breazeale; (fifth row) Clem Parker, James Singleton, J.B. Ledbetter, Eugene Tollison, Reid Sherard, and William Cobb. Baccalaureate services were usually held at the First Baptist Church.

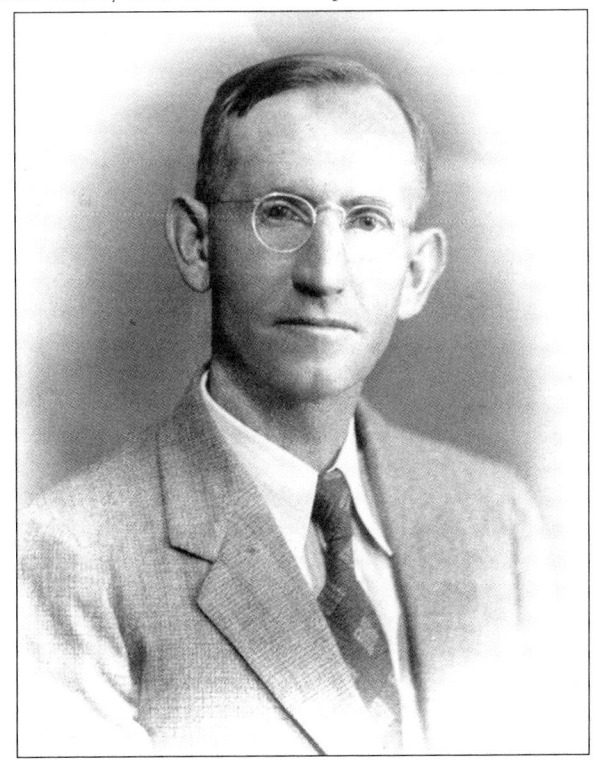

BROOKS MARSHALL, BELOVED SCHOOL SUPERINTENDENT. In 1926, Stanmore Brooks Marshall came to Belton to assume the duties of superintendent of schools. He became a member of the First Baptist Church where he taught the Marshall Bible Class for many years. After a fishing trip to the Lowcountry, Marshall succumbed to a short attack of pneumonia and died at his home in 1939. He was known as a wise administrator and, when problem children were brought to his attention, he worked diligently to create better opportunities for them. In 1954, Marshall was honored by having the new primary school named for him.

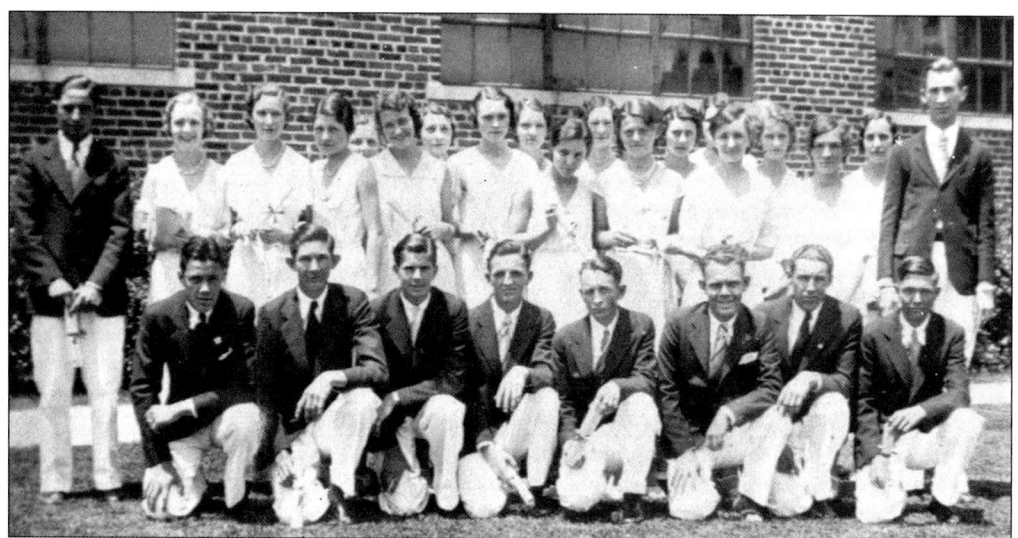

BHS CLASS OF 1932. The Depression certainly doesn't seem to have affected this class, since the men are all dressed in their finest and the women have on white dresses and pearls. They each hold the diploma for which they have worked 11 years to obtain. The following are pictured from left to right: (front row) Tate Horton, Marion Kay, James Geer, Nim Harris, Mortimer Poore, Kenneth Henderson, John Roe, and Harris Wardlaw; (back row) Jacob Ivester, Annie Sue Bramlett, Frances Burnette, Beaufort McCuen, Eleanor Hobson, Ruth Murphy, Lucille McCuen, Lois Carroll, Carolyn Cobb, Trudy Shearer, unidentified, Ruth McMahan, three unidentified, Frances Poore, unidentified, Estelle Green, and James Todd.

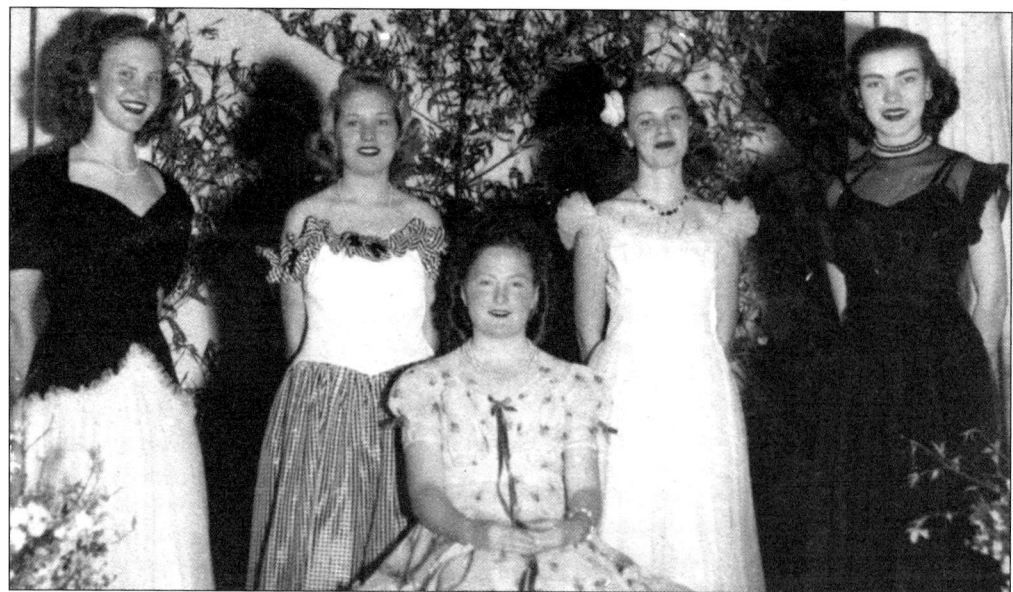

BEAUTIES OF 1945. The Junior-Senior was held in the school's auditorium and these five friends posed for a picture. The patriotic theme was carried out in the decorations of red, white, and blue streamers and centerpieces made up of flags, which recreated a USO Canteen feel. Dates danced to the music provided by records. Pictured here are Betty Jean Acker (Padgett), Leila Rogers (Thompson), Jeanette Land (Eskew), Geraldine McMurray (Evans), and Bobbie Jean Anders (Ford).

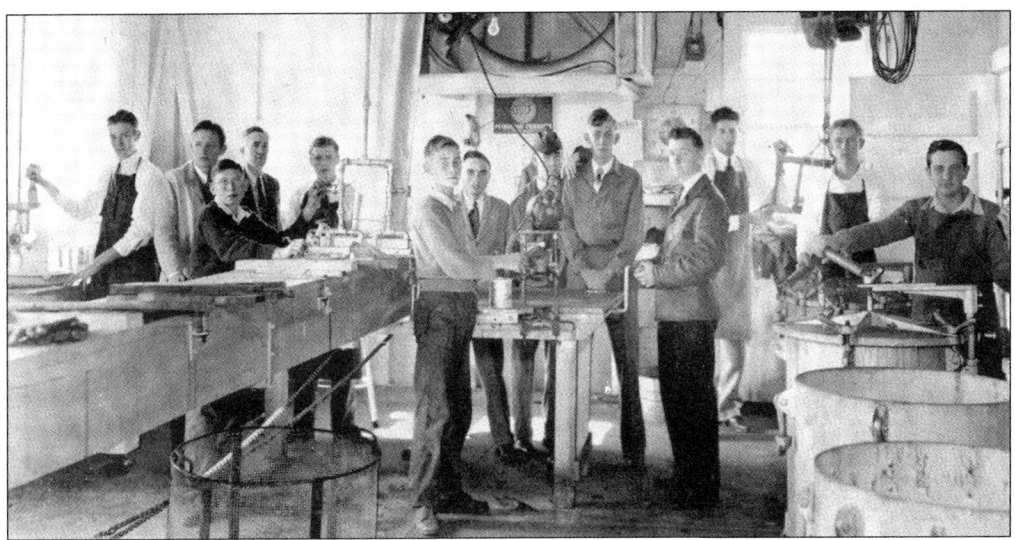

THE BHS CANNERY, 1946. Belton High's Future Farmers of America class meets in the cannery for a picture. Pictured here, from left to right, are members Kenneth Knox, Loyd Collins, Guy Ray Watson, agriculture teacher J.M.H. Clayton, Vernon Boswell, Ray Wilson, Thomas Hill, Kipling Acker, Ernest Tollison, Don Watson, Bill Cole, Bobby McCoy, and David Pruitt. During World War II, community members would take their vegetables and fruits to the cannery to have them processed for a small fee of 2–3¢ a can, which were then shipped to soldiers overseas. Even beef and pork were canned at this facility. Bill Norris ran the cannery throughout the 1940s, and Matthew Breazeale maintained the operation until it was shut down in the mid-1960s.

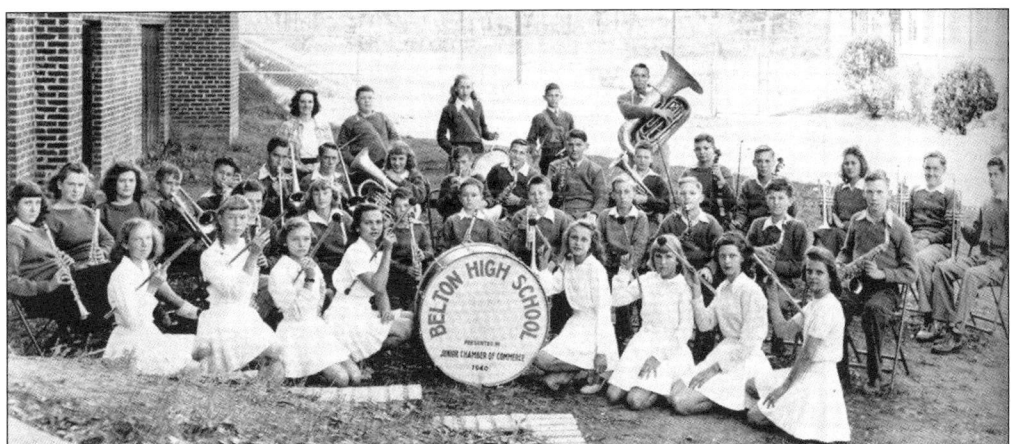

BHS BAND, 1947. Performing for ballgames, concerts, and special events, the Belton High School Band gave students an opportunity to develop their musical talents. Musicians include, from left to right, (first row) Dorothy Haynie, Louise McIlwain, Sara Haynie, Delores Norwood, Joyce Hall, Kitty Blake, Dorothy Cox, and Nadine Sarratt; (second row) Rochelle Montague, Peggy Campbell, Charles Cox, Henry Clinkscales, Wilton Holliday, Jimmy Martin, Larry Smith, Billy Hughes, and Toppie Haynie; (third row) Joan Session, Dorothy McIlwain, Ann Cox, David King, Dan Malone, William Bowen, Gerald Banister, Billy O'Bryan, Wallace Hicks, Billy Malone, Archie Morgan, Bradley Rice, Ronald Moore, Plumer Craft, Nellie Holliday, Thomas Lynch, and Wesley Hughes; (fourth row) Jean Tollison, Larry Craig, Ruby Martin, Everette Rampey, and A.C. Hannah.

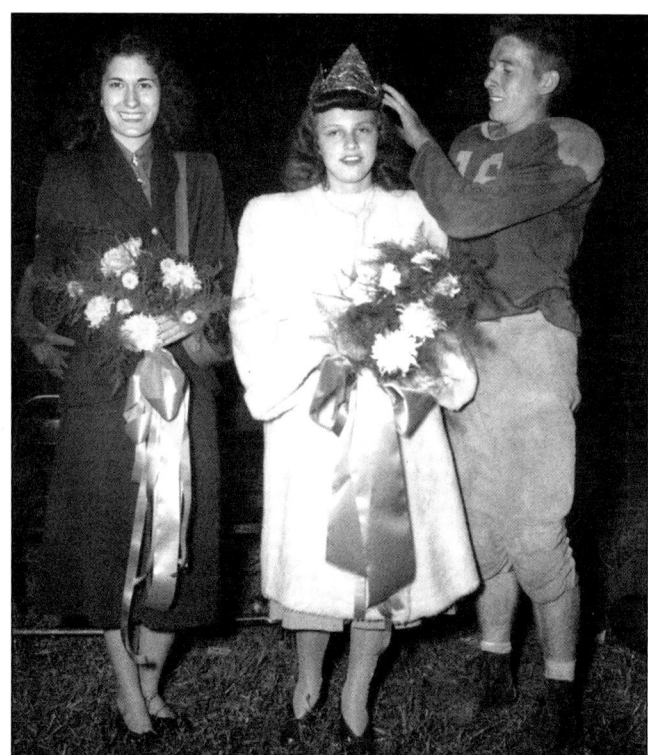

YOUNG LOVE. Outstanding football player and captain of the team Ray Stephens crowns his sweetheart Jane Coward as Homecoming Queen in 1948 as Margaret Turner (King) looks on. Coward was a seventh grader, but since she was Stephens's girlfriend and the football team chose the Homecoming Queen, she was a shoo-in. They have been married 51 years.

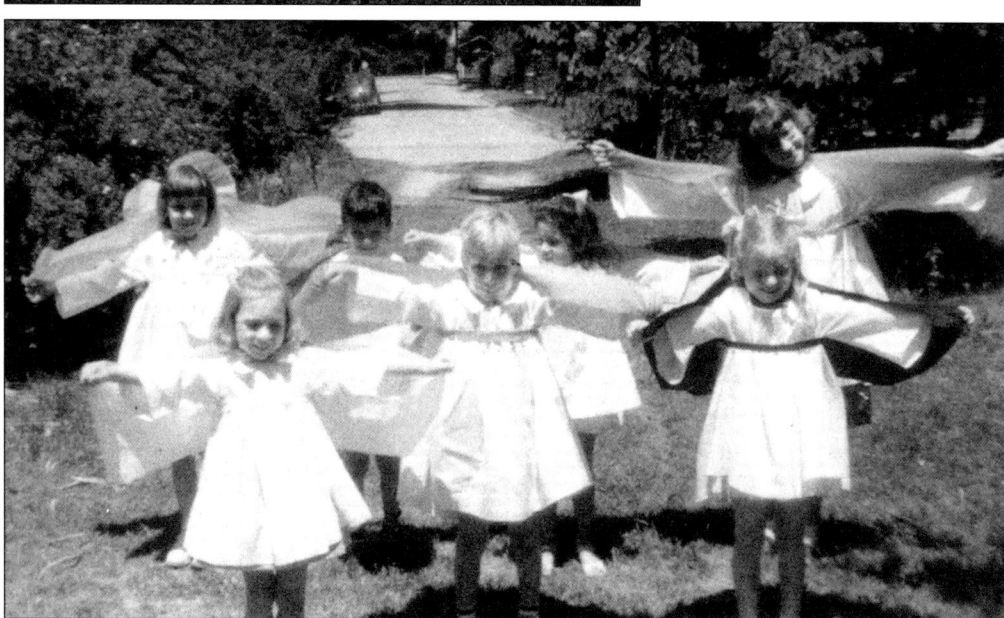

PRETTY BUTTERFLY. Grace Hobson provided young children with a kindergarten experience unparalleled in the 1940s. In a big Victorian on O'Neal Street, the children met each day to enhance their academic and social skills before entering first grade. Here, the kindergartners perform the butterfly dance. They are, from left to right, (front row) Betsy Middleton, Tolly Pruitt, and Mary Walker Roberson; (back row) unidentified, Malloy Evans, Frances Mattison, and Hilda Bruce.

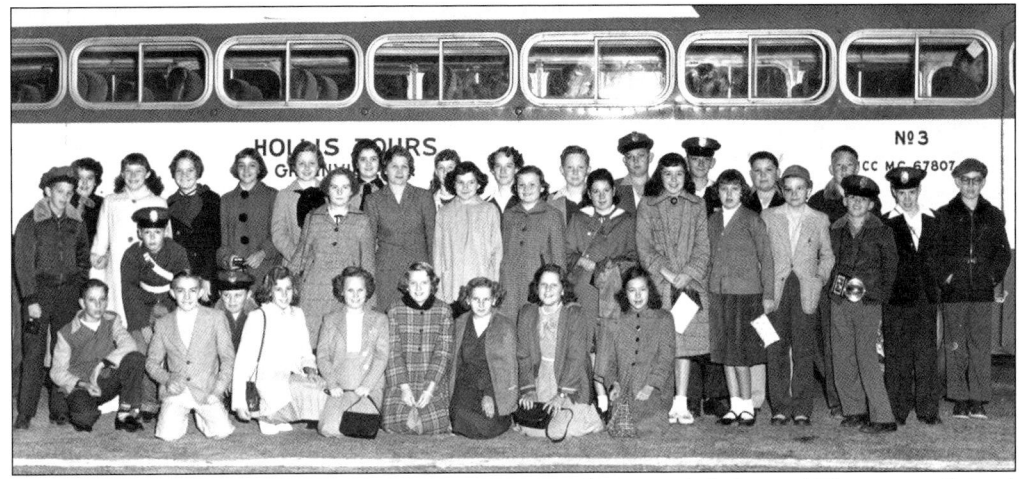

ANNUAL SIXTH GRADE CHARLESTON TRIP, 1954. The group left Central Elementary School at 6:40 a.m. on Wednesday, March 17, and returned on Thursday, March 18, at 9:15 p.m. after a whirlwind tour of South Carolina's historic sites. First they stopped in Columbia, toured the State House and legislative chambers, the Governor's Mansion, and the Confederate Museum. They travelled on to Charleston, where they went to Magnolia Gardens, St. Andrew's Church, Charleston Museum, Hampton Park, and the Battery. After a good night's rest at Folly Beach, they toured St. Michael's Church, St. Philip's Church, Fort Sumter, and Cypress Gardens before returning home. Students include, from left to right, (front row) A. Burris, G. Sharpe, B. Lowe, E. Mattison, M.W. Robinson, C. Hembree, L. Shirley, and G. LeCroy; (middle row) M. Evans, F. Wright, F. Burton, B. Hawkins, R. Drake, B. Fant, V. Grubbs, F. Mattison, G. Lollis, B. Vaughn, C. Hunter, C. Smith, T. Pruitt, and G. Thompson; (back row) S. English, J. Davis, A. Blake, J. Blake, C. Maynard, P. Tollison, J. West, I. Thompson, J. Little, S. Ashley, D. Hamby, L. Carter, and J. Greer.

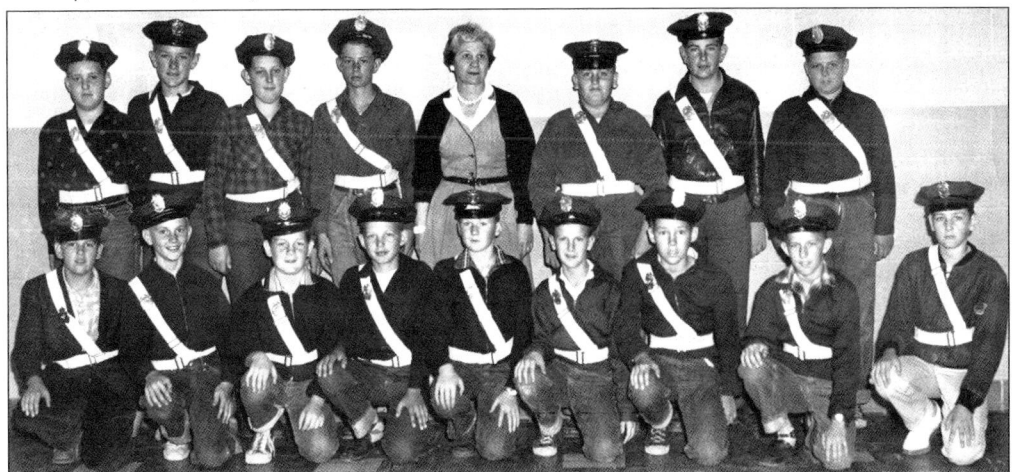

CENTRAL PATROL, 1956. The schoolboy Safety Patrol directed traffic and helped students at crosswalks before and after school. The Belton Police Department provided the uniforms and caps and each year treated the members to a trip to the County Fair. The members are, from left to right, (front row) Steve Shaw, Steve Wilson, Roger King, Jimmy Lollis, Jimmy Strickland, Joe Chandler, Jermal Jackson, Russell Hawkins, and Michael Foxworth; (back row) Mickey Meeks, Charlie Wilson, Freddie Stalcup, Wesley Woods, Ruth Drake (advisor), Wilton Johnson, Johnny Clamp, and David Sarratt.

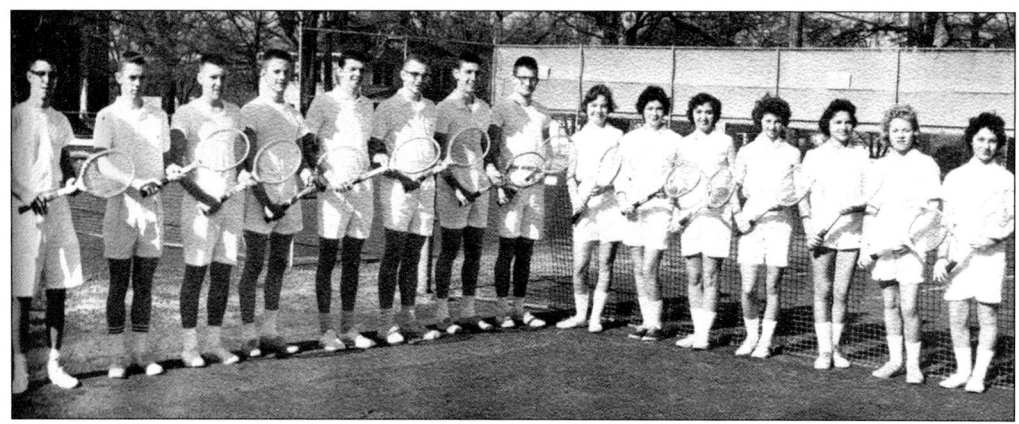

SOUTHERN CHAMPS. The Belton High School tennis teams swept the State High School Tournaments and then went on to take regional victories. The boys' team captured the Southern High School Championship by edging out one of the biggest high schools in the south, Carlton Fuller in Atlanta. Members of the 1960 tennis teams were Palmer Kirkpatrick, William Poore, Mickie Meeks, Steve Wilson, Malloy Evans, James Ledbetter, Skipper Maynard, Julian Kirkpatrick, Ann Blake, Frances Mattison, Julia Blake, Jean Evans, Nancy Haynie, Shirley Holliday, and Ann Cheshire.

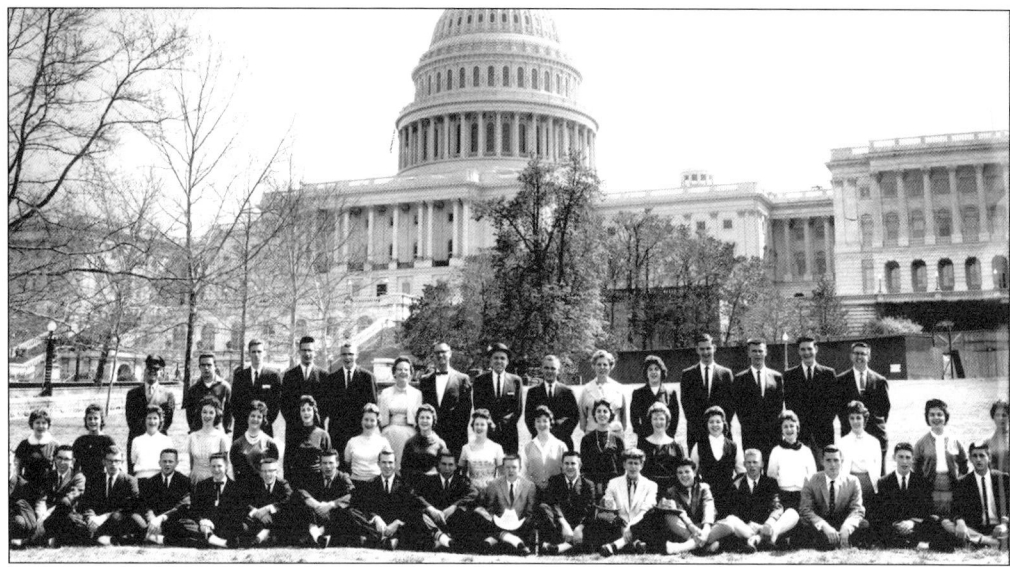

A CAPITOL EXPERIENCE. The Belton High School Class of 1961 went on a three-day trip to Washington, D.C., in April. They toured the White House, Capitol Building, Washington Monument, Arlington Cemetery, Mt. Vernon, Museum of Natural History, and the Smithsonian Institute and took a moonlight cruise on the Potomac River. Students included, from left to right, (front row) W. Poore, T. Lollis, J. Thomas, D. Bryant, E. Martin, R. McClain, J. Workman, D. Heller, R. Poore, R. Smith, J. Elgin, R. Pruitt, unidentified, J. Vaughn, M.Webb, C. Hawkins, and G. Hilliard; (middle row) M. Fant, B. Parker, F. McClennon, S. Vickery, K. Wilson, M. Ledbetter, C. Davis, A. Shirley, S. Allred, S. Knight, N. Martin, D. Moore, F. Houston, H. Blackwell, P. Jordan, M.L. Cunningham, and S. Burton; (back row) bus driver S. Clayton, W. Ledbetter, J. Kirkpatrick, J. Ledbetter, Mrs. Bratcher, Mr. Bratcher (principal), guide, L. Polatty (band director), E. Anderson (teacher), D. McGee, J. Ellison, J. Hill, D. Burgin, and J. Robinson.

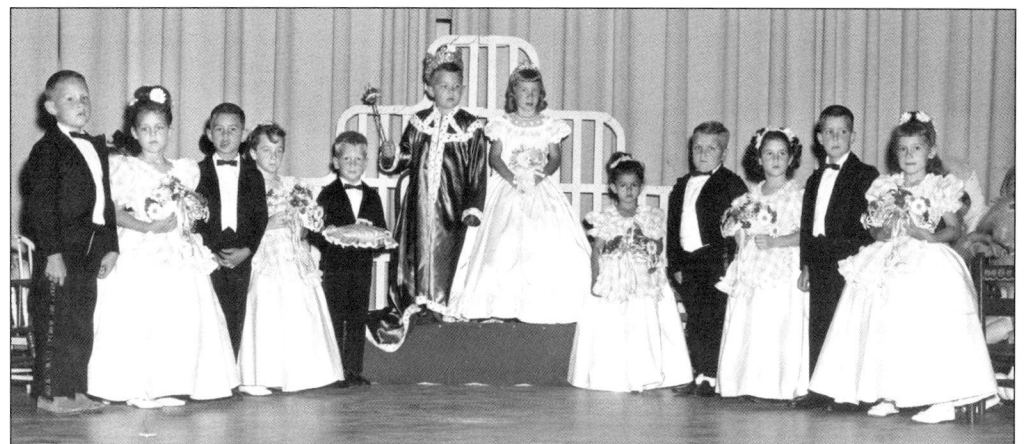

HOW MUCH IS THAT DOGGIE IN THE WINDOW? Alice in Wonderland Kindergarten class of 1965 puts on a pageant entitled "Choose a Pet for the Queen of May." It was the 18th annual recital held at the Belton High School Auditorium. Pictured here, from left to right, are David Haynie, Pam Craft, Wayne Baskin, Royce Rollison, Stanley Gibson, Roe Watkins (King), Connie Mattison (Queen), Angie Rollison, Keith McCoy, Jill Kirpatrick, Robbie Douglas, and Cheryl Pulliam.

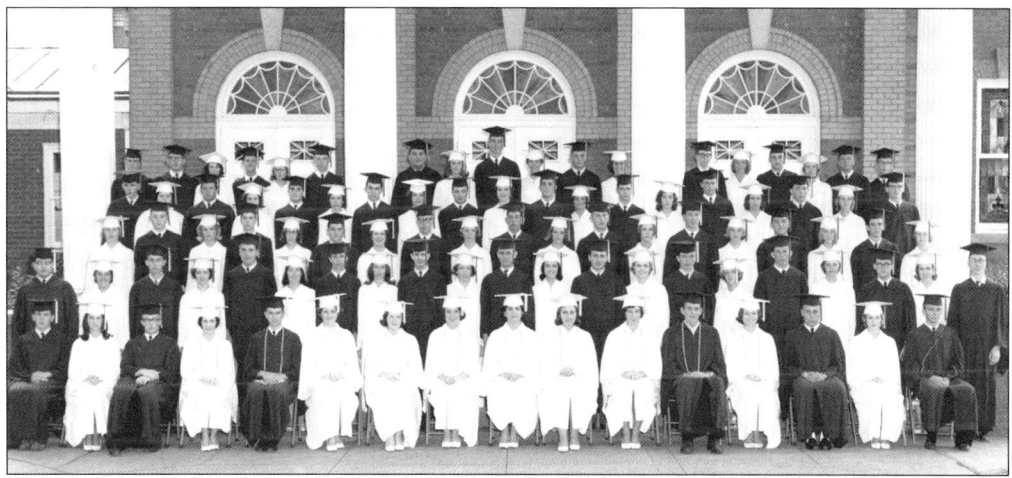

END OF AN ERA. The Class of 1966 was the first class to attend the new Marshall Primary School and the last class to attend Belton High School. This class included, from left to right, the following: (first row) A. Bridges, B. Brooks, E. Shirley, G. Webb, L. Deanhardt, T. Rice, P. Land, M. Clinkscales, B. Cox, J.A. Horton, C. Garrett, G. McGee, D. Wilson, M. Whitt, A. Milford, and J. Autry; (second row) R. Davis, P. Mitchell, D. Horton, J. Lowe, B. Ferguson, M. Sheriff, S. Hunter, A. Jordan, H. Hopper, J. Ladd, T. Bratton, N. McKinley, R. Holliday, P. Beeks, B. Baldwin, C. Madden, D. Riddle, S. Vickery, D. McKee, B. Smith, and G. Smith; (third row) T.A. Hayes, P. Burgess, B.L. Timms, R. Cox, C. Pruitt, L. Hawkins, P. Bannister, M. Pruitt, D. Mills, R. Chandler, D. Spearman, L. Carmen, J.M. Gibson, T. Jordan, F. C. McCoy, D. Hawkins, M. Marshall, J. Arflin, and C. Bryant; (fourth row) J. McDowell, B. Gambrell, C. Ellison, D.e Holtzclaw, C. Eberhardt, J. Finley, R. Strickland, M. Little, M. Davis, B. Mize, R. Henderson, S. Snipes, I. Parnell, V. Rudd, W. Lowe, G. Trotter, K. Anderson, B. King, and B. Key; (fifth row) M. Teague, M. Hanley, G.B. Woodson, A. Garrett, K. Riley, B. Hammond, J. Stoner, S. Bryant, P. Hendrix, S. Strickland, M. Patterson, P. Rice, D. Timms, M.J. Smith, T. Lawson, R. Hawkins, L. Jordan, and R. McCoy.

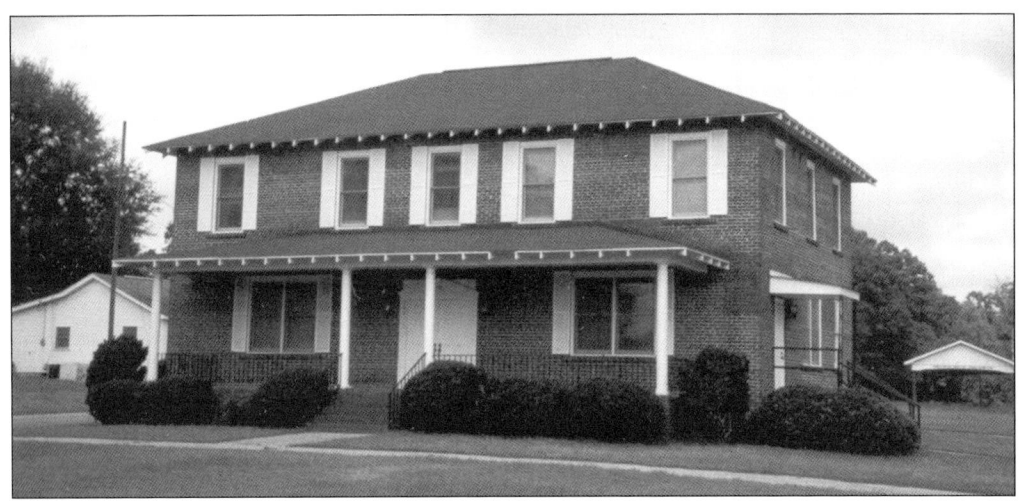

UNION HIGH SCHOOL, 1917–1937. This building served as classroom space and dormitory for the black Union High School. Students from Anderson, Abbeville, and Greenville Counties attended the school for a small tuition, but one that most families during that time had little extra funding for. Even food products such as potatoes and corn meal were taken as payment on tuition. Courses in English, general math and algebra, zoology, botany, and health issues were offered. The school was originally comprised of five buildings, but a fire in the mid-1930s destroyed all but the brick structure shown here. The school could not recover from the loss and closed in 1937. Refurbished and renovated in 1991, the building is now the headquarters of the Rocky River Baptist Association.

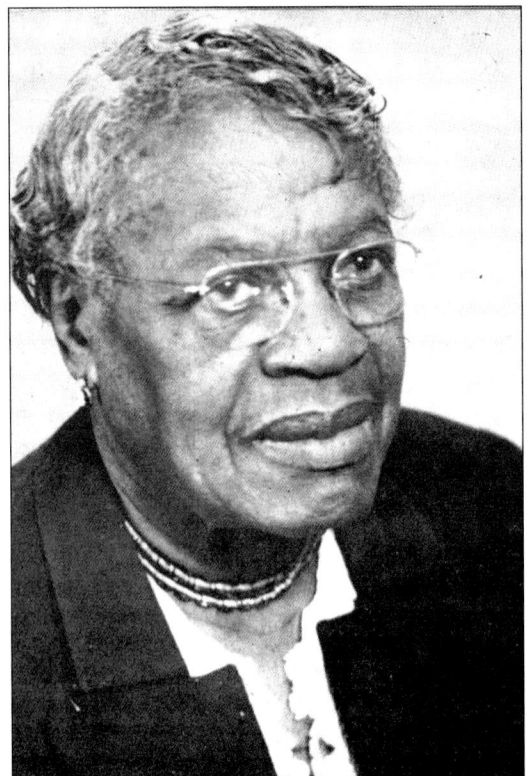

THE POWER TO EFFECT CHANGES. Corrie Watkins, a teacher at Union High School and later Anderson County schools, influenced countless young African Americans during her long career as an educator. She also began the Woman's Missionary Union of the Rocky River Baptist Association and served as its president for a half-century.

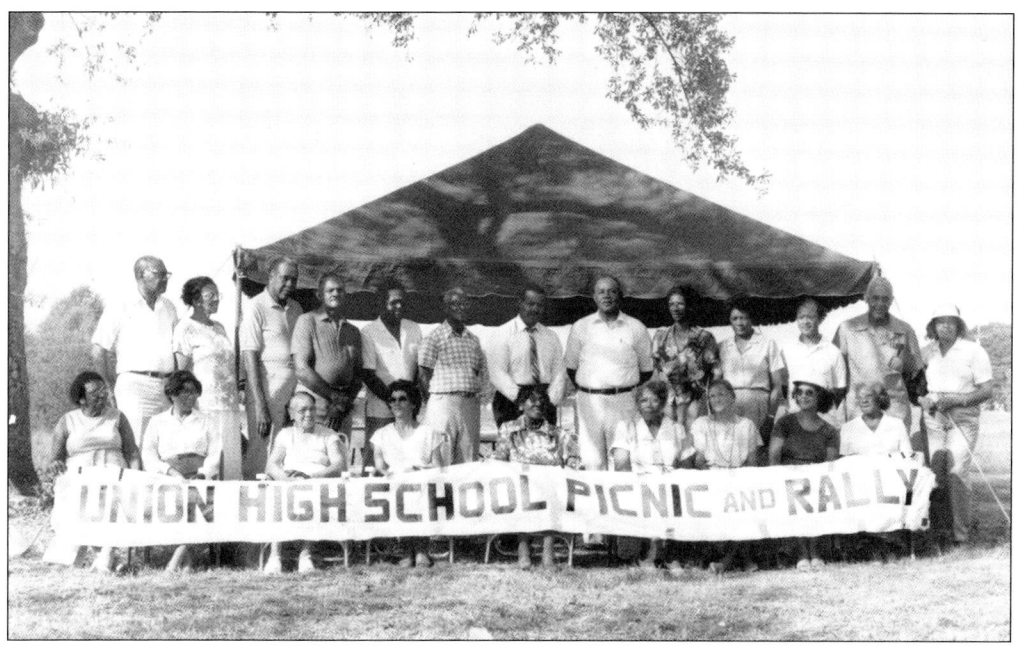

SUPPORTERS GATHER TO DEDICATE RENOVATED BUILDING. In 1991, alumni and friends of Union High School met for a picnic and dedication ceremony marking the renovation of the building and its new use as home of the Rocky River Baptist Association. Attendees included, from left to right, (front row) Annie Bell Rice, Margie Boseman, Hallie Green, Ruth Cunningham, Polly Yeargin, unidentified, Malona Williams Rice, Ida Johnson, and Bertie Mae Mattison; (back row) William Shaw, Ida Mae Shaw, Charles Clement, Cleo Clement, Herman Keith, unidentified, Wendell Cox, Furman Martin, unidentified, Ruth Lindsay, Hattie Green Ligon, Joseph Clement, and Malley Clinkscales Hatten.

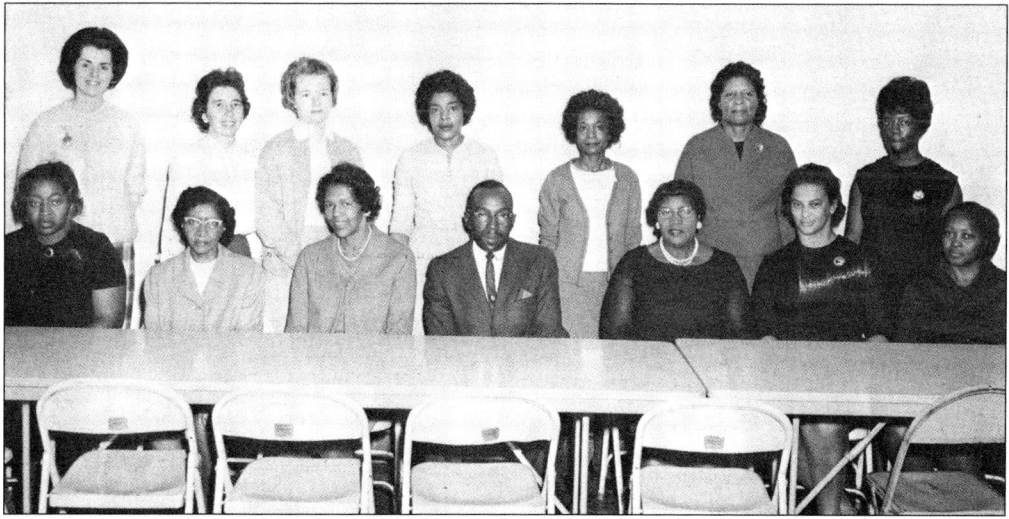

FACULTY, 1968. Geer Rosenwald Elementary School serviced the black community until integration in the fall of 1968. Shown here are, from left to right, (front row) Helen Aiken, Margie Boseman, Ida Shaw, Luther Johnson (principal), Synola Robinson, Hattie Robinson, and Venezuela Billups; (back row) Lynn Finley, Martha Bagby, Louise Clinkscales, Ruth Thompson, Costina Bobo, Sallie Sherard, and Annie Stewart.

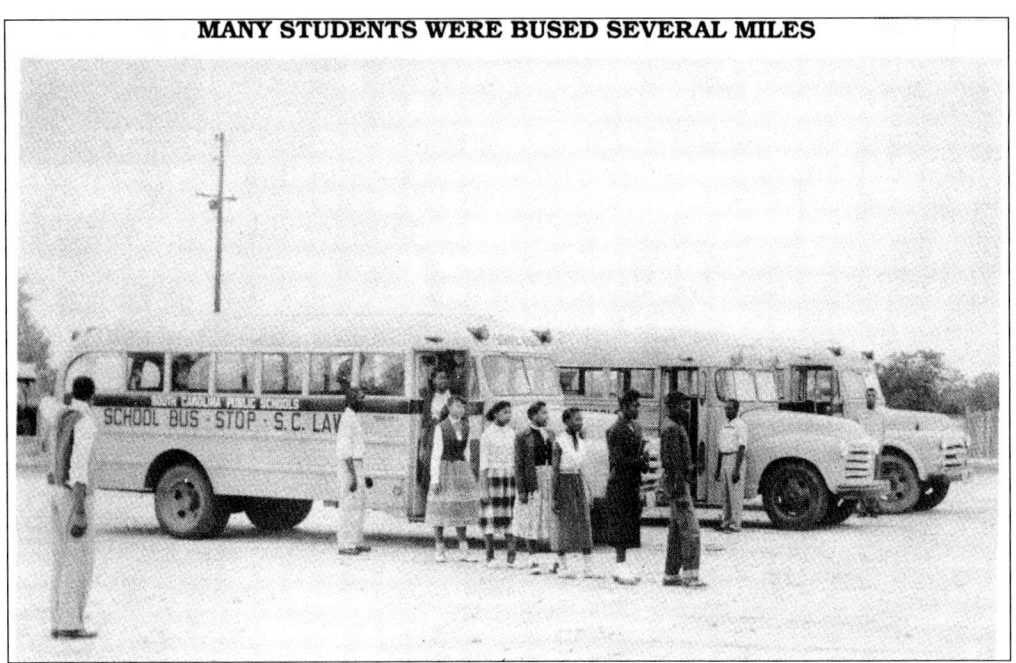

TRAVELING MANY MILES EACH DAY. To attend Geer-Gantt High School, the present home of Belton Middle School, teens were bussed from all over the area in order to receive an adequate education. Students were given the opportunity to attend the newly opened Belton-Honea Path High School for the 1967–1968 school year or remain at the school one more year. The school was closed in 1968 when the entire district was integrated.

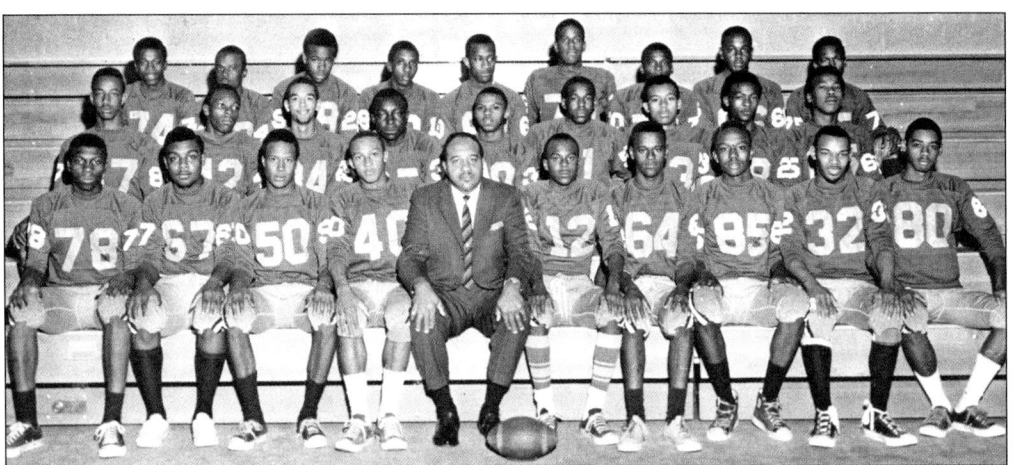

A LAST HURRAH. Known for its powerhouse football teams, the 1968 team went all the way to the state championships and captured the coveted trophy. Players are, from left to right, (front row) Albert Henry, Donnie Harper, Cornelius Bolden, Jimmy Ellis, Matthew Crayton (coach), Jackie Clement, George Wilkerson, Johnny Davis, David Dooley, and Henry Leverette; (middle row) Jerry Davis, James Donald, Larry Leverette, Harold Geer, Charles Brenson, David Brenson, Clinton Anderson, Henry Latimer, and Joe Groves; (back row) James Davis, J. Walter Agnew, Charles Latimer, Richard Leverette, Mason Gordon, Andrew White, Eddie Henry, Willie Peterson, and John Edwards.

Five
ARTS, ENTERTAINMENT, AND CIVIC ORGANIZATIONS

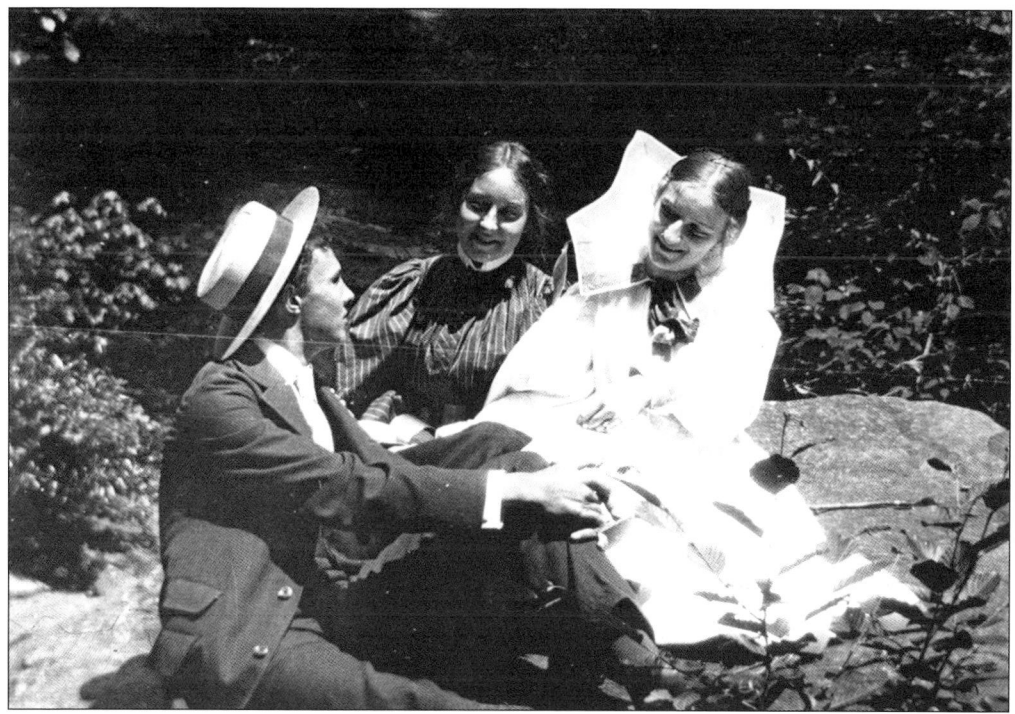

OLD MAN RIVER. The Saluda River basin provides many recreational opportunities, such as fishing, camping, hiking, and picnicking. In 1896, these three young people—W.C. Latimer, Jesse Dean, and Effie Blake—enjoy a relaxing Sunday excursion.

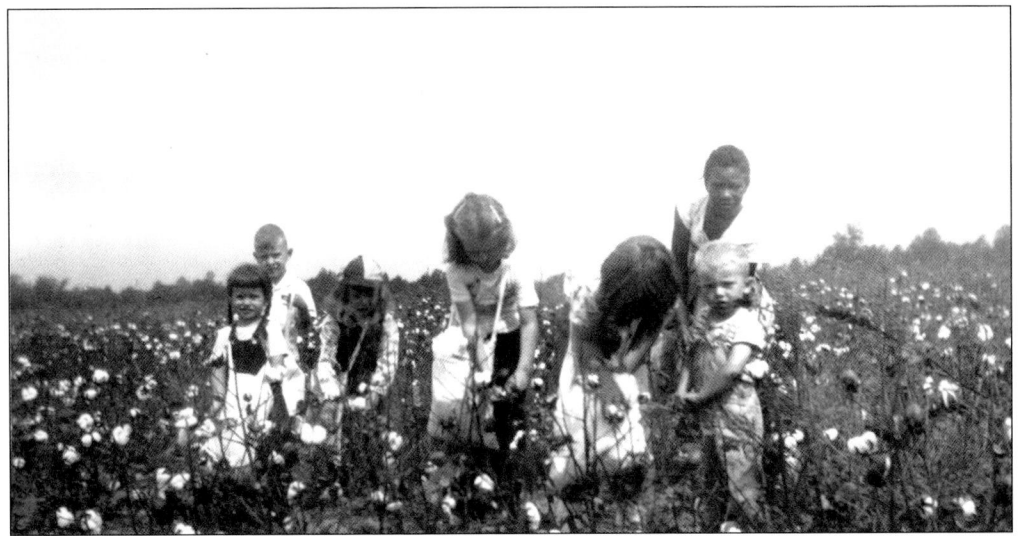

A COTTON PICKIN' GOOD TIME. In 1947, Jim Horton had an unusual birthday party: a cotton picking party. Each child was given a sack and sent to the fields under the tutelage of the unidentified black girl. After filling their sacks, the children were given a payout for their labors by Big Jim. Pictured here, from left to right, are Caroline Grubbs, Skipper Maynard, Margaret Clayton, Vicki Grubbs, Cary Maynard, unidentified, and Jim Horton.

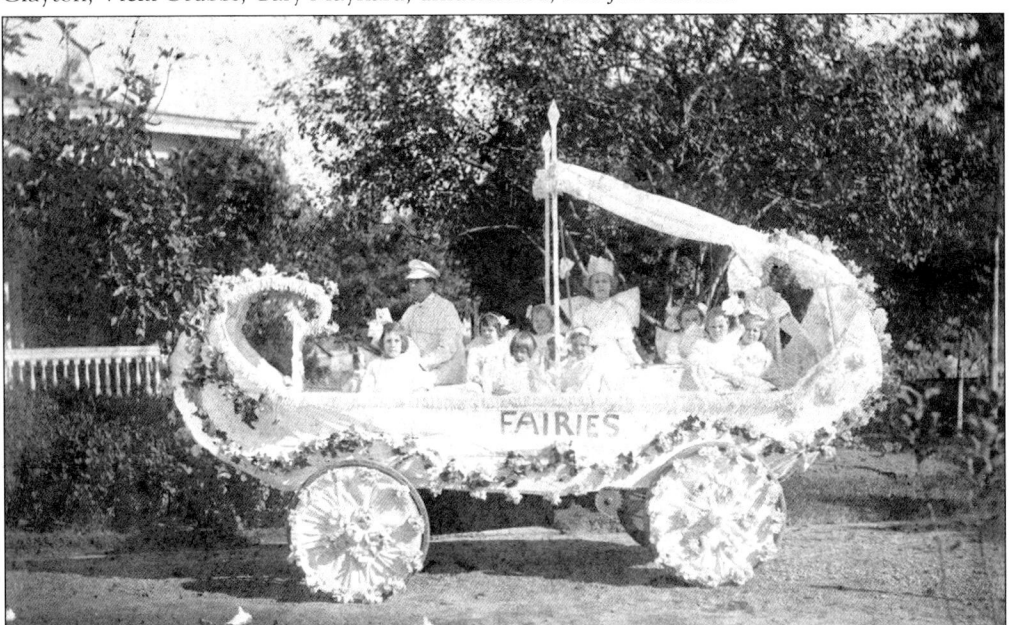

THE QUEEN OF THE FAIRIES, 1911. Belton held a community fair from 1909 to 1927 and a fair for black residents during the 1930s. Donated merchandise and cash prizes were awarded for the fastest horse, the prettiest crocheted item, the biggest gourd, the fanciest chicken, and the best apple streudel, among other items on display. The fair was held during the third Wednesday in October, and thousands of people gathered to enjoy the festivities and carnival. A parade and pageant preceded the judging. Also, the big football game between the Belton Warriors and the Honea Path Stingers always created quite a furor. Here, the Fairy Queen and her court await the beginning of the parade in front of the Stringer House on River Street.

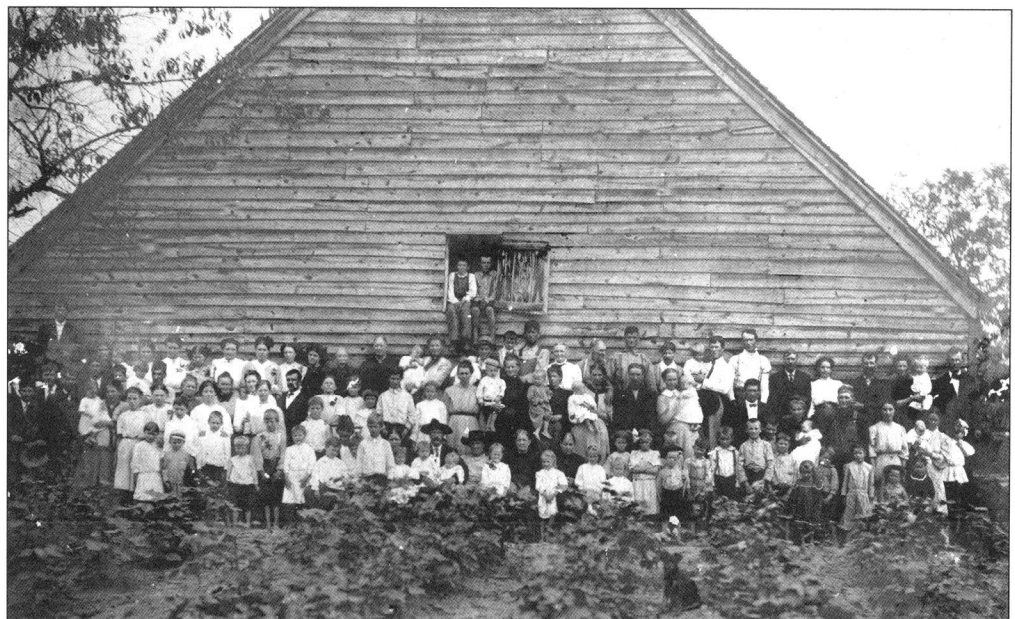

RAISING THE ROOF. A pleasant and productive pastime during the late 19th century was the annual barn-raising. A time for socializing, eating, and meeting new people, barn raisings were sometimes considered the highlight of a community's year. Here, the entire Long Branch community gathers to erect a barn for one of their neighbors.

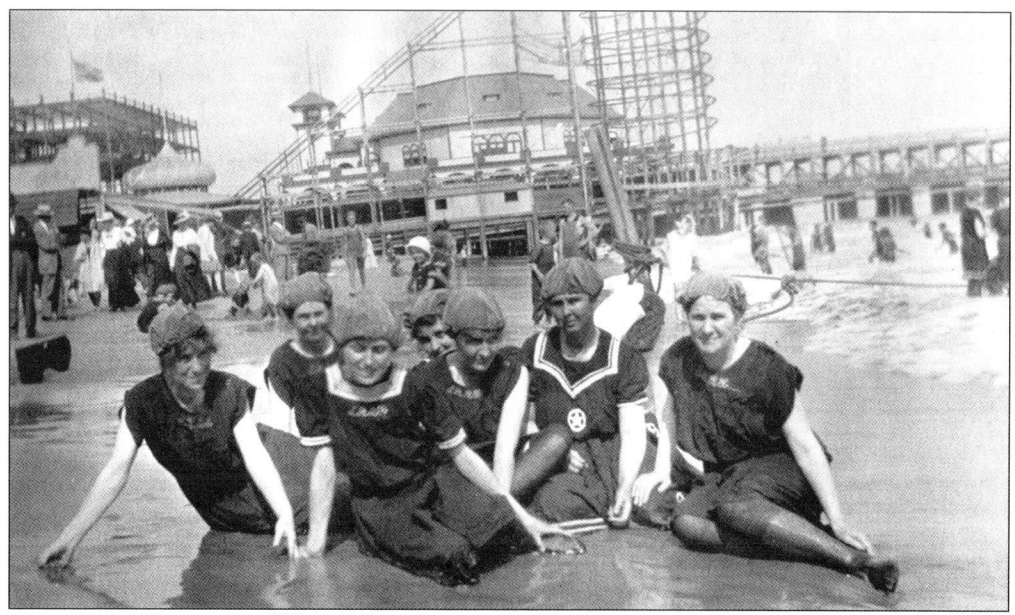

BATHING BEAUTIES. Leda Poore was a great traveler, spending two summers on tour in Europe and meeting her friends from college out West and in New York. She kept diaries of her trips; they can be found in the Belton Area Museum. Here, Poore (center) and six of her Greenville Female College buddies bask in the sun and pleasant waters of the Great Salt Lake in 1915.

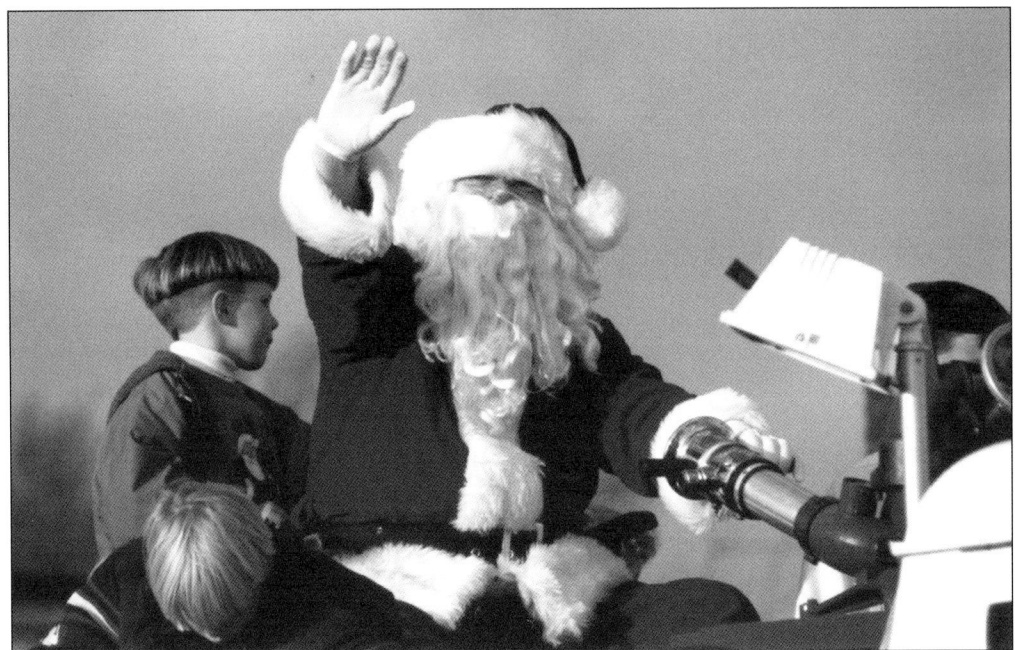

SANTA CLAUS (ALSO KNOWN AS CHARLES BERRY) IS COMING TO TOWN. Santa leaves his reindeer at the North Pole and hitches a ride on the Belton Fire Truck. The Belton Parade has been held for over 50 years, usually on the Sunday after Thanksgiving, and heralds the advent of the Christmas season. Children ride on decorated bicycles, church floats proclaim the birth of Jesus, and the local beauties are presented as bands entertain the crowds.

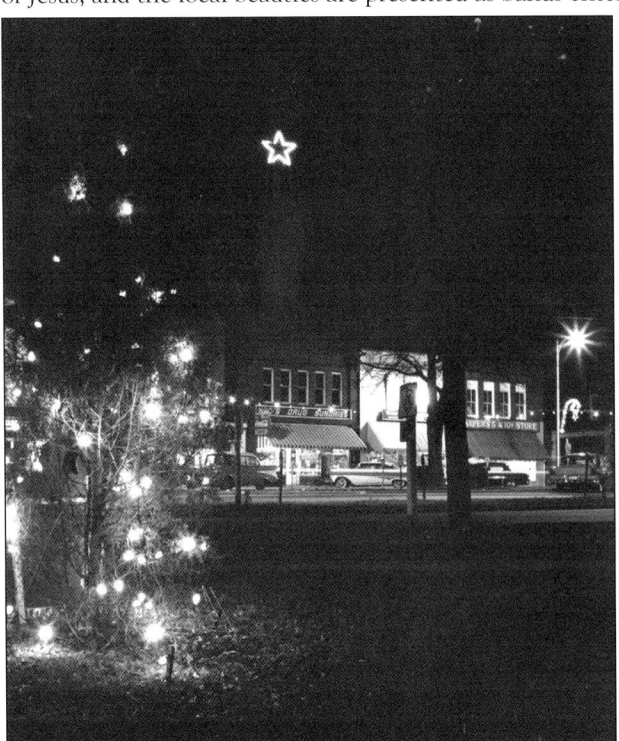

STAR LIGHT, STAR BRIGHT. The star shines brightly over the Belton Square in this 1961 Christmas scene of downtown. Originally a lighted Santa Claus was placed atop the Standpipe in 1938 and 1939, but in 1940 the star was lit and became a Christmas tradition. However, during the decades of the 1950s and 1960s, the star was not turned on, and weather damage frayed the electrical cables, making it unsafe. After renovations were made to the Standpipe, the star shone brightly again. Mac's Drug Store, Western Auto, and Harper's 5 & 10 are seen in the background.

ANOTHER DALE EVANS. Just like the goat carts of the 1930s, traveling photographers arrived in a neighborhood to document the cute children who were excited to hop on the pony. Here, Janice Ruth (Edwards), smiles for the camera in 1950. She owns and operates Classic Cuts.

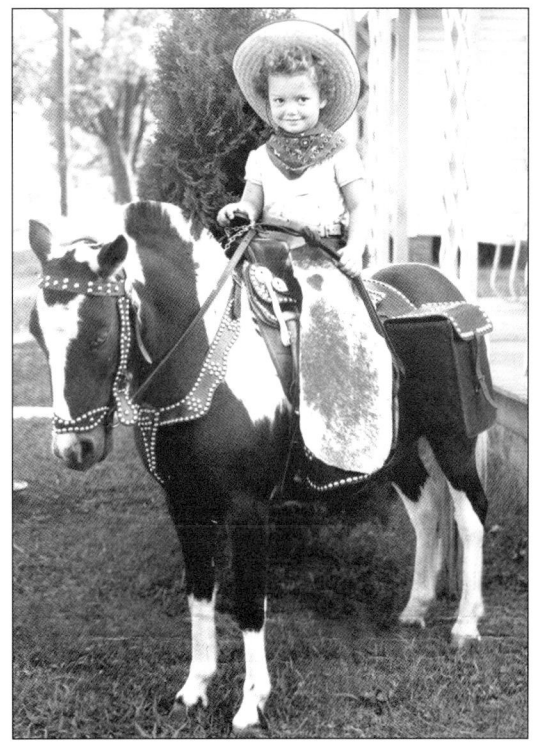

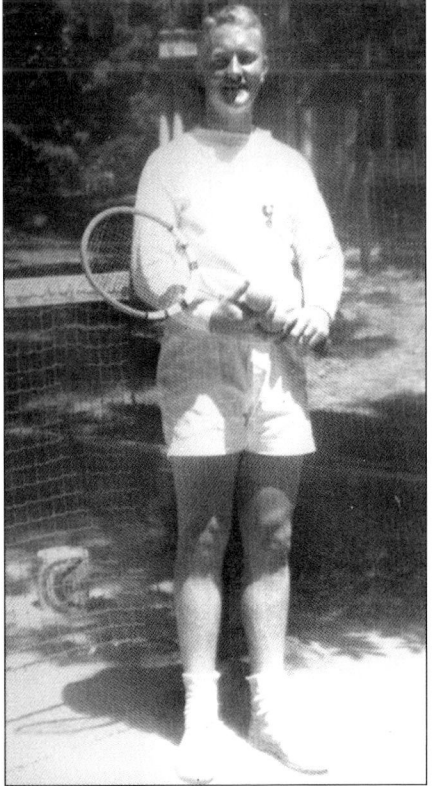

MOST RESPONSIBLE FOR BELTON AS THE TENNIS CAPITAL OF SOUTH CAROLINA. E.B. "Fluffy" Rice, shown here as a high school tennis champion, is known not only for his skill on the court, but also for his leadership and support of local and state tennis programs and tournaments. At six years of age, he began playing tennis on the court behind his home. Rice helped to form the Belton Tennis Club in 1954. During his tenure as president of that organization, he helped raise $10,000 to convert the town courts to rubico and personally financed a third court. "It was not uncommon in the 1950s," said a junior tennis player, "to find businessmen like Fluffy Rice out on the court during the middle of the day, giving tips and pointers to us teenagers, and challenging us to a game." In 1955, Rice helped organize the first Piedmont Championships, which became the Palmetto Championships two years later, and assisted with the tournaments in some capacity until his death. In 1991, he spearheaded a project to build two more courts and a tennis clubhouse. Raising over $180,000, the facility was dedicated in June 1992, with Rice having the honor of receiving the first serve on the new courts. He was inducted into the South Carolina Tennis Hall of Fame, located in the historic Depot.

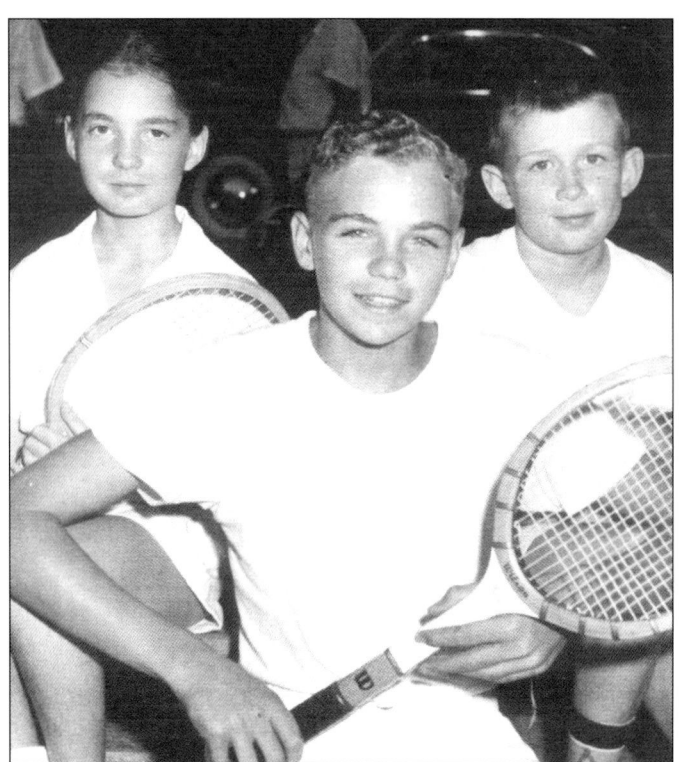

THREE WINNERS. The Wachovia/Palmetto Junior Tennis Championships originated in the Piedmont Championships, begun in 1955. Here, James Ledbetter (center), poses as the winner of the 13 and under division. Flanking him on the left is Ann Cheshire and on the right is David Wilkins. They were the youngest players in the tournament. Although not a native of Belton, David's grandmother lived here, so he spent most of his summers on the courts. He now serves as the speaker of the South Carolina House of Representatives. Today, the tournament is the official South Carolina junior qualifying tournament for 18 and under players.

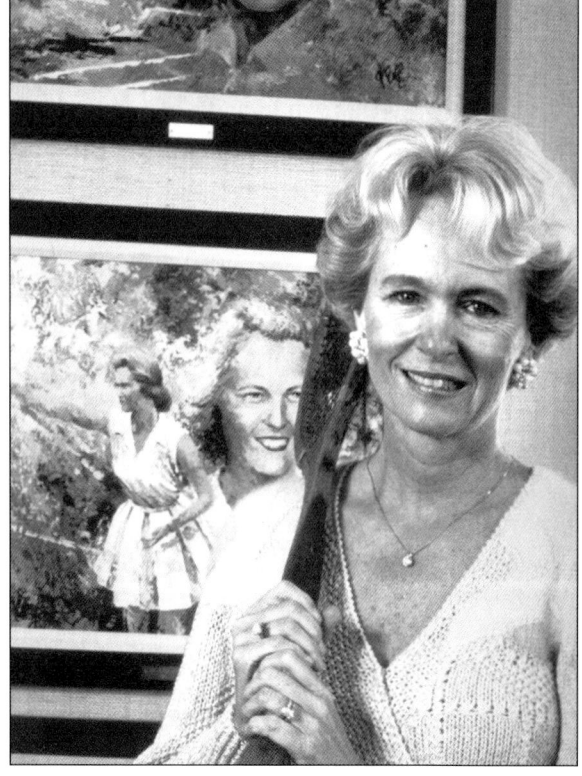

A TENNIS AFICIONADO. Considered the most impressive player ever to have come out of Belton, Janie Haynie Hentz won her first state girls' high school championship as a seventh grader. She played No. 1 on the Southern Junior Wrightman Cup Team and captained that team for two years. She won over 20 championships during her playing career, including the Palmetto Championships, the North Carolina Open, and the Southern Championships. She eventually attained a No. 8 ranking in the nation. She is an inductee to the South Carolina Tennis Hall of Fame.

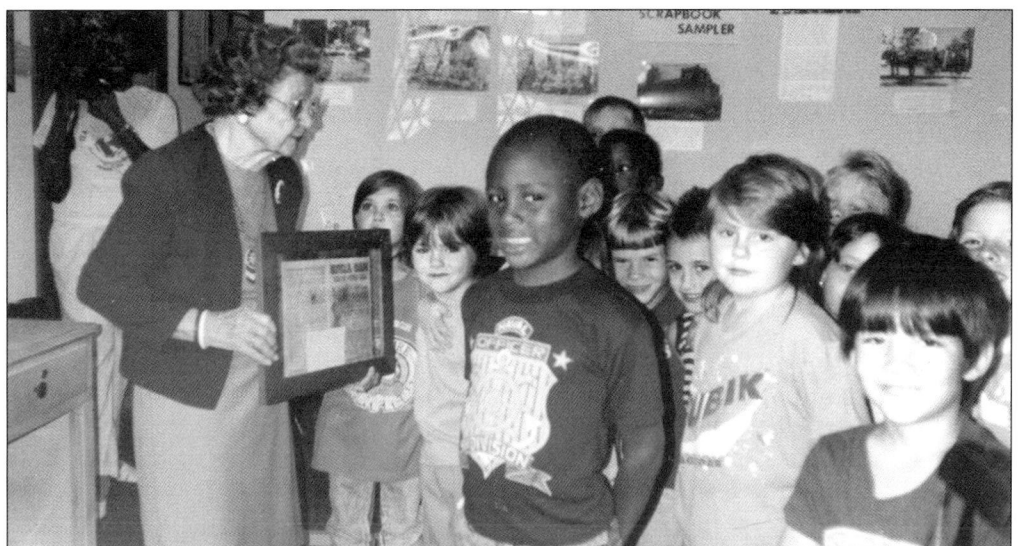

AN ARTIFACT AND A STORY. A schoolteacher for over 30 years, Ruth Drake was passionate about sharing history with children. After helping to establish the museum, first in the basement of the library, then in the city hall, and next in the renovated Depot, Drake began giving personal tours to school children who visited the museum.

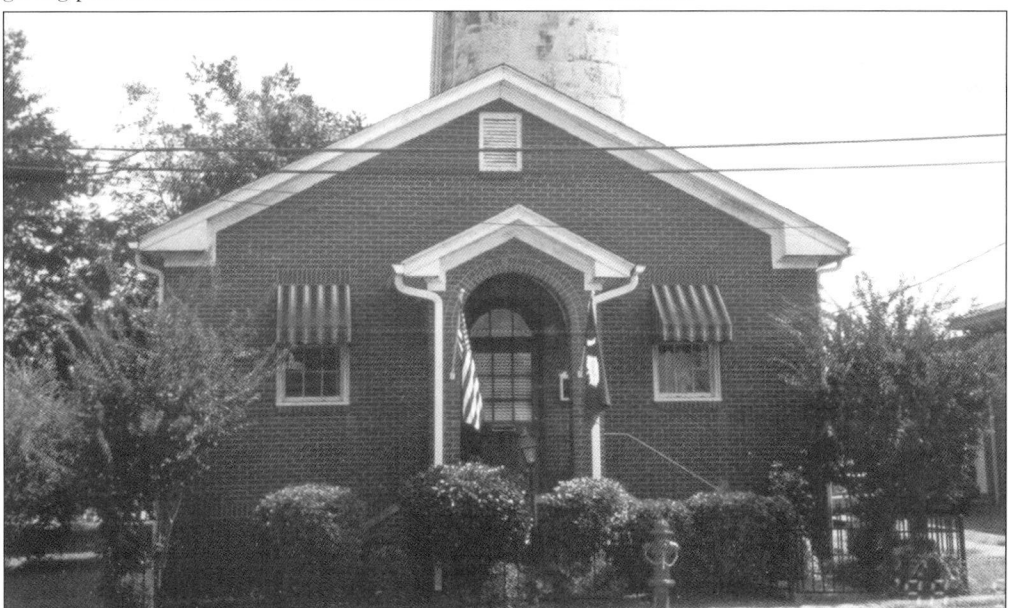

A FACILITY OF CIVIC PRIDE. A very important project of the Women's Civic League was to provide a public library for the citizens of the town. In 1914, under the leadership of Jessie Lewis, the Civic League agreed to give $50 a year to fund a library. W.K. Stringer offered a room in his store, rent-free, and 352 volumes helped to open the Belton Library. Membership fee was $1 per year, and members of the League volunteered their services when the library was open on Thursdays and Saturdays. In 1938, this facility was built to house the library. In 1947, a city tax was levied to support the library and its collection. It has since become part of the Anderson County Library System with a new $1.2 million facility with room for 27,000 volumes being constructed to replace the cramped space in the Depot.

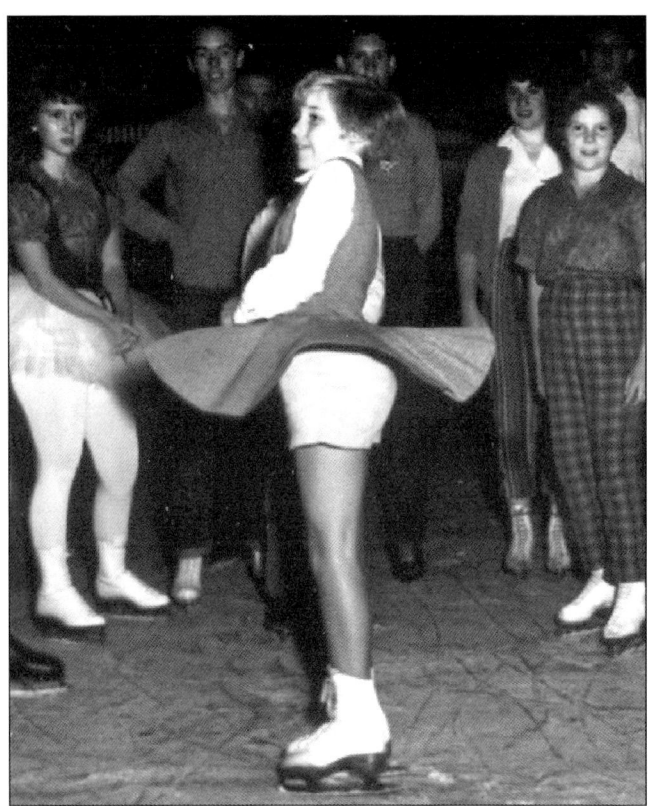

FIGURE EIGHTS AT COX'S SKATING RINK. Originally there was a Cox Swimming Lake off Calhoun Road, which operated from about 1921 to 1937. Built by J.M. Cox, the manmade lake was equipped with dressing rooms, canteen, and dancing pavilion. Bathing suits were rented. In 1959, Charles M. Cox built and operated a swimming lake in the Cheddar Community. His lake measured 100 feet across and ranged from a depth of one foot to 10 feet. Picnic facilities, snack bar, a grassy area for sunbathing, and a small dancing area were provided. In 1962, Cox opened an ice-skating facility, which operated in the fall and winter. Jim Durham was the instructor, and skates could be rented. Here, Shirley Cox (Grant) shows off her twirls in 1963.

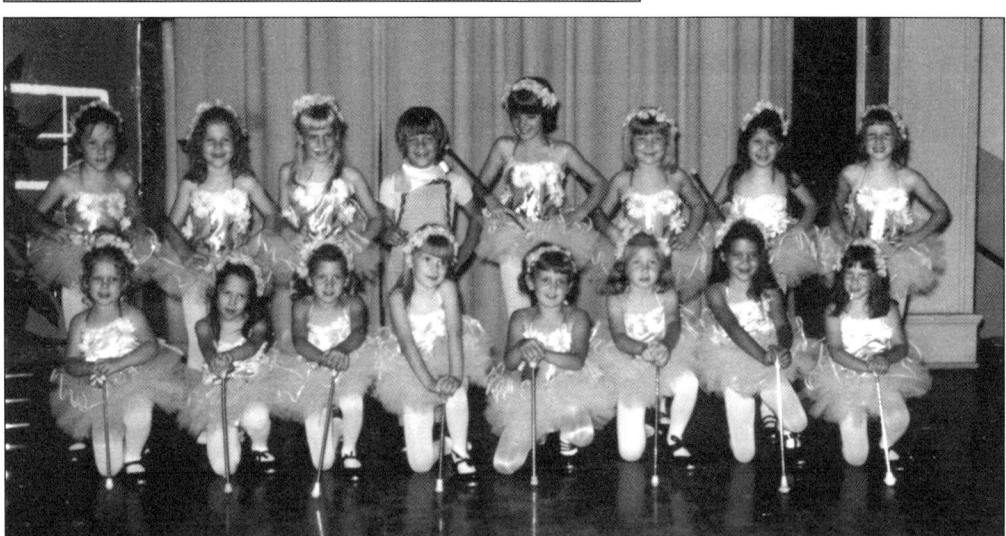

"LAVENDER AND LACE." This recital exhibited the talents of June Horton's dance classes and was held on May 26, 1972, at the Belton Elementary School Auditorium. From September to May, the class met every Friday afternoon for one hour. Tap, baton, and ballet for students up to the third grade were offered. Performers included, from left to right, (front row) Julianna Bolton, Malura Mulligan, Kim Pruitt, Teresa Bratton, Dixie Pruitt, Julie King, Melissa Henderson, and Karen Kay; (back row) Jana Holliday, Melissa Boatwright, Eva Smith, Anthony McAlister, Martha Hart, Allison Hunter, Franny Russell, and Ginny Kay.

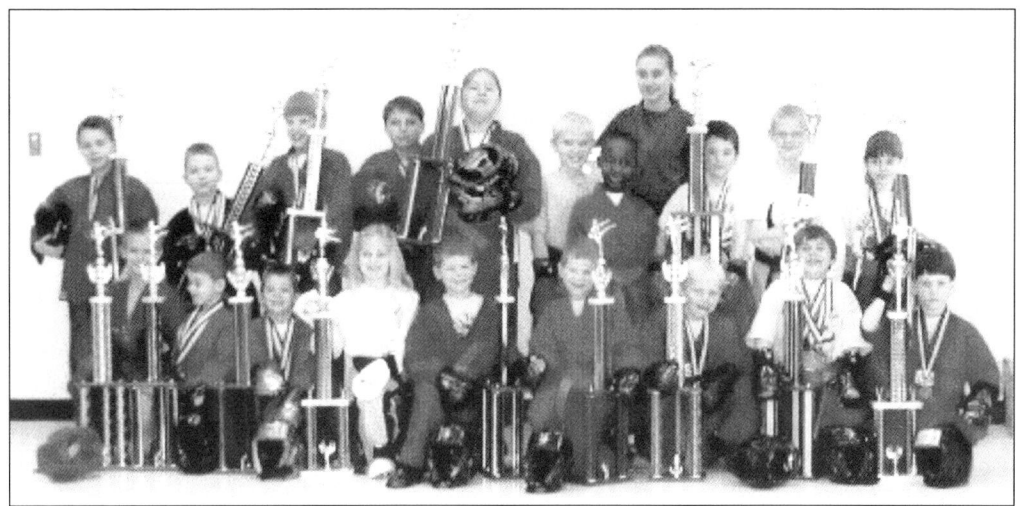

DEVELOPING DISCIPLINE. Marty Knight, two-time world karate champion, provides instruction in karate and the martial arts two days a week during the school year at Belton Elementary School gym. His students succeed consistently in competitions. Here, trophy winners pose for a photograph, from left to right: (front row) Chip Hunter, Seth Oglesby, Parker Peeples, Amber McCurry, Garrett McClellan, Grayson McClellan, Zachary Edwards, Aaron Tucker, and Tyler Phillips; (back row) Jeffrey Bishop, Dylan Southerland, Curtis Easton, Storm Avery, Emily Loudermilk, Allen McGee, August Davis, Alexandria Soto, Brooks DeVore, J.D. McCurry, and Miranda Cooley.

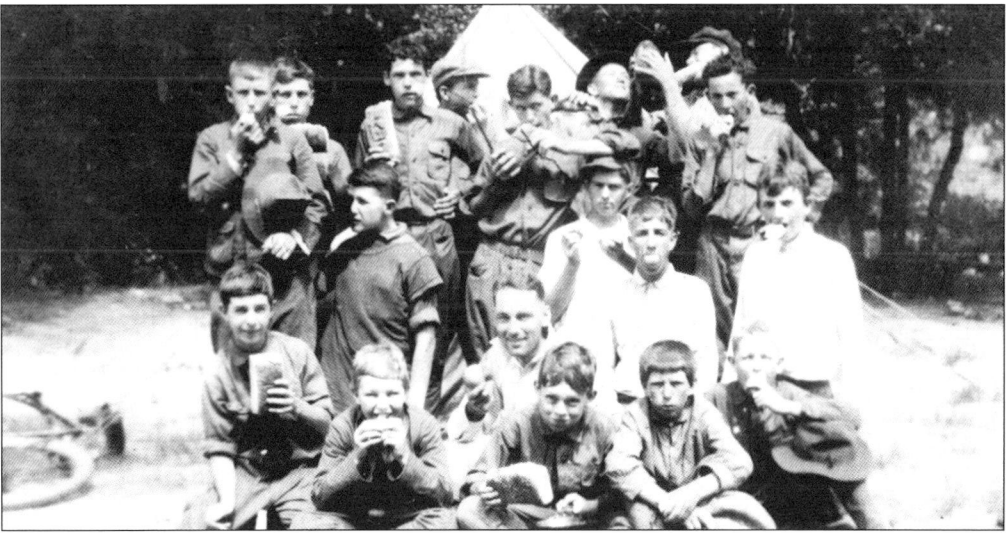

EARNING BADGES, 1916. Traveling in mule-drawn wagons to the campsite, the year-old Boy Scout Troop enjoys a camping trip at Erwin's Mill. Members included Luther Cox, Clarence Cox, Jim Bowen, Calvin Shaw, Kay Griffin, Lee Major, Herbert Cox, Louis Seel (Scout Master), James Clement, Joe Harris, Joe Grubbs, Charlie Cox, and Joe King. The troop was organized in 1915 by Blair Rice and Lewis Cox and originally met in the Masonic Lodge above the Farmer's Bank. Later, a house at 304 Brown Avenue was supplied for their use and still later a log cabin was built for the troop's meeting place. Throughout their history, Belton's Boy Scout Troops have been disbanded and reorganized at least five times into Troops #31, # 32, #33, #34, #187, and #310. Cub Scout Troops were begun in 1950.

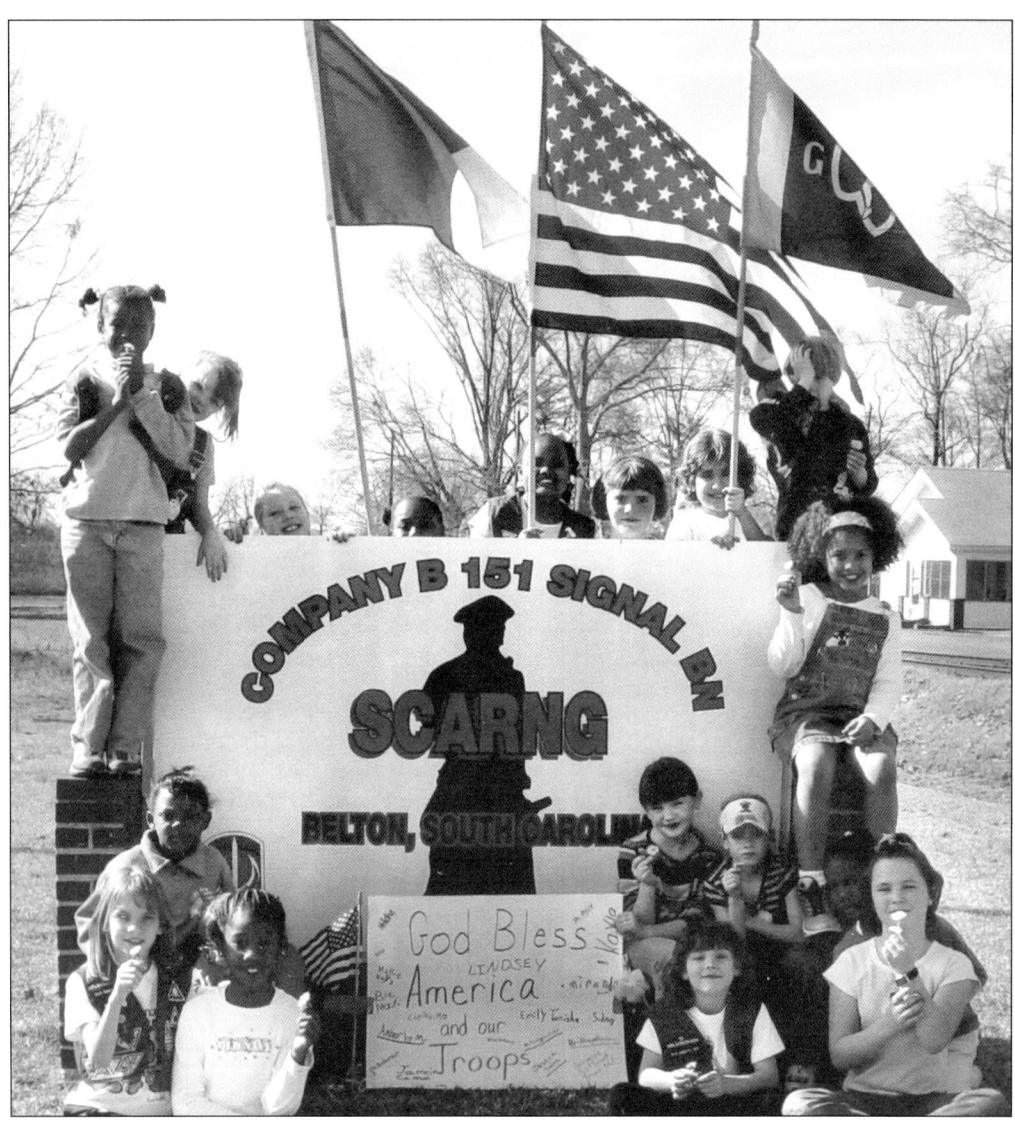

GOD BLESS AMERICA AND OUR TROOPS. The Brownie Troop #561 of Marshall Primary School salutes the 151st Signal Battalion after they were deployed to Iraq in the spring of 2003. The young girls marched from the school to the armory carrying their flags and posters. News Channel 4 followed the girls and interviewed a few for that night's broadcast. Pictured here, from left to right, are Sidney Dean, Lindsey Clem, Jameika Cannon, Tanisha Jones, Miranda Keys, Haley Keys, Holisha Coleman, Kelsey Latimer, Brittany Trevino, unidentified, Emily Eaton, Amberly Matthews, Jessica Smith, Kayla Dean, Hannah Waters, Brittany Shiflett, and Miranda Gray. Not pictured is Christina Burgan. The troop leader is Linda Anderson.

SWEET ADELAIDE, 1959. Variety shows called minstrels were popular during the 1940s and 1950s. A comedian, dancers, and even barbershop quartets would perform for the community. Here, Bill Ellett, Gaston Poore, Charles Davenport, and Glenn Coward break out into a melody, much to the enjoyment of the audience at Belton High School Auditorium.

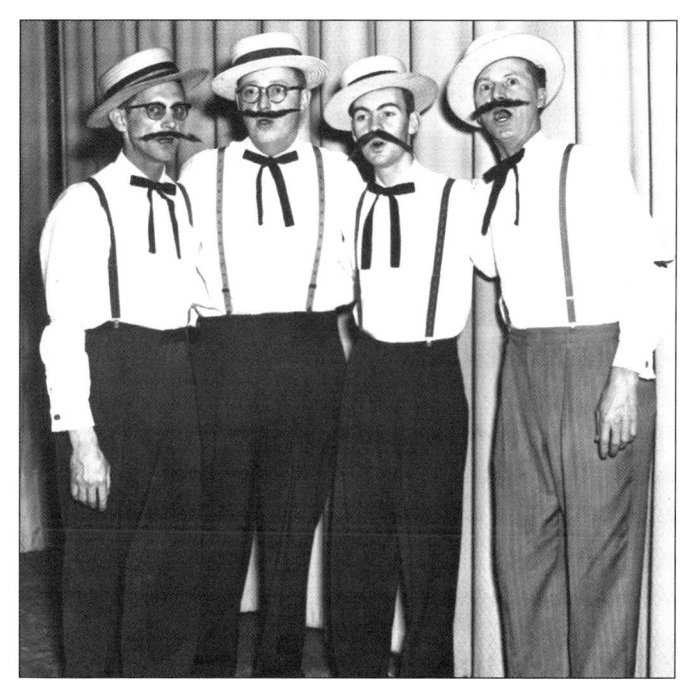

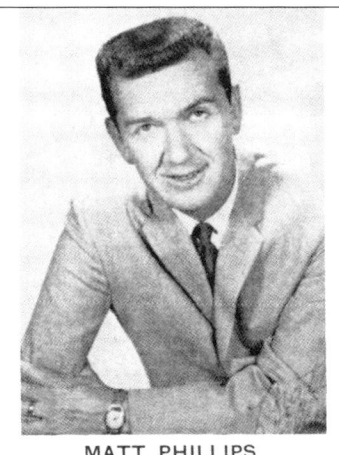
MATT PHILLIPS
NEWS
MUSIC
SPORTS

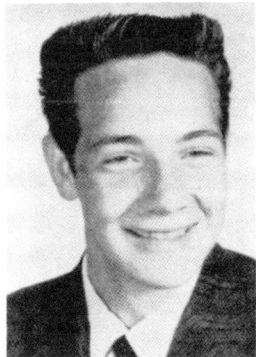
DOUG BURGIN

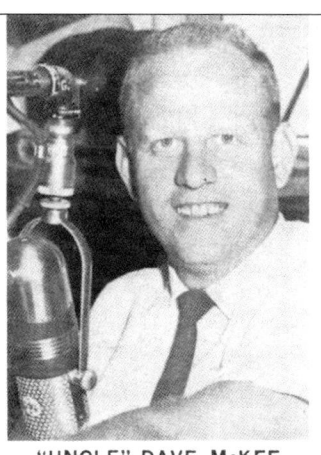
"UNCLE" DAVE McKEE
NEWS
MUSIC
SPORTS

WHPB 1390 KC BELTON, S. C.

ANDERSON COUNTY'S MOST POPULAR RADIO VOICE

THIS IS WHPB. WELCOME, FOLKS. WHPB, the official radio station of Honea Path and Belton on AM 1390, began in 1945. Known for reporting the top news stories, playing music, and sponsoring talk shows featuring area personalities, the station reached out to the community over the airwaves. During the 1940s, Leland Cox had a program called "Radio Recess" in which he made civic announcements and conducted special interviews. Matt Phillips of WRIX fame worked at the radio station during the 1960s. In 1978, Bonnie Fleming changed the format to a Christian broadcasting station. The station made its last broadcast in 2000.

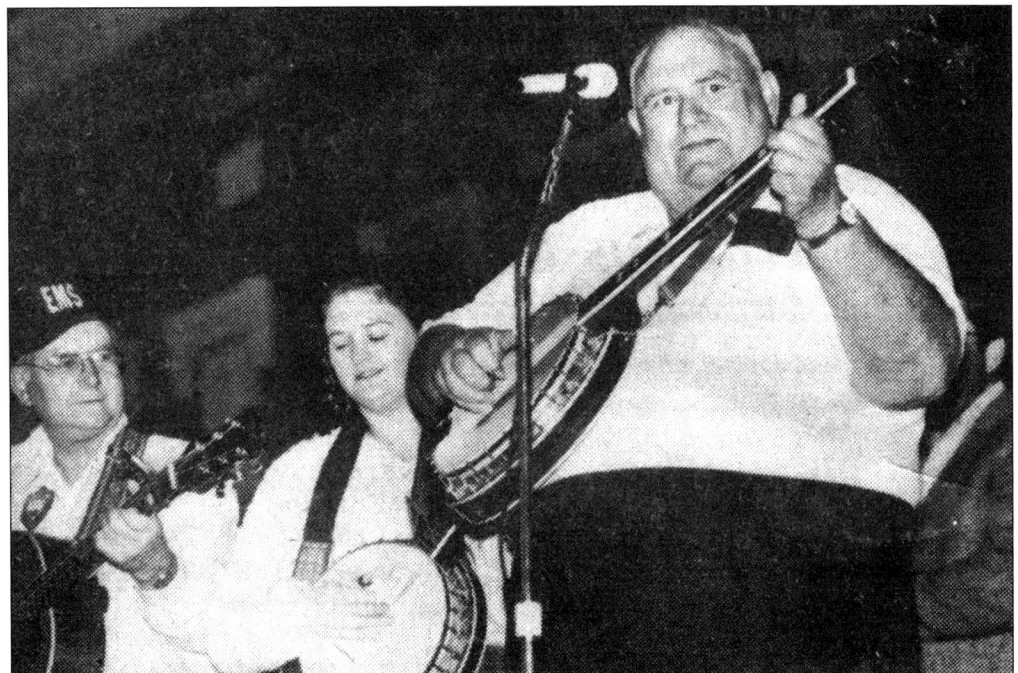

MONDAY TO SATURDAY. Monday Night Pickers Dennis Brock, Lynn Ellison, and Ed Campbell pick and grin at a jam session at the Depot during the mid-1980s. The impromptu gatherings to play and sing got so popular that the night was changed to Saturday even though the group retained its name. People from all over Georgia and South Carolina descend upon the Depot on the second, fourth, and fifth Saturdays of the month to listen to the old-time bluegrass music.

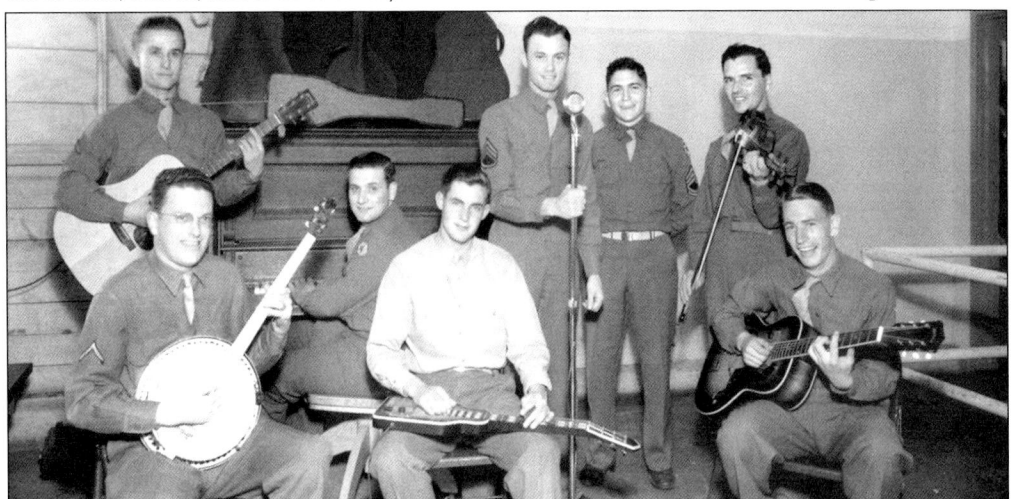

AN AMERICAN ICON. Ralph D. Smith, center, and the Army Mess Hall Band perform for the enlisted men in San Antonio, Texas, in 1942. Throughout the war in Europe, Smith kept his guitar slung across his back and entertained the troops whenever there was a lull in the fighting. Prior to and after the war, he was famous for playing the Dobro, a resophonic lap guitar, which is one of the few American-invented instruments. His son Alda Smith is carrying on the family tradition by holding a Dobro convention in Belton to honor the heritage of this unique instrument.

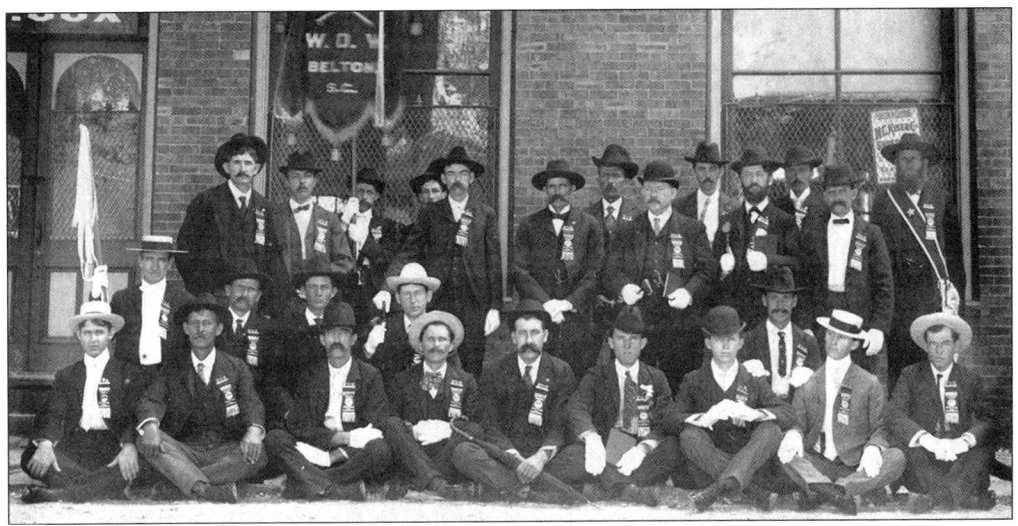

MYRTLE CAMP, #69. The Woodmen of the World Chapter was begun in 1898 with B.A. Wilson, consul commander, and M.E. Geer, clerk. W.B. Deanhart was secretary from 1923 to 1958. The chapter was very active throughout the early part of the 20th century and a meeting place was built by the Mill. There was also a chapter at Shirley's Store in the Long Branch Community. If one walks through the Belton Cemetery, many a marker will be found with the Woodmen of the World insignia since membership dues also covered a death and burial insurance policy. These distinguished gentlemen sit for a photograph in front of I.W. Cox's store about 1910.

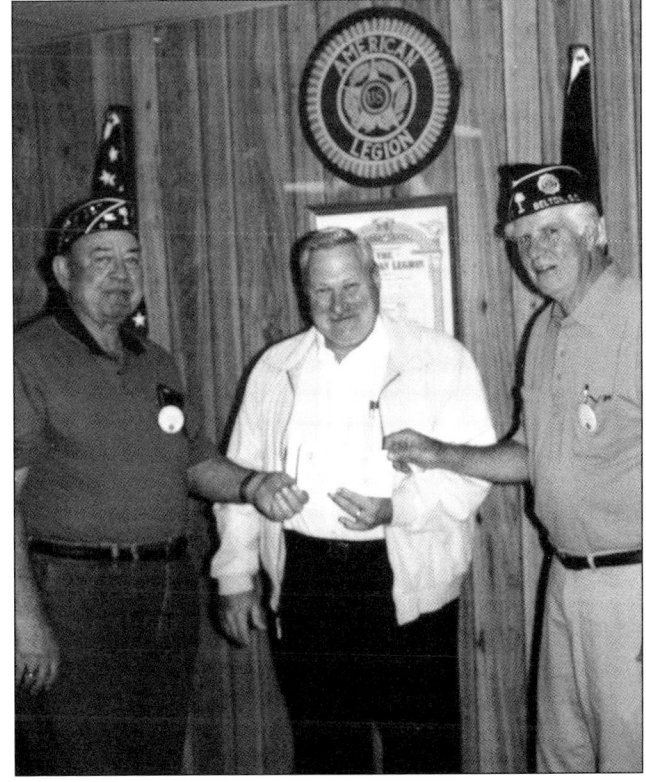

AMERICAN LEGION POST #51. Charles Campbell, Veterans Park chairman, and Joe Coward, post commander, receive a $700 check from Anderson County councilman Larry Greer in 2003 to be used for upkeep and maintenance on the park. In addition to maintaining the park and other projects, the post pays the expenses of three boys to attend Boys' State each summer.

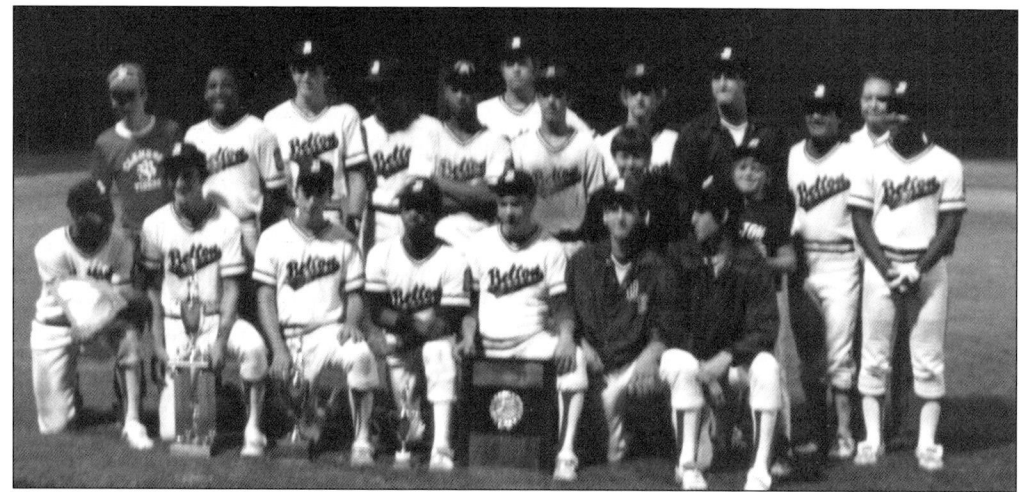

STATE CHAMPS! One of the most long-lasting programs that the post has sponsored is the American Legion baseball team. Each year, Belton's Post #51 succeeds in providing entertainment for the crowds and a proving ground for young talent. Members of the 1982 State Championship Team are, from left to right, (front row) Rufus Huffman, Bill Poore, Will Garrison, Tony Miller, Terry Griffin, Doug Brock, Tommy Crowe, and bat boys Shanon Burke and Joey Lance; (middle row) ? Lowe, Sidney Rucker, Charlie Jackson, Carroll Parker, Daniel Martin, Danny Weber, Phillip Vaughn, David Howells, Coach Dave Delgado, and Ernest Valentine; (back row) Coach Butch Hopkins and Post 51 Athletic Officer Charles Meeks; not pictured is Timmy Crowe.

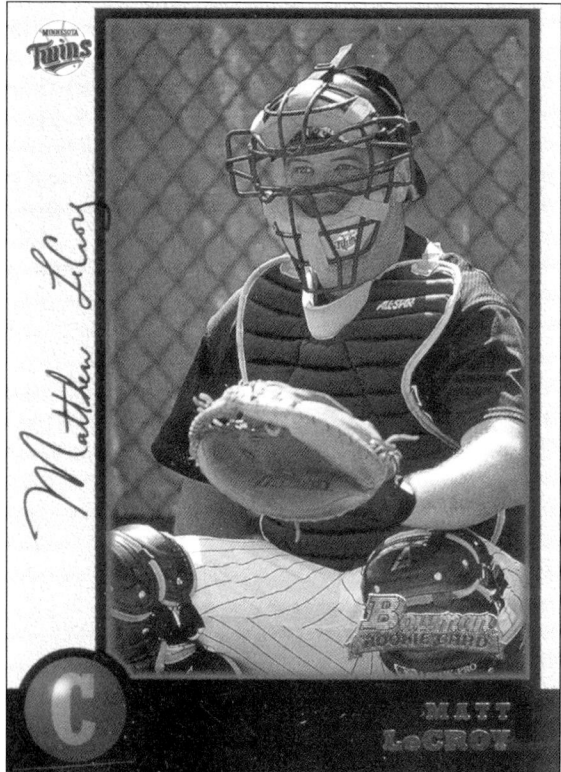

ROOKIE CARD. Matthew LeCroy, who was an outstanding baseball player for the Belton-Honea Path High School Bears, the American Legion Post #51 team, the Clemson Tigers, and the U.S. Olympic team, has provided hometown baseball fans with a local man to follow. LeCroy signed with the Minnesota Twins in 1997 and in 2003 finished his first season in the Major Leagues. As a designated hitter, he finished the season with 17 home runs and batting average of .287 and helped to lead the Twins to the American League Division Series.

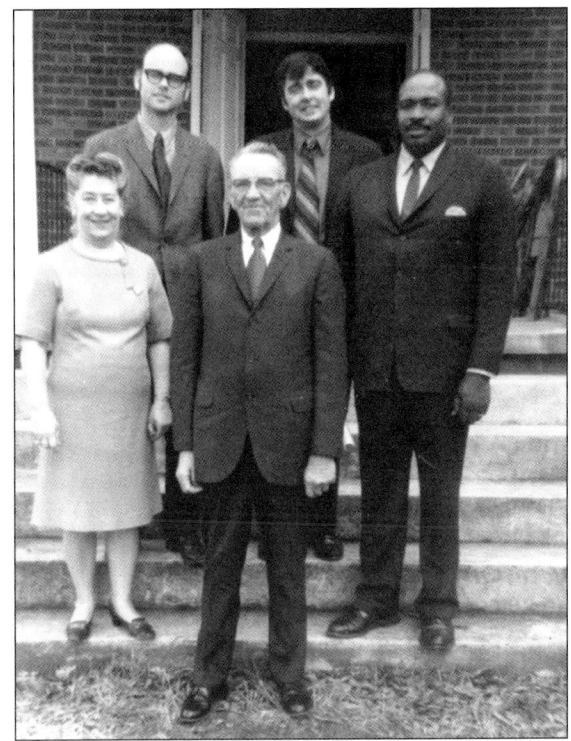

NEWLY ORGANIZED SENIOR CITIZENS GROUP. With the motto "Stop the world, I want to get on" and an energetic array of organizers, the group was bound to take off. The organization began meeting in 1970 and found a home at the old Abney Chapel off North Main Street in 1971. Persons aged 55 or older were encouraged to attend the bi-weekly meetings. They planned and enjoyed trips, held informational meetings, and met just to sing, play checkers, and talk about the old days. Group treasurer Sybil Vann, president W.D. McMurray, and three area pastors, Dr. T.E. Clarke, Rev. Mr. Bundy, and Rev. Mr. Mathis, stand on the steps of the new meeting place in April 1971.

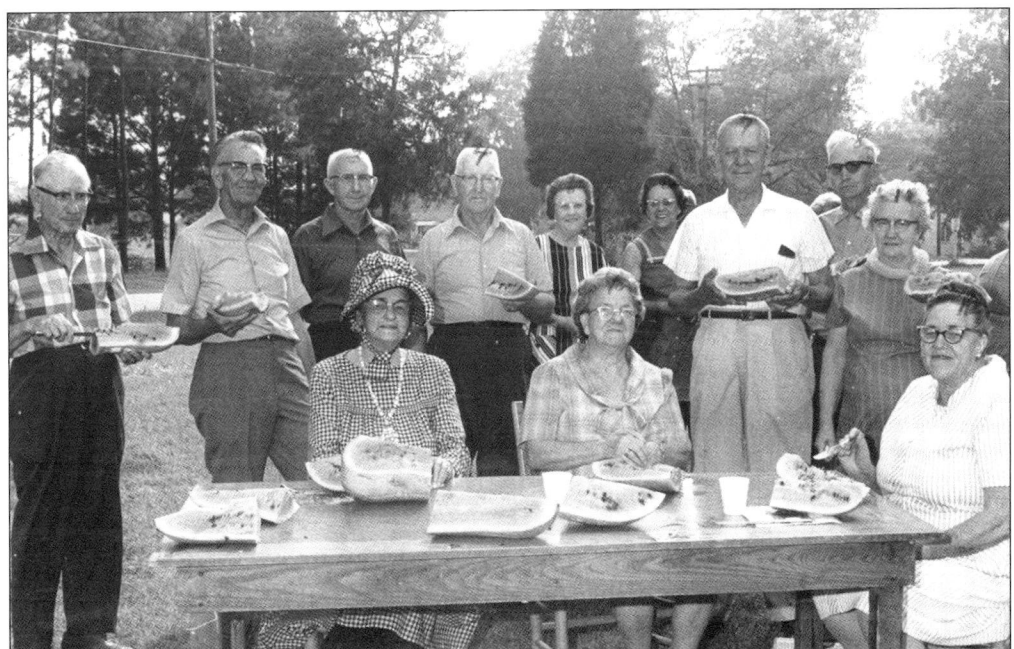

THAT JUICY RIPE WATERMELON. Over 50 members attended a melon slicing party at the Belton Senior Action Center in 1971. Pictured here, from left to right, are (seated) Mrs. C.E. Massey, Lucille Campbell, and Mrs. J.E. Mullinax; (standing) W.A. Snead, W.D. McMurray, Reese Thomas, Mr. and Mrs. Louie Campbell, P.M. Willingham, Henry Lowe, Kate Hanks, and Louie and Daisy Campbell.

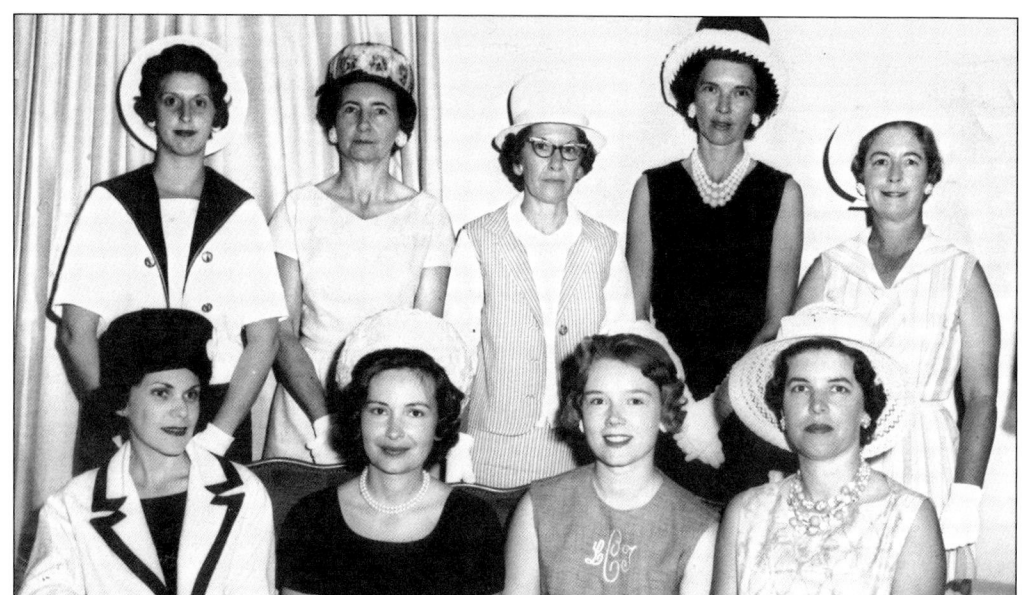

A WORTHY CIVIC GROUP. The Belton Woman's Club was formed in 1961. The officers for 1964–1965 included, from left to right, (front row) Mrs. R.E. Watkins, Mrs. Lewis Haynie, Mrs. Henry Clinkscales Jr., and Mrs. Walter Newman; (back row) Mrs. Dean Miller, Mrs. J.L. Turner, Mrs. Troy Timms, Mrs. James McClain, and Mrs. Albert Maynard. Throughout its existence, the Belton Woman's Club provided a teen canteen, provided college scholarships, conducted beautification projects, assisted with eye and ear screenings at the elementary schools, and started a children's story hour at the library. The club was disbanded in 1983.

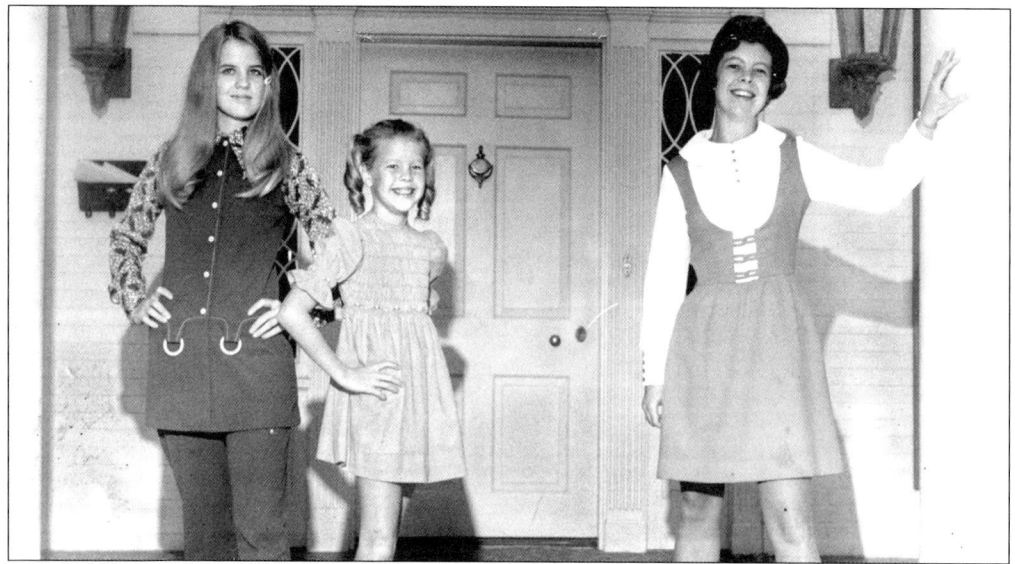

AN ENJOYABLE PROJECT. Each year, the Belton Woman's Club held a fashion show to raise money to fund their projects. Myers Arnold furnished the fashions for the show, which was held at the Belton Armory on November 10, 1971. Tickets were on sale for $2. Turner Rice, daughter of C.T. and J.T. Rice and a recording artist for Capitol Records, was scheduled to perform her most popular vocal numbers during the intermission. Joy Ellison, Cyndi Cox, and Susie Cox model some of the latest fashions that were to be featured in the show.

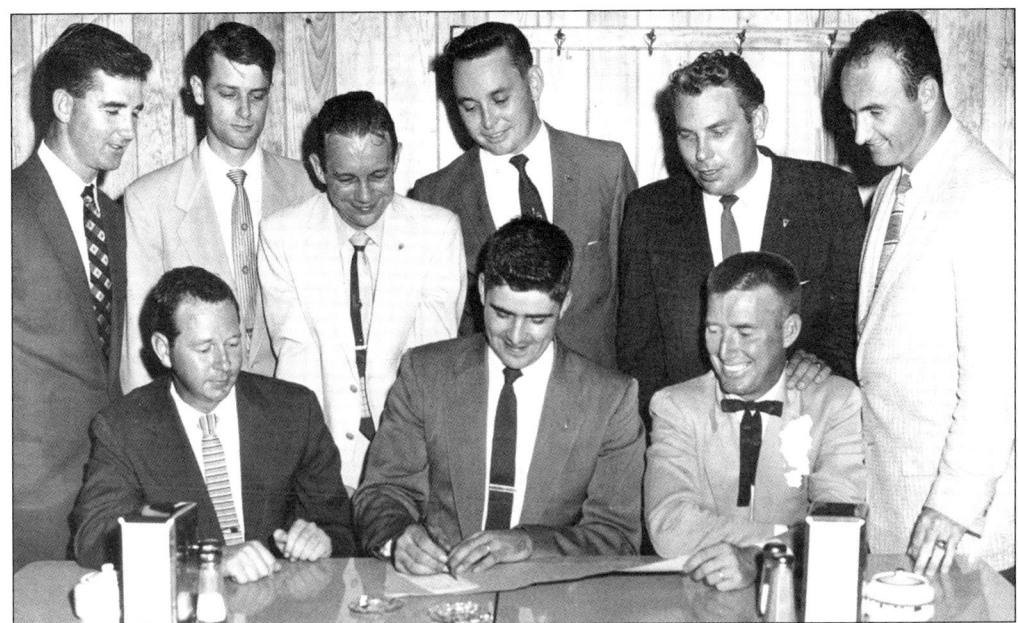

JAYCEES, 1958. Organized in 1939, the Belton Jaycees have improved the community in which we live. During their years of community service, the Jaycees and the Jaycee-ettes have assisted the Haven of Rest Children's Home of the South, held a children's Christmas festival on the Square, sponsored a shooting education program for boys and girls, sold Christmas trees and firewood, and funded the Jaycees Ball Park. Members include, from left to right, (front row) Alton Finley, Joe Coward, and Ray Stephens; (back row) Bill Brissey, James Daniel, Bob Folk, Charles Meeks, Dick Plyler, and Dan Malone. These men watch as treasurer Joe Coward writes a check to fund construction on the new Jaycees Ball Park.

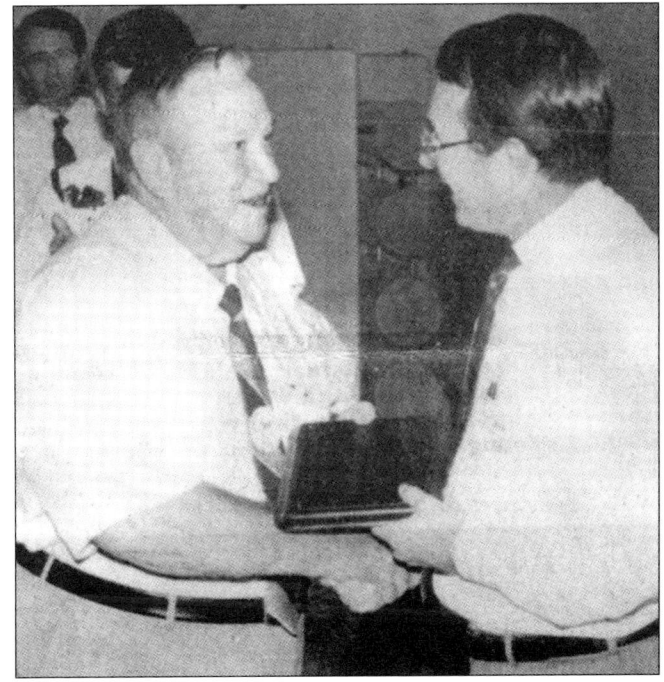

LIONS RECOGNIZE THEIR OWN. J. Ed Horton was inducted into the Belton Lions Club Hall of Fame during awards ceremonies in 1990. Horton was chief magistrate for Anderson County and had been a member of the Belton Lions since 1946. Presenting the award was Jim Fowler, awards chairman. Others receiving awards that year were Bill Eaves, "Lion of the Year"; and Rex Maynard, "Belton Citizen of the Year." Six Belton Men have been posthumously inducted into the South Carolina Lions Hall of Fame: Louis Seel, Nathan Coward, Walter T. Cox, Clyde Murdock, J.J. Pruitt, and Herbert L. Corder.

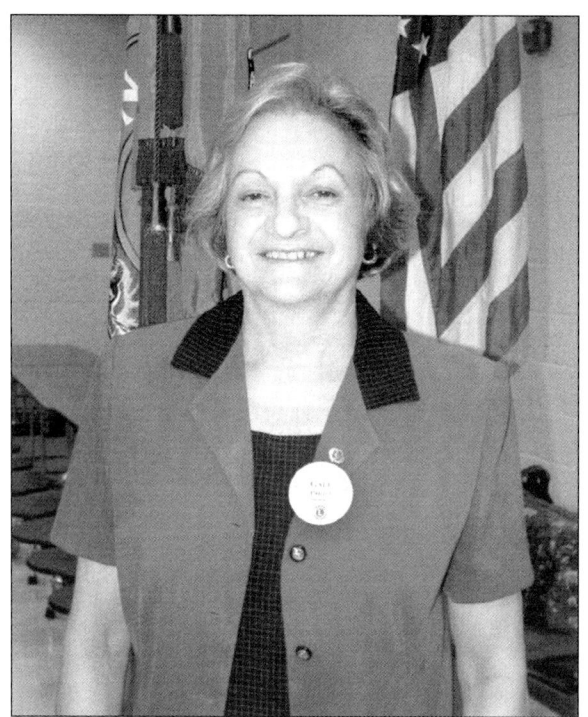

HISTORIC OCCASION, 2003. Women have been admitted to the Lions Club since 1998, but this year the club took that much further: they elected Gale Pruitt to serve as president. The Belton Lions Club was chartered in 1935. From their fundraising efforts of selling brooms, candy, and local community calendars, the Lions are able to fund sight conservation projects. Over 50 Belton residents received eye exams and new glasses in 2002, funded entirely through the Lions' fundraising efforts. In this picture, Gale Pruitt stands in front of the Lions Club and American flags.

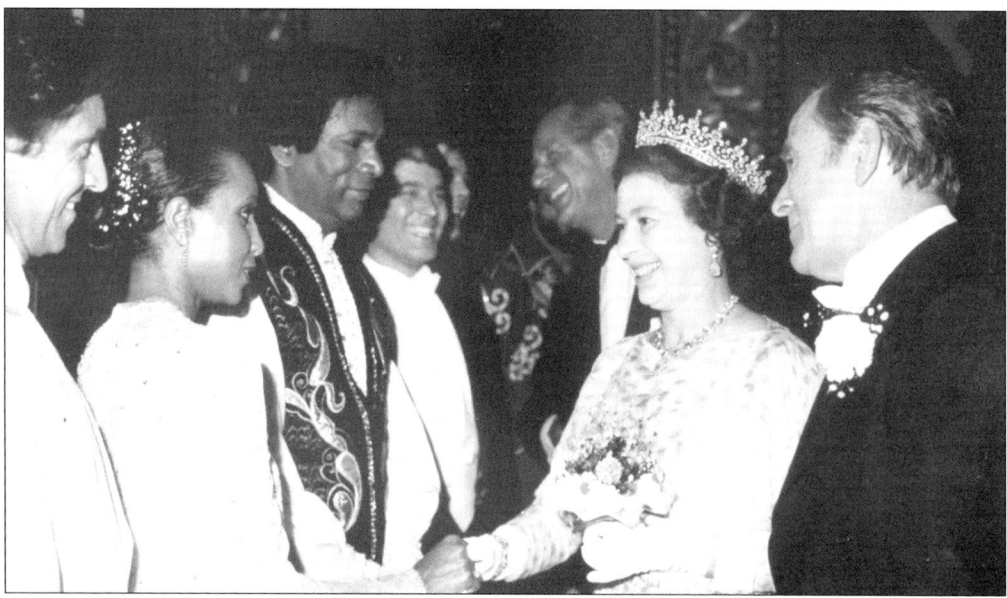

A ROYAL PERFORMANCE. Wearing a white designer original gown by Fernando Pena, Loretta Holloway headlined the entertainment for the 1982 Commonwealth Games in Brisbane, Australia. This Royal Command Performance was broadcast around the world. Queen Elizabeth and Prince Philip visited with Holloway immediately after the performance. During her active career, Holloway has sung the theme song for the movie *BlackJack*; has shared the marquee with stars such as Bill Cosby, Whoopi Goldberg, Jay Leno, Don Rickles, and Garry Shandling; and has appeared in movies such as *Pure Country*, *Elvis and Me*, and *Indecent Proposal*. She currently has a CD out entitled *Loretta Holloway . . . Quietly*.

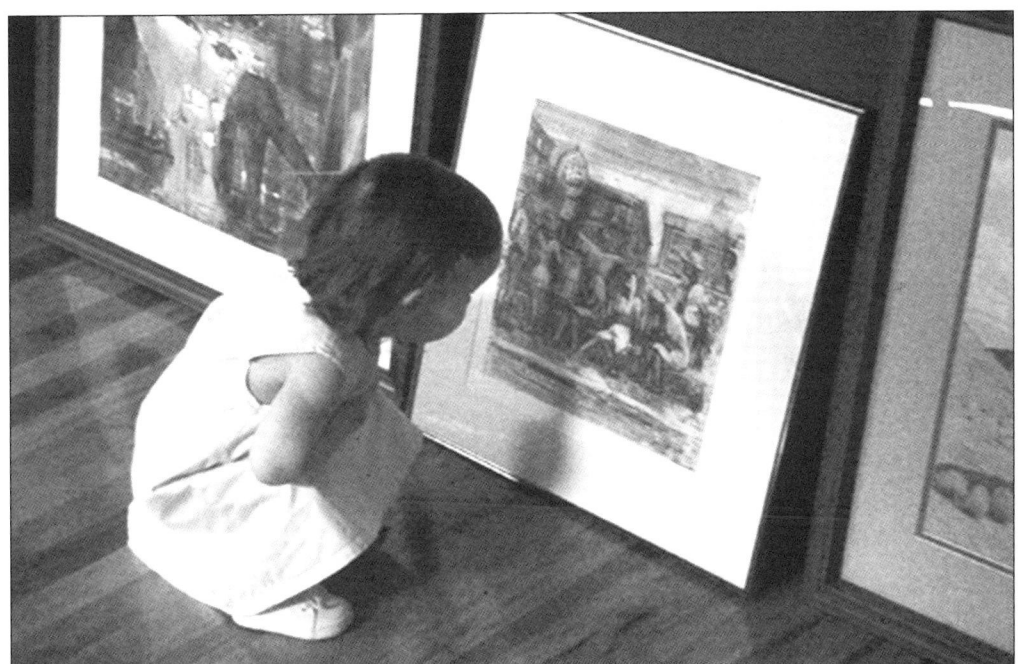

LITTLE TOWN, BIG ART. Begun in 1999 with a handful of determined and energetic citizens and artists, the Belton Center for the Arts now has a staff of two who curate shows, teach art lessons, and assist in the coordination the Arts in Education program for the school system. This year it held its fifth annual Standpipe Festival Juried Art Show. With over 350 pieces submitted, the judge had a difficult time culling the presented art to a mere 149 hung pieces. Here, Callie Williamson, daughter of director Kristy Williamson and Belton native Tim Williamson, examines a piece of work by local artist Jose Acaba.

HUNKA, HUNKA BURNING LOVE. Elvis, also known as Chad Lowe, wows the crowd at the Standpipe Festival in 2001. The Standpipe Festival was first held in 1987 to help fund renovations to the historic Standpipe. Thousands of people came that first year, so the event organizers have brought in bigger and better attractions. In 2003, the festival featured free art classes in raku, the juried art exhibit, the box washers tournament, a petting zoo, dobro seminars, bluegrass music, heritage craft exhibits, vintage auto show, and a 5K fun run/walk.

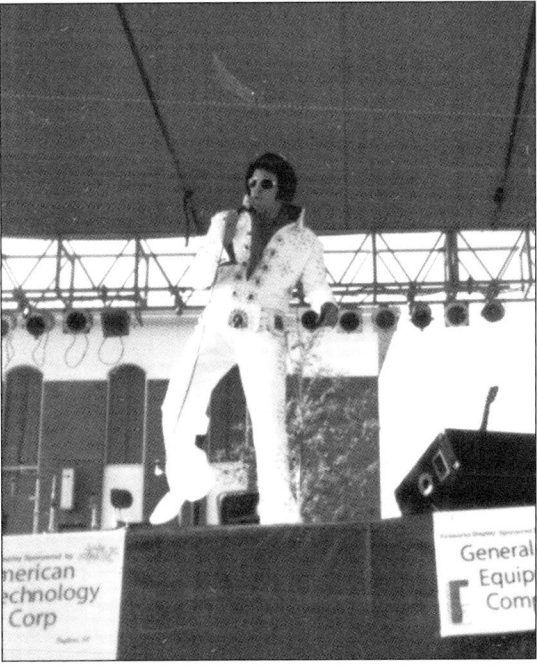

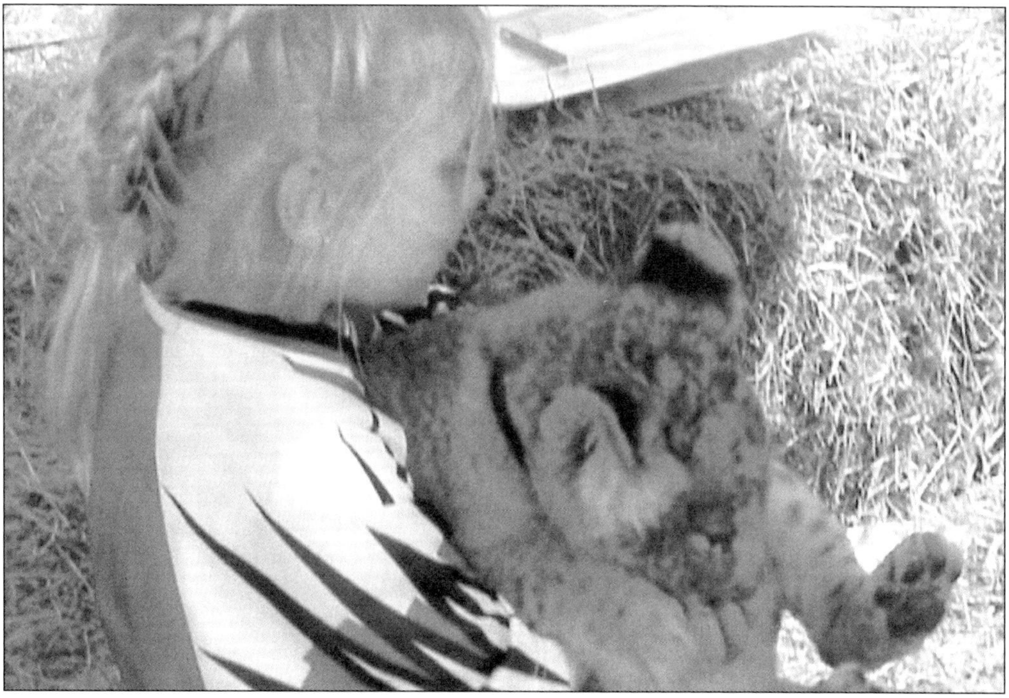

WHAT A BIGGGG CAT! Anna Kelly McGonigle snuggles up with a tiger cub that was brought by Hollywild to the 2003 Standpipe Festival. For a small fee, children could hold the cub and have a picture taken. The Standpipe Festival is organized each year by the Belton Area Partnership under the project leadership of Gina Ballard.

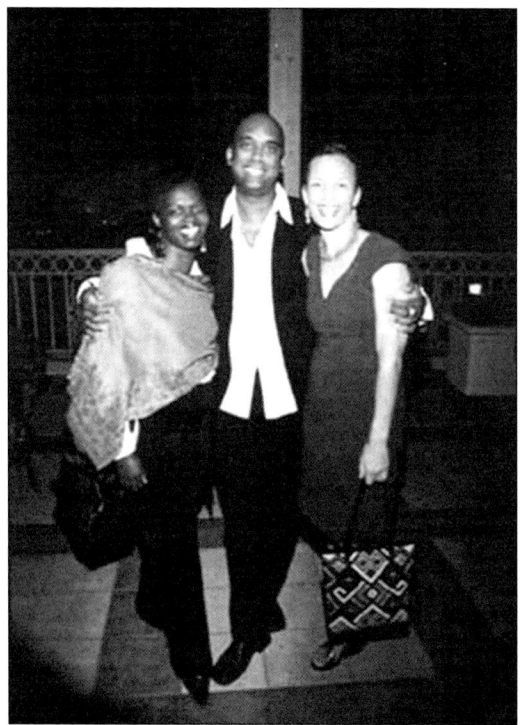

AWARD-WINNING AUTHOR. Belton native Dwight McBride has become a famous author and lecturer during his tenure as a college professor at Northwestern University. Chair of the Department of African American Studies at the Illinois school, McBride is pictured here with Prof. Judith Jackson Fosset of the University of Southern California and Prof. Caroline Streeter of UCLA on the rooftop of the Wyndham Bel-Age Hotel in West Hollywood after receiving the Lambda Literary Award for best fiction anthology for his latest work. (Picture by John Nicolaro.)

Six
GOVERNMENT AND POLITICS

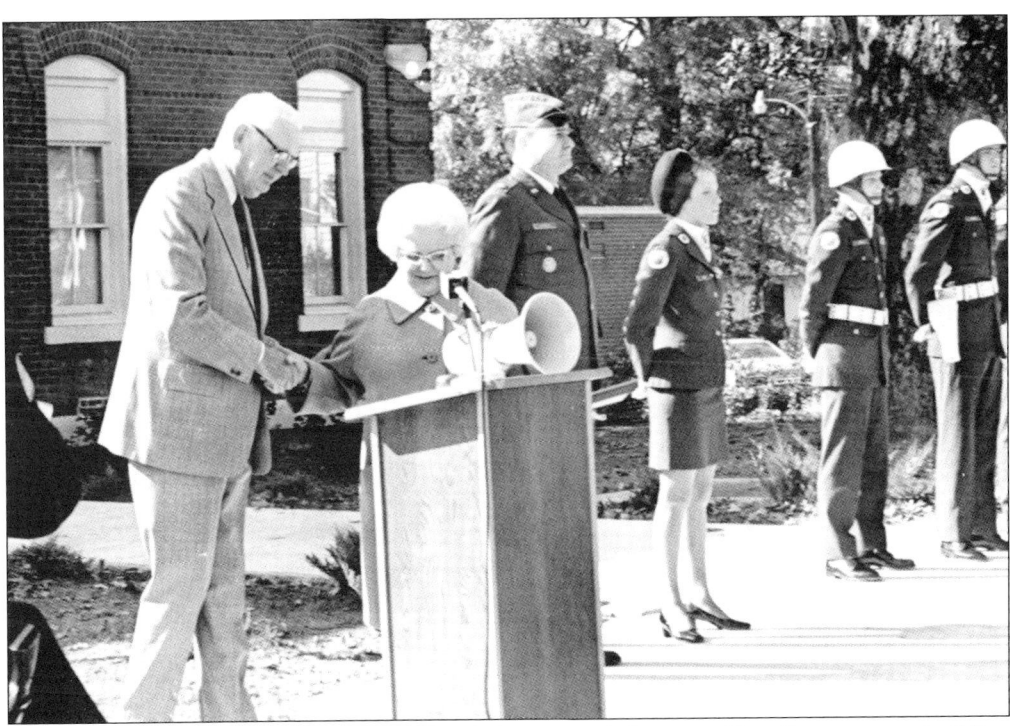

CITY HALL DEDICATION, 1976. At the dedication of the new City Government building on Anderson Street, Mayor Jones Ellison accepts the time-capsule to be placed on the grounds from Miriam Corder, representative of the Belton Area Museum and Daughters of the American Revolution, while Maj. Roger N. Anderson and the ROTC Honor Guard stand at attention. The City Hall was dedicated on May 23, 1976, after extensive renovations to the old Central school building. Rep. Butler Derrick was on hand to make a speech about this historic occasion.

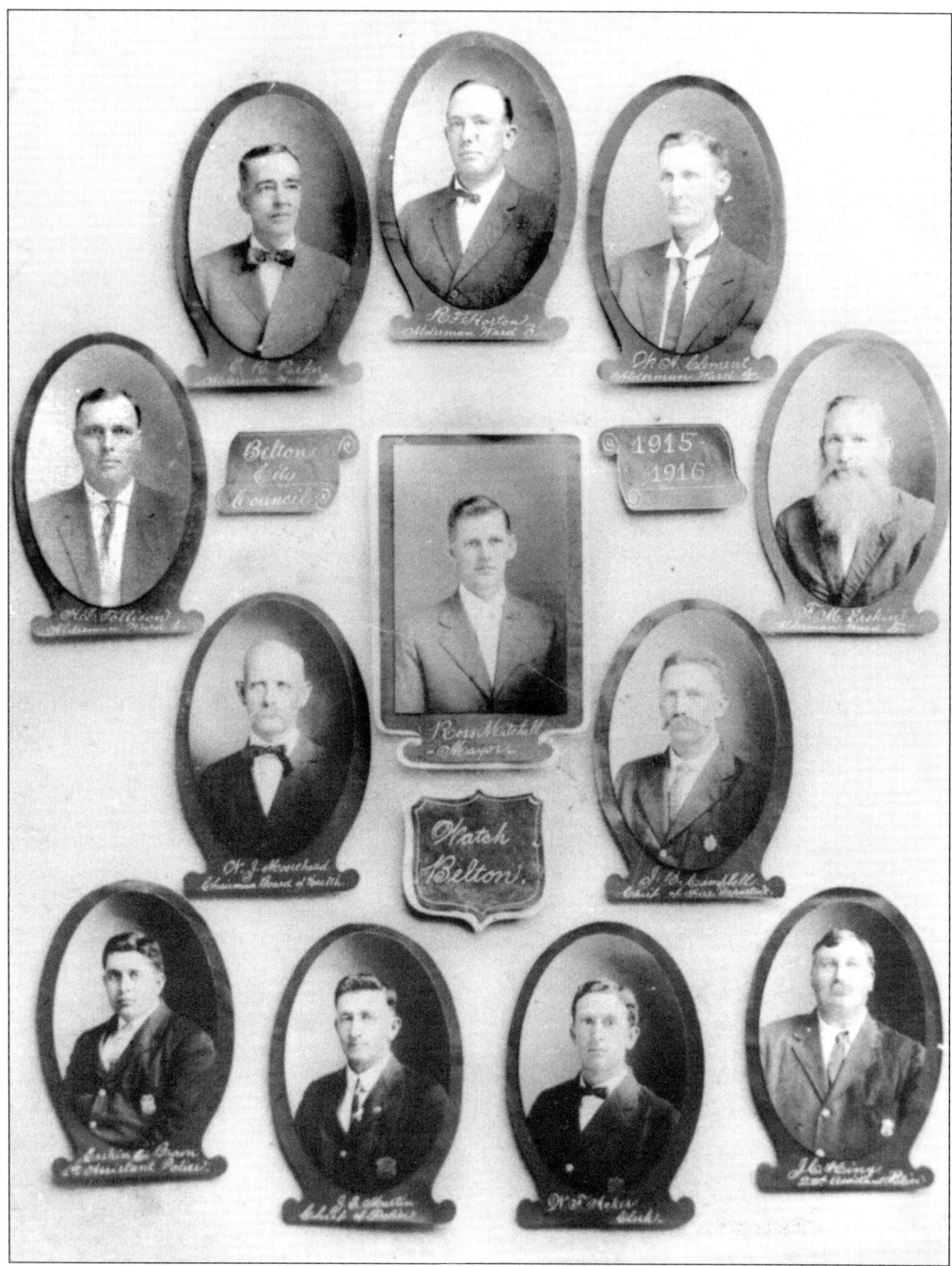

WATCH BELTON, 1915. Mayor, aldermen, and police and fire chiefs are shown in this postcard of the period. Elected every two years, Belton had five wards represented by M.L. Tollison, C.B. Parker, R.F. Horton, W.A. Clements, and F.M. Eskew. The mayor was Ross Mitchell, who served in this capacity from 1914 to 1927, with the exception of the 1919–1920 period, when the office was held by E.T. Breazeale. M.J. Moorehead was the chairman of the Health Board, J.B. Martin was chief of police, J.B. Campbell was chief of the fire department, and W.F. Acker was city clerk. The "Watch Belton" motto was adopted and placed atop the Belton Standpipe.

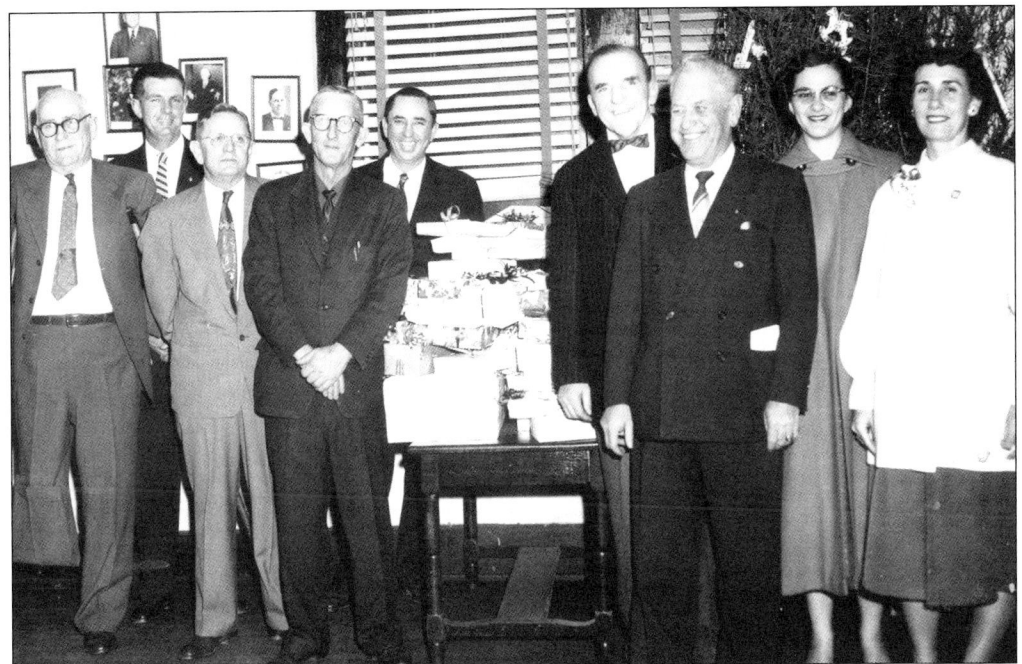

SWAPPING NOEL, 1952. Every Christmas, City Hall held a party for the staff and council. Here, Mr. Kirk, Mr. Kay, Clayton Jones, Nelson Davis, Charles Haynie, Gene Haley (lawyer), Mayor Jimmy Guthrie, Audrey Coleman (clerk), and Mae Minyard (clerk) pose before swapping presents.

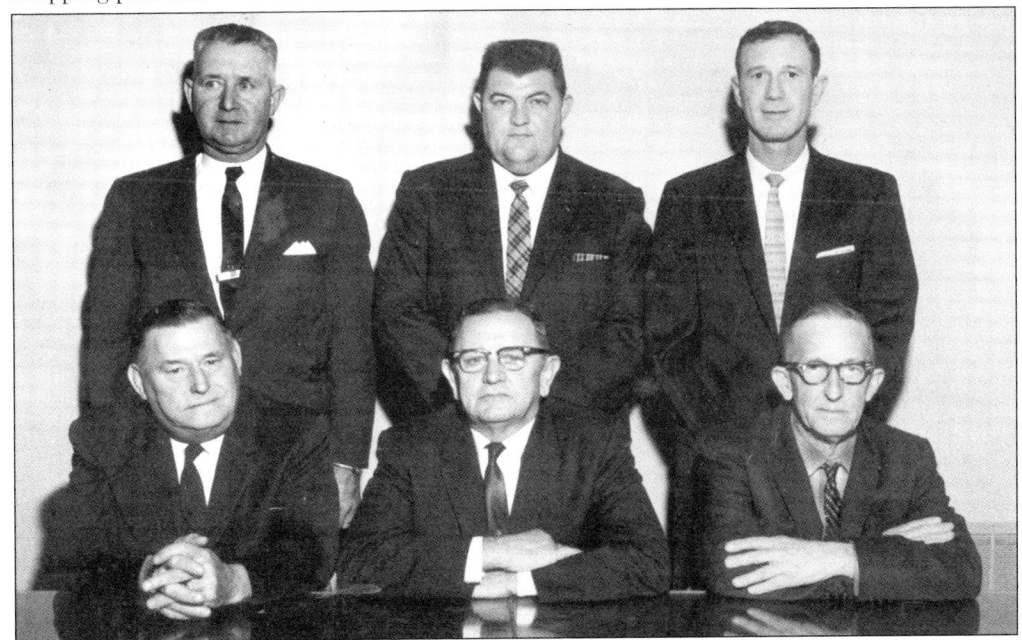

IT GETS IN THE BLOOD. The 1962–1963 Council sits for a promotional picture. They are, from left to right, (front row) Bill Stephens, Mayor Clayton Jones, and Nelson Davis; (back row) Gary F. Thomas, Jamie Mattison, and Leo Fisher. Jamie Mattison (1964–1967) and Leo Fisher (1980–1985, 1988–1998) served as mayors also.

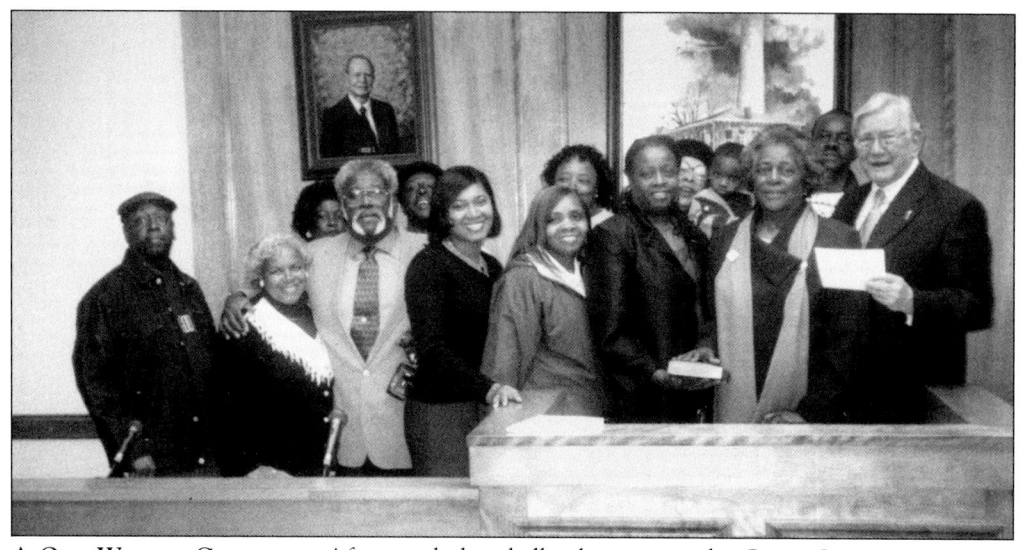

A One-Woman Crusader. After single-handedly cleaning up the Green Street area, Hattie Green was encouraged to run for the City Council. In 2000, she was elected as the first black council member in Belton. Here, she is shown with her family at her swearing-in ceremony. Shown from left to right are (front row) Gilbert Green, Sweetie Sullivan, Reid Sullivan, Yolanda Black, Vermell Green, Viola Black, Hattie Green, and Judge Ross Anderson; (back row) Lelar Black, Jonathan Green, Wanda Green, Dora Thompson, Antoine Green, and Howard Green.

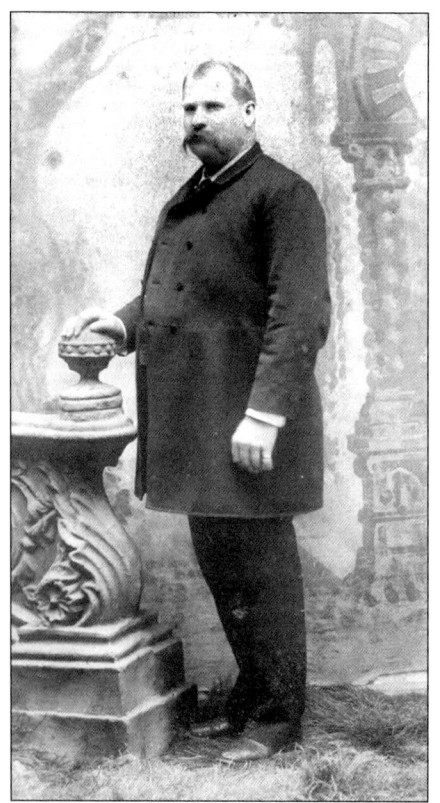

Senator Asbury Churchwell Latimer, 1851–1908. Denied a formal education except in the field schools of Abbeville County, A.C. Latimer nonetheless rose to high status and regard as a businessman and U.S. congressman and senator. At the age of 25, he became interested in politics and took part in the Red Shirt action to support Wade Hampton as governor. The next year, he married Sarah Alice Brown; they moved to Belton in 1880 to begin farming. Employing the latest technological advances and innovative agricultural practices, he prospered as a farmer. In 1892 with no prior running experience, he endeared himself to the people while stumping for the congressional race against George Johnstone of Newberry and was sent to Congress. Subsequently, he was elected for four more terms to that office. In 1902, he ran for the Senate. During his career he was most interested in improving roads and rural mail delivery and served on the Senate committees of Agriculture and Public Lands. He served in this office until his unexpected death of peritonitis following surgery in February 1908. Congressman Finley of South Carolina remarked: "To my mind there is no public man of recent years whose career is so rich in lessons of hope and inspiration to struggling youth as that of our lamented friend."

ORGANIZED ENFORCEMENT. By 1930, the city had a new City Hall complete with fire department, police department, and jail located in the same location under the Standpipe.

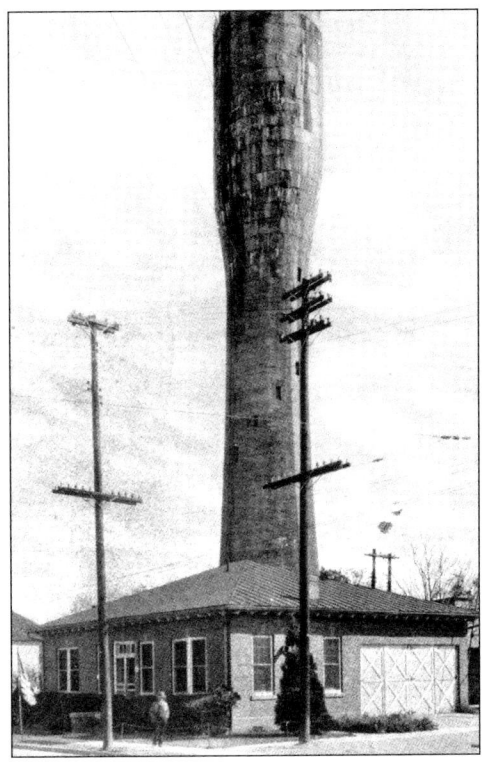

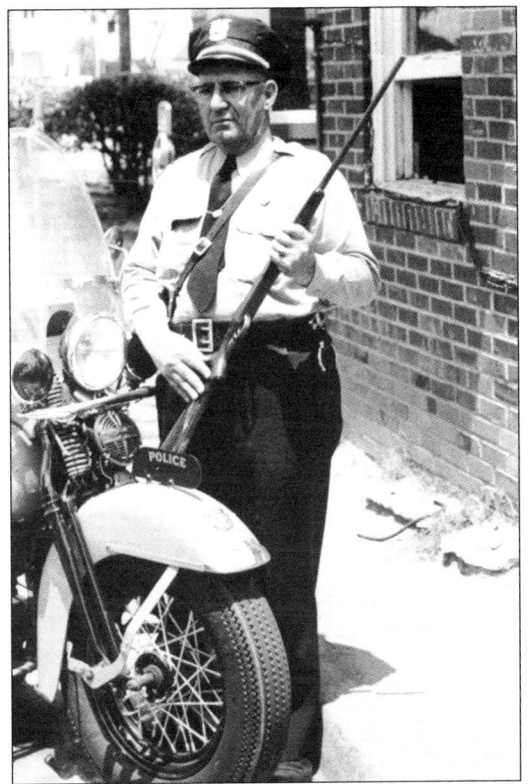

STRAY DOGS BEWARE. In May 1955, the Belton streets were ravaged by rabid dogs. A 30-day quarantine was instituted to end serious rabies outbreaks. Six children and one adult were bitten by dogs that proved rabid and received the 14-day shot regimen required to overcome the disease. Over 37 rabid dogs were destroyed between April 30 and May 12. Belton Officer H.T. Mathis is shown with the 410-gauge shotgun that was used to rid the town of the pestilent dogs.

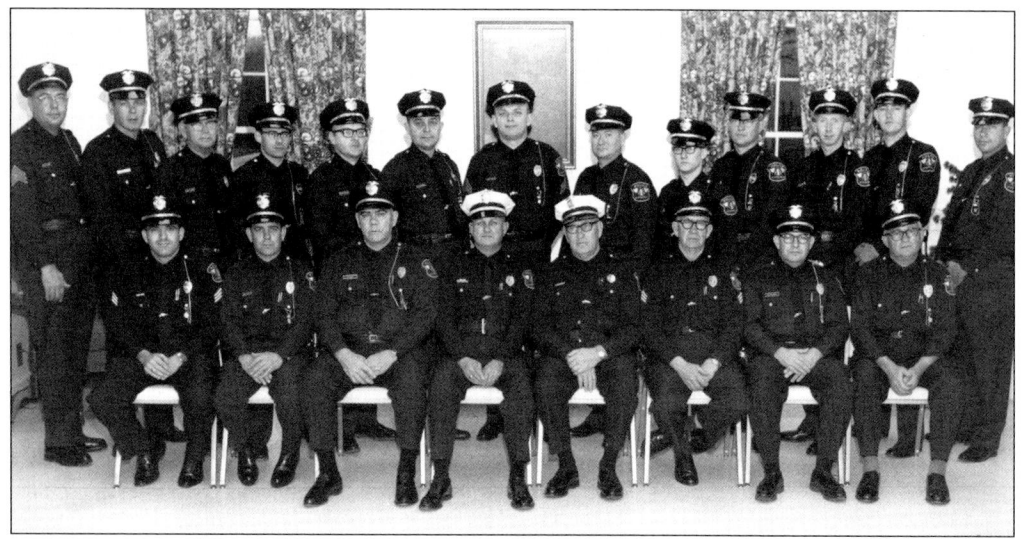

WE'VE GOT THE BEAT COVERED. Both volunteer and full-time police forces were needed to patrol the streets of Belton in 1966. Here, from left to right, the regular force (front row) was comprised of Dean Bannister, Rock Nation, J.T. King, Chief J.B. Lindsey, Lt. Broadus Clamp, Sgt. Jack Kay, Dave Franklin, and Kenneth Parnell; the reserve force included (back row) Sgt. Calvin Ellison, Charles Kelly, Charlie Snider, Ken Mize, Norman Phillips, Jeff Campbell, Sgt. Parker Shirley, Truman Williamson, Danny McKee, William Henry Norris, James Thomas, Fred Norris, and Jim Hines. The reserve forces walked regularly scheduled beats.

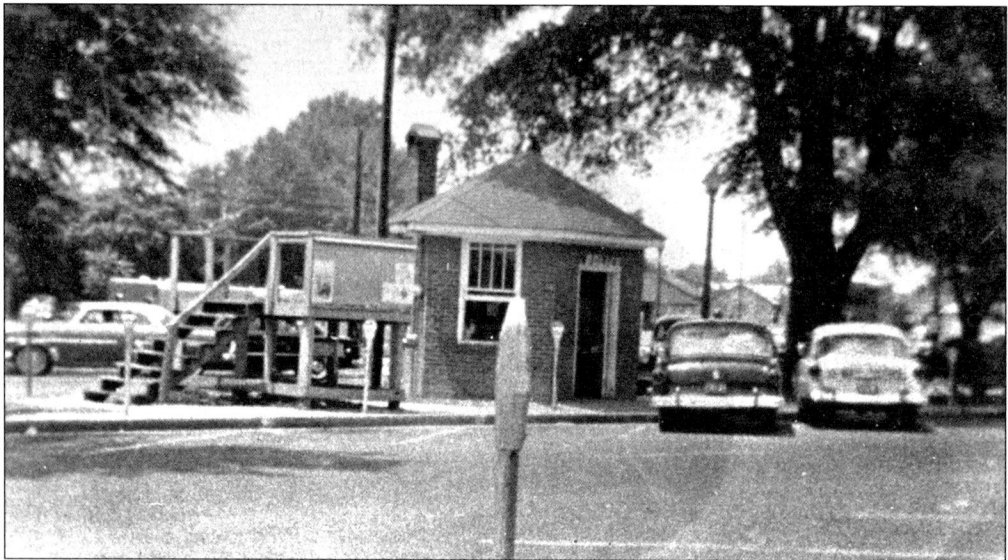

THE POLICE SUBSTATION, C. 1950. Demolished in the first renovation of the Square in 1973, the octagonal building served as a police sub-station for three decades. According to the memories of policemen on the force mid-century, only a few people could fit in the tiny building at a time. Little boys who thought of doing misdeeds were told that the station covered the old town well so that floorboards could be taken up and the miscreants thrown down into the hollow. This deterred many a prank. The wooden platform beside the station was used by the merchants for the weekly drawings and as a platform for the band when square dances were held in the streets.

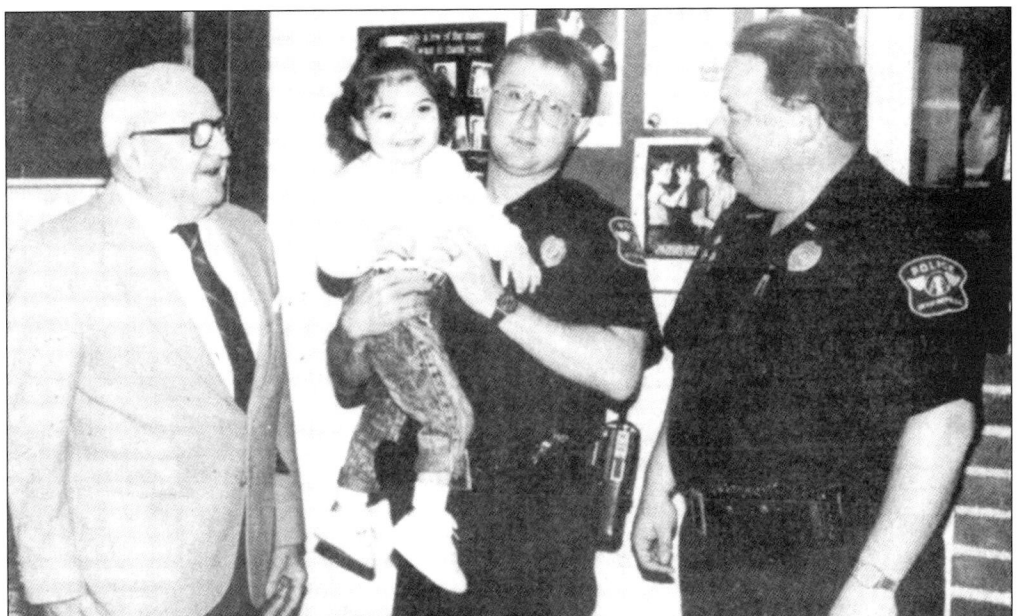

BUCK-A-CUP PATRON. Belton police kicked off the Buck-a-Cup campaign in 1991 with a visit to the Easter Seal Center in Anderson. Pictured with two-and-a-half-year-old Heather Black, a patient at the center, are Wilbur Hunter of Belton, founder of Buck-a-Cup, patrolman Eddie Webb, and Police Chief David Dockings. The center, located on Ella Street, provides help for crippled children and adults for the Easter Seal Society of South Carolina. Belton's goal in 1991 was $8,500.

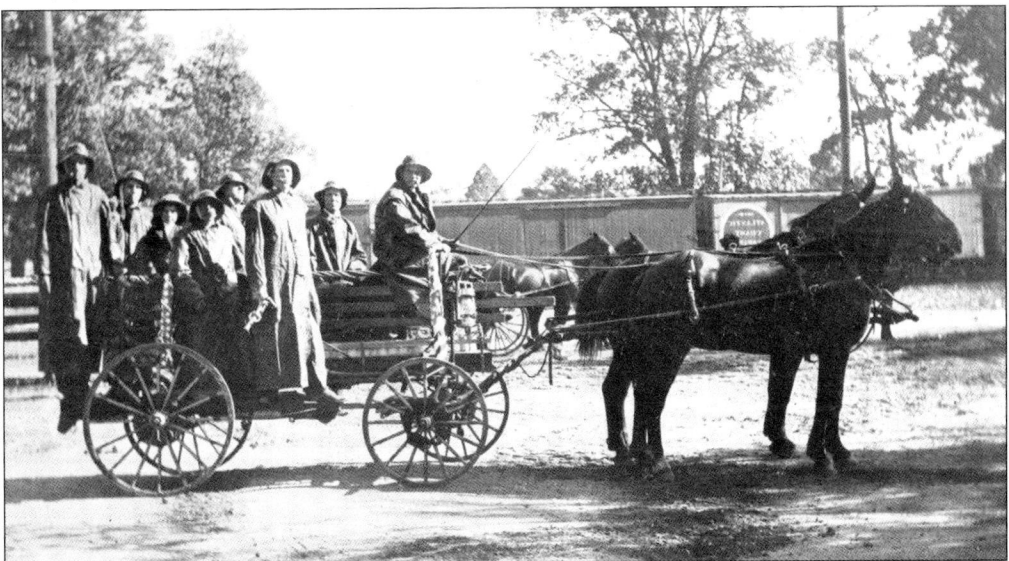

THE BELTON FIRE DEPARTMENT, C. 1910. Volunteer firemen donned raincoats and hitched up their horses when the alarm sounded that a fire had broken out. DeWitt Ledbetter quipped that by the time the men had gotten hold of the horses, gathered their gear, and raced to the scene of the blaze, they got there just in time to douse the other structures to prevent the fire from spreading. By 1930, three different locations of fire departments were posted within the city limits. Two were located near Belton Mill and the third was under the Standpipe.

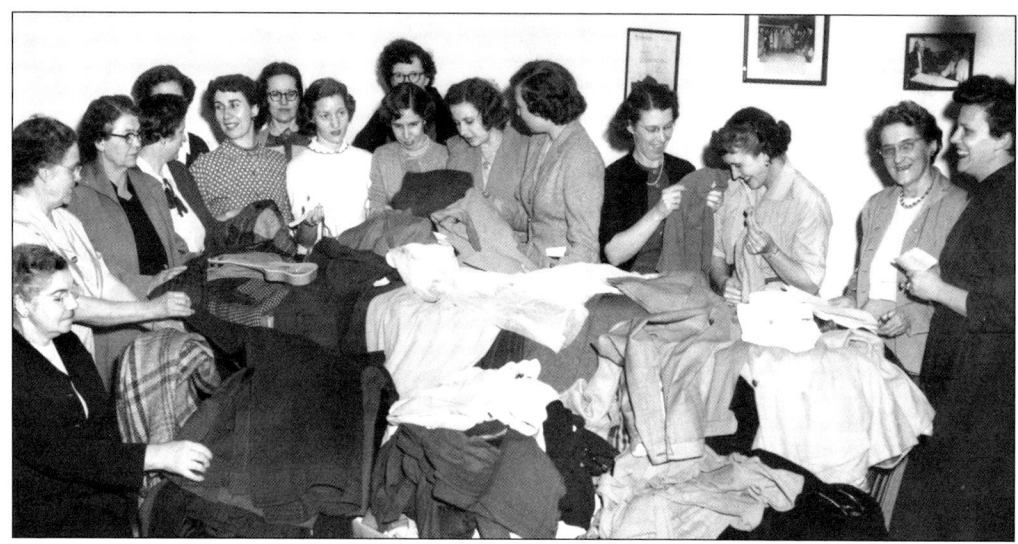

BELTON'S VOLUNTEER FIREMEN ENLIST ASSISTANCE FROM WIVES FOR CHARITY DRIVE, 1954. The annual charity drive brought in hundreds of items of clothing and toys to be sorted before distribution by their husbands before Christmas Eve. Over 40 persons gathered in the City Hall building to enjoy an oyster stew supper before sorting the items for needy families in the area; $225.26 was also contributed to help buy food and coal. Assisting with the sorting are Mrs. Henry Mathis Sr., Mrs. Mack Singleton, Mrs. C.M. Bollinger, Mrs. Joe Bannister, Mrs. Charlie Coleman, Mrs. Charles Minyard, Mrs. Roscoe Willingham, Melba Fleming, Mrs. Nelson Davis, Mae Mathis, Mrs. James Thomas, Mrs. Jeff Campbell, Mrs. Gary Thomas, Mrs. N.A. Coward, Mrs. J.E. Sullivan, and Mrs. Jimmy Guthrie Jr.

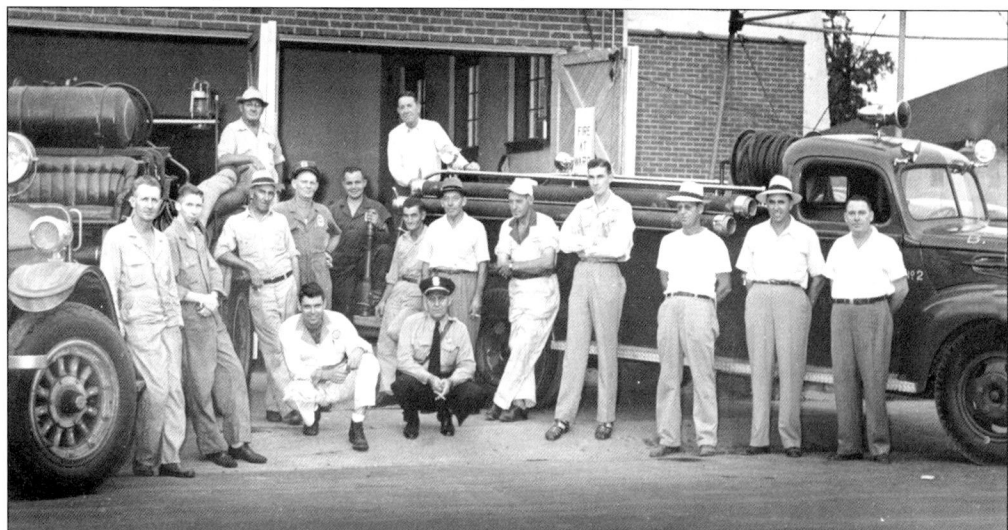

READY FOR THE ALARM, 1947. Volunteer firemen included, from left to right, Gary Thomas, James Thomas, Joe Bannister, S.J. Kay, Jeff Campbell, Jabus Brooks, Mac Singleton, Harold Townes, Ray Mattison, Roscoe Willingham, Charles Haynie, John Bill Simpson; (kneeling) Julius Cox and Henry Mathis; (standing on truck) Alvin Greer and Carl Bollinger. James Thomas stated that the old 1923 American La France engine was hard to get started, but once it sputtered, you could get 75 mph or more out of her. The new fire truck purchased in 1947 could climb no higher than 60 mph when racing to a fire.

Postal Retirement, c. 1950. To show appreciation for his long years of service, a retirement dinner was hosted for John Dow Hunter (seated), rural mail carrier. Joe King (house-to-house city carrier) and George Singleton joke with Hunter about his exploits as a carrier.

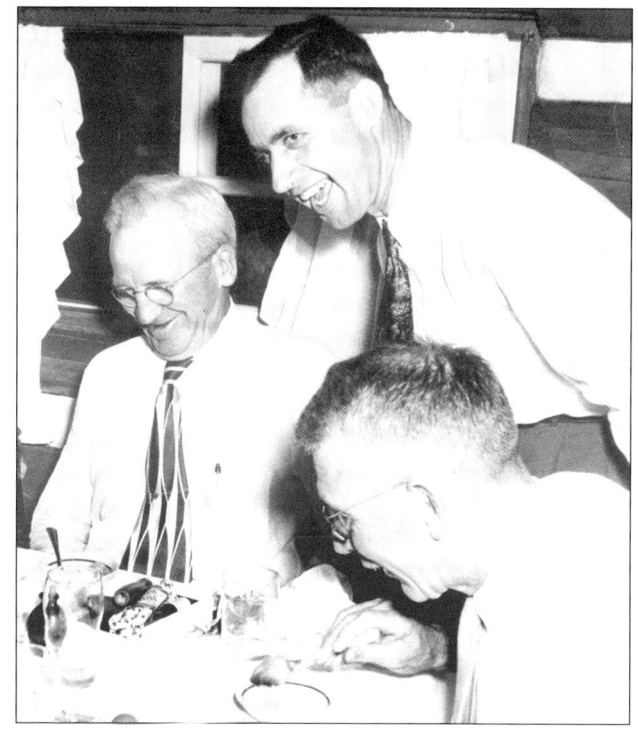

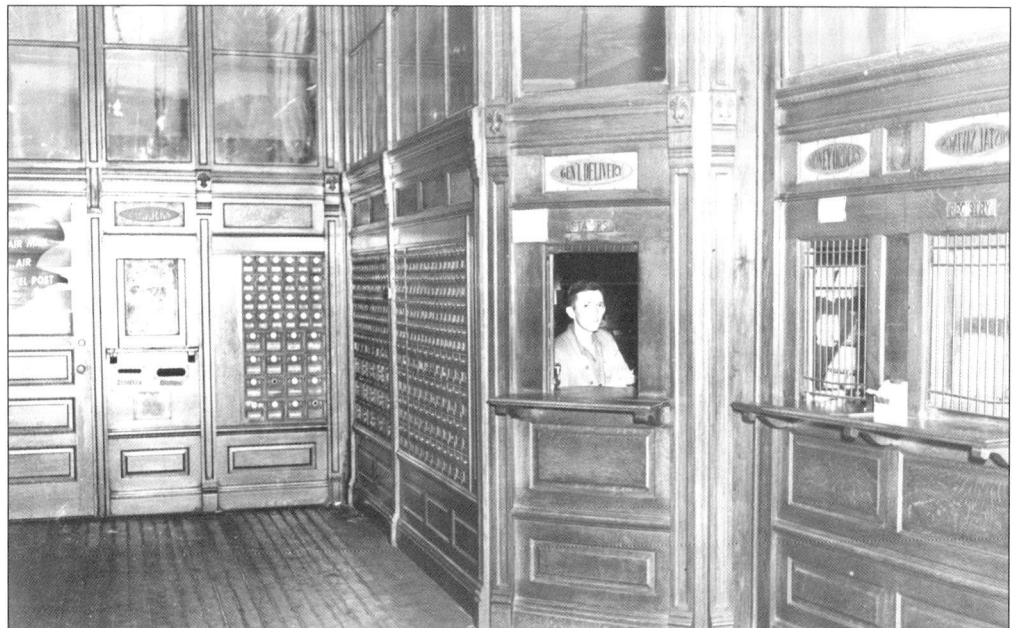

The Wood and Stained Glass Architecture of Days Gone By. Louis Vickery, for years the city walking route deliverer and lino-type operator for the *Belton News*, peers from the stamp window in the old post office before moving to the new post office in 1958. This post office was located on O'Neal Street where it had been since 1908. The post office has been located in 13 different places since Jonathan Berry Lewis established mail delivery in 1851. Note that one of the stained glass windows was installed backwards.

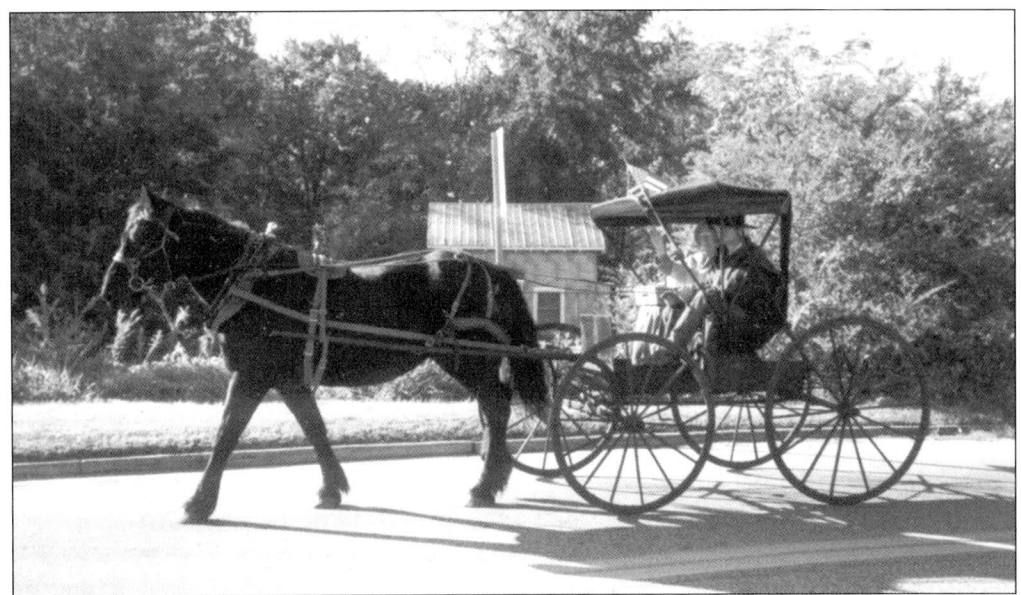

ONE HUNDRED YEARS OF RURAL DELIVERY OBSERVED. The Belton post office marked a century of rural delivery with fanfare, a time capsule, speeches, and horse and buggy-delivered letters in October of 1996. Dressed in period costume, Lucille Vaughn Mattison arranged for a driver (Mosie Munn) and horse (use donated by Dr. Pogue Reid of Pendleton) and carriage (use provided by Sonny Clinkscales) to help her run her route. A special cancellation stamp to commemorate the occasion was designed by Connie Mattison Price (Caldwell).

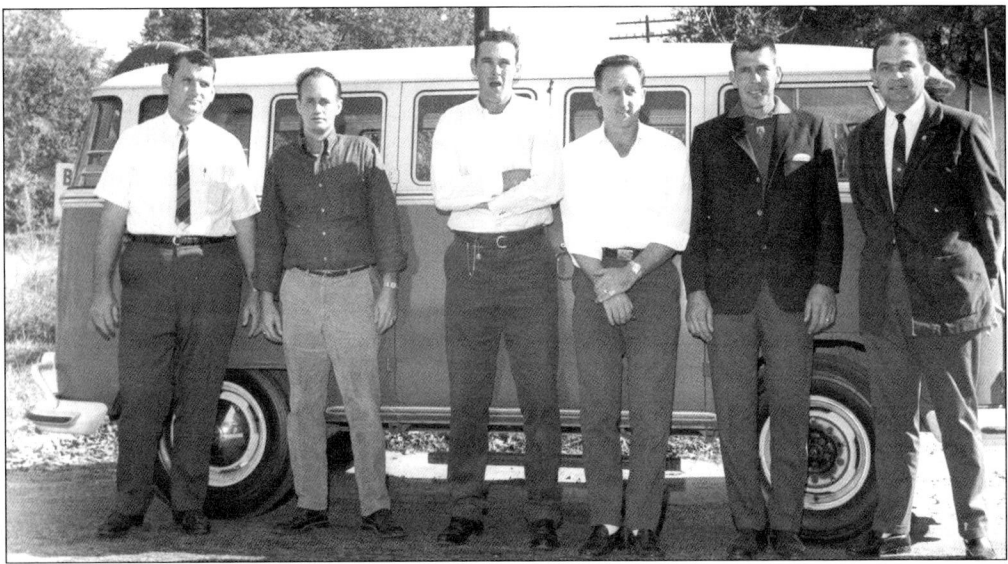

WHEN DUTY CALLS. In 1964, the Belton Rescue Squad was founded as the first of its kind in Anderson County. In 1966, the squad poses, from left to right, in front of their converted bus: Archie Morgan, Maurice Bowie, Tom Tolly, Jim McCullough, Bill Woodson, and Jim Brown. A metal building was dedicated for use in May of 1973 and has since housed the unit. From the completely volunteer and donated services to the budgeted enterprise, sophisticated equipment, and paid employees of today, the Rescue Squad has served the community well for almost 40 years.

Seven
Churches and Religious Activities

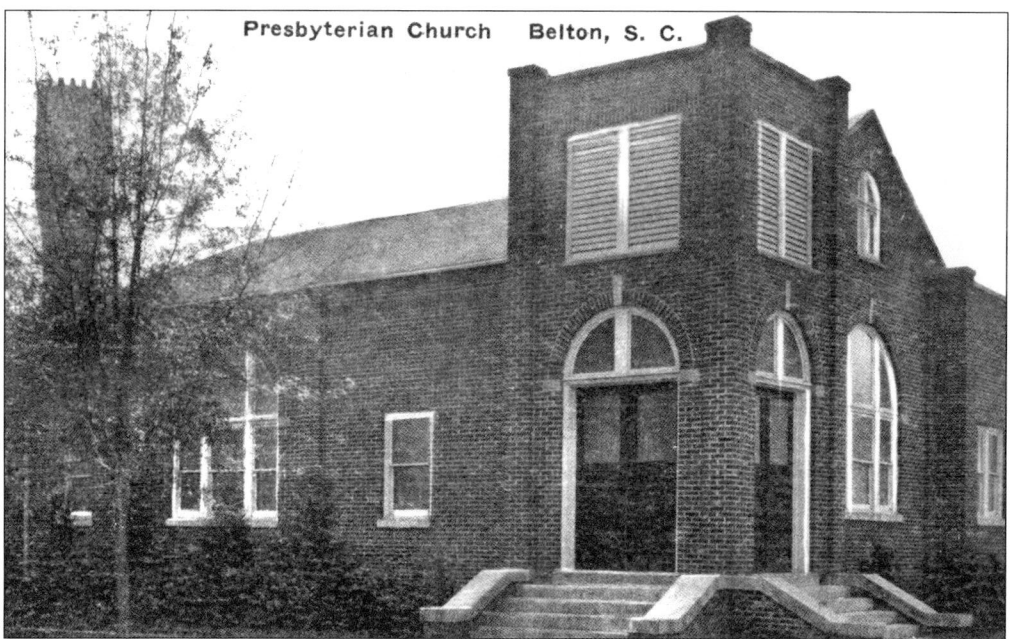

BELTON PRESBYTERIAN CHURCH, C. 1925. In 1851, Dr. George Brown donated a town lot to relocate the Broadway (Bradaway, Broadaway) Presbyterian Church. The old structure was dismantled and re-erected on the bequeathed site (the present site of Kentucky Fried Chicken). This church has the distinction of being the first church within city limits to be erected to the worship of God. The name was changed to Belton Presbyterian Church with the Rev. T.H. Reid dedicating the building with three days of communion. Built in 1925 at a cost of $12,500, the building shown here on the corner of Green and River Streets is the third building of worship for the Presbyterian church. The first service held in this building was on November 1, 1925, and when the building debt was satisfied, the church was dedicated on November 3, 1935. It was vacated in lieu of a new building erected on Brown Avenue in 1983.

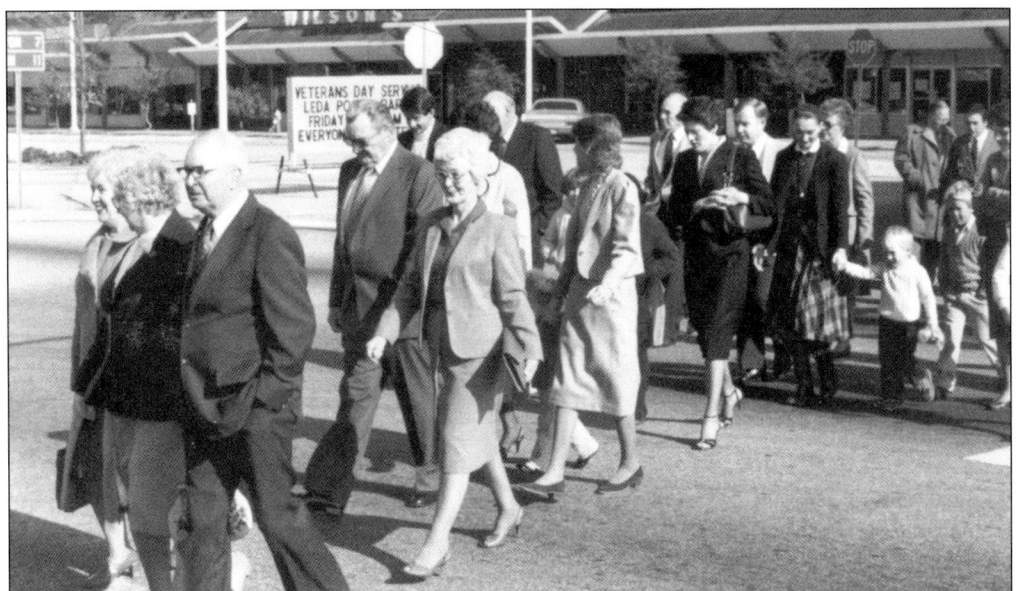

A HISTORIC MARCH. In October of 1983, the congregation of Belton Presbyterian Church walked the half-mile from its old location to its new sanctuary on Brown Avenue. Lewis "Bootsie" Blake and his wife Alice, Vivian Buchanan, Bill and Frances Gerisch, and other church members stroll through the City Square on their way to the new site. The church was under the leadership of the Rev. Jim Foil at the time.

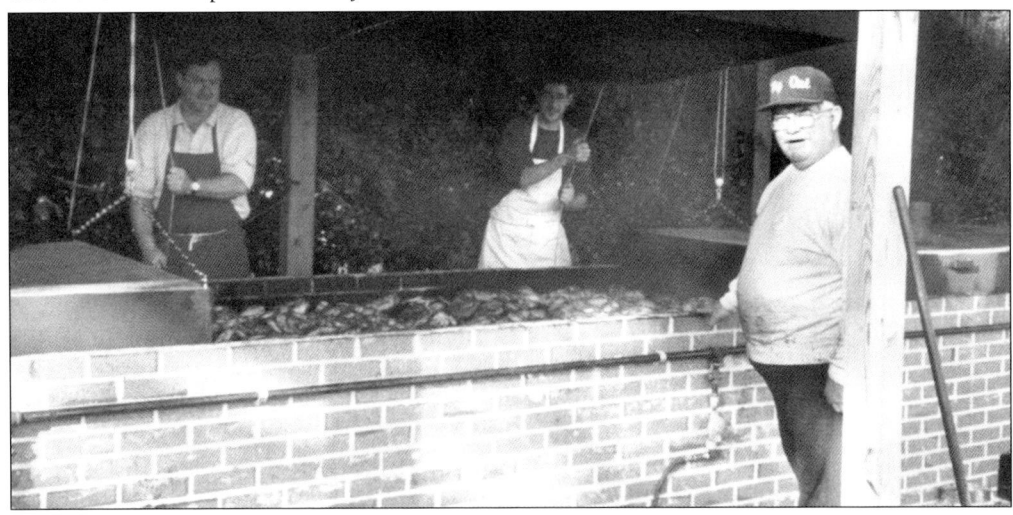

PIGGIN' OUT WITH THE PRESBYTERIANS. Every October since 1984, the Presbyterians have offered the absolute best barbecue for sale. When the smoke starts wafting over the Square, townspeople eagerly await the barbecued pork and chicken that will make up their lunch the next day. From its meager beginnings when they had to borrow all the utensils and ran out of barbecue to the smooth operation of today, the organizers have perfected the process. This year alone they barbecued 2,500 pounds of pork shoulders and 700 chicken halves, grossing $11,000 in sales. "Big Jim" Russell spearheads the project with the help of almost every member of the church. Here, John Broadwell, Benson Mattison, and David Bolton tend the chicken pit in 1999. The profit of this fundraiser has helped pay off the debt of the new church building and now funds donations to area charities such as Habitat for Humanity and the Hospice House.

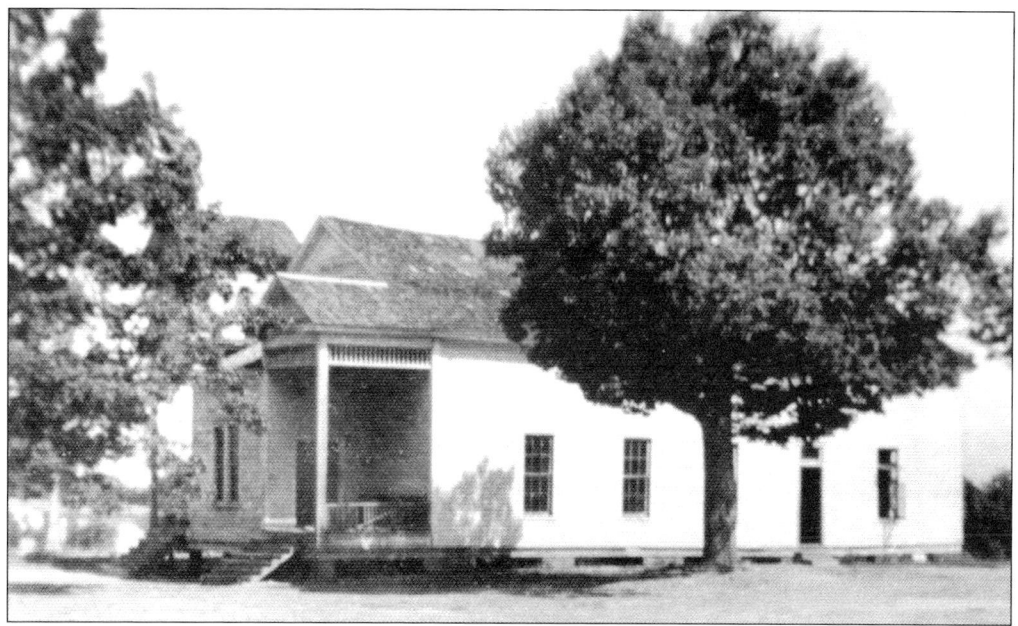

SERVING THE COMMUNITY FOR OVER 170 YEARS. Shady Grove Baptist Church of Christ was organized by 14 residents and two slaves of the Calhoun Community in 1833. The Broyles family gave the original building and land for the church, and the structure shown here was the third building erected by the congregation. It was built in 1853 under the pastorate of Rev. Alexander Acker. It was razed in 1939 after the present sanctuary was constructed.

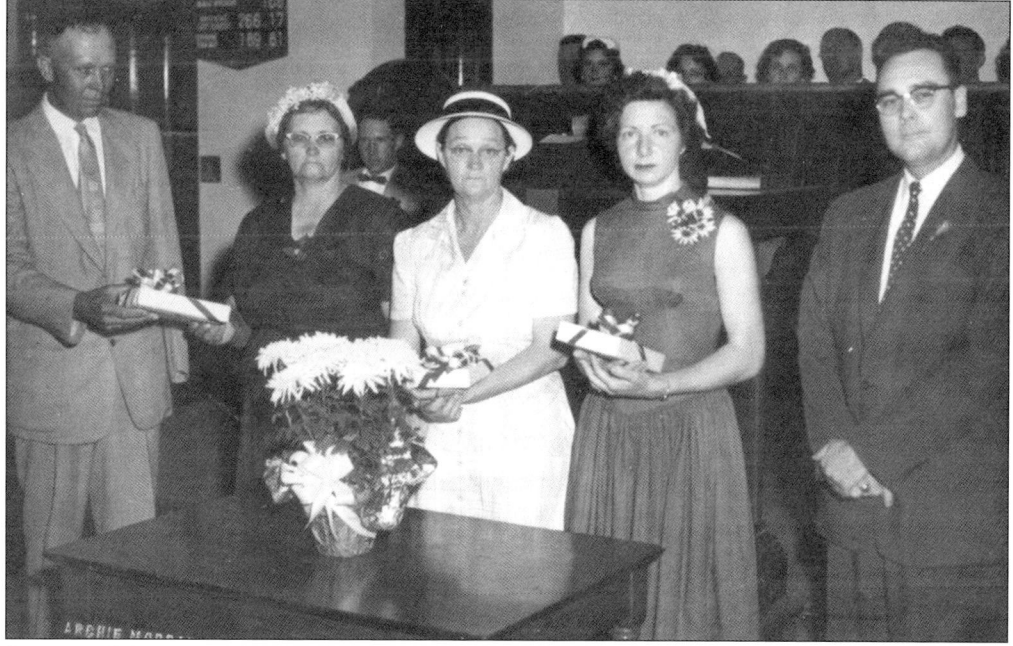

SAINTED MOTHERS. On Mother's Day in 1956, these Shady Grove Baptist Church mothers were recognized by the congregation: Blanche Arflin (most children), Maude Browning (oldest mother), and Ruth Caldwell (youngest mother). Buren McDowell and the Rev. David Lucas (pastor from 1954 to 1958) stand on either side of the honorees.

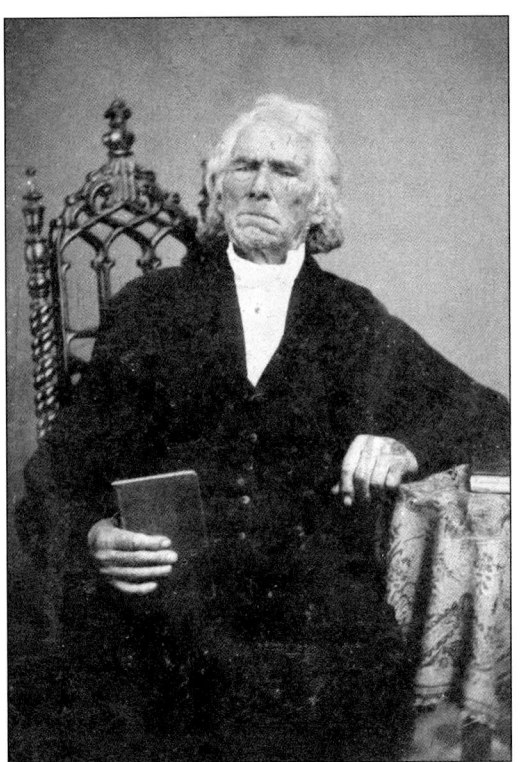

MISSIONARY ZEAL. In the 1840s, Rev. Alexander Acker and Rev. Robert King served as missionaries, evangelists for the Domestic Mission Board of the Saluda Baptist Association. They made tours through the mountain region of Oconee, Pickens, and Greenville Counties, distributing Bibles and religious literature and holding meetings. One legend says that on this tour in the Long Creek section of northwest South Carolina, the Rev. Bobby King, shown here, left his newly shined shoes on the front porch of the cabin in which he was staying. He had polished his shoes with tallow, or beef fat. The next morning when he went to search for his shoes, he found that the dogs had eaten them during the night, so he had to preach his appointed sermon barefoot that day. A person attending the religious meeting took pity on the forlorn gentleman and purchased a pair of shoes to replace those destroyed by the dogs. Later, after spending some time with the grateful minister, the patron was converted to the heavenly fold.

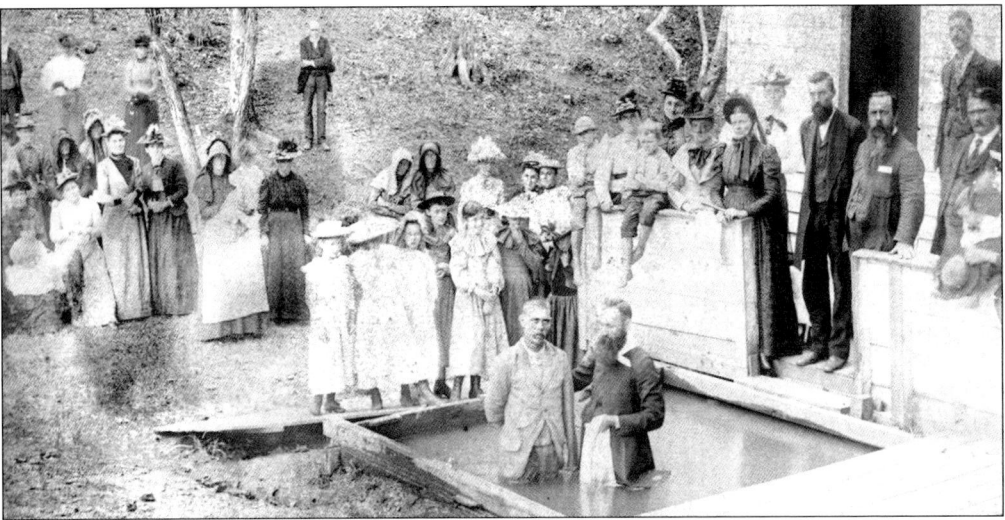

POOL BAPTISM, C. 1890. Dorchester Baptist Church was organized May 3, 1832, by about 40 members of the Big Creek, Neals Creek, and Hopewell Churches. Originally worshipping at the Rock Creek Brush Arbor, the church built a small wooden structure and gathered to worship once a month under the leadership of Rev. Bobby King. Even though most baptisms were held in creeks or rivers during the 19th century, this church was prompted by a great revival held in 1854, in which 40 persons were saved, to build a permanent structure. Water would be carried in large barrels to fill the pool for each baptismal occasion. Eventually filled in and covered over with dirt after the new church building housed an indoor baptismal, the pool was restored and dedicated on September 26, 2000.

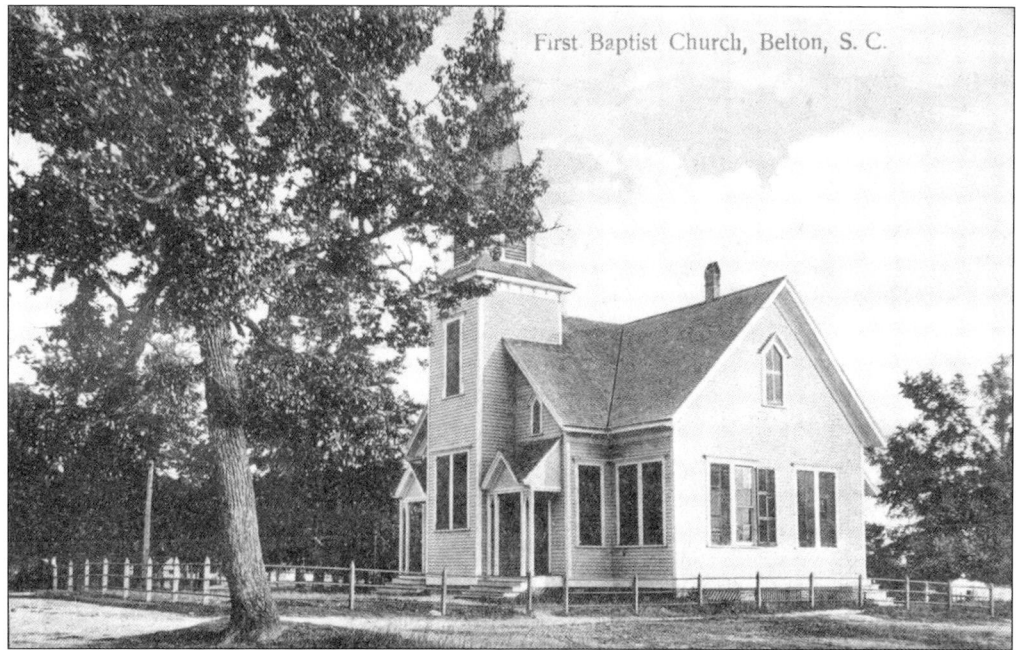

THE CHURCH ON THE PLAZA. In 1861, the First Baptist Church was conceived when 19 members met in Belton Academy to organize a church. John W. Harris donated three acres of land where the Belton cemetery now stands, and a one-room church of logs was built of wood donated by Billy Holmes. The Rev. Amaziah Rice was called to be the first pastor. In 1888, the church membership had outgrown the log structure, so a new frame church was constructed for $2,300 on what was known as the Plaza (present site of the Belton Tennis Center). A larger sanctuary was built in 1911 at the cost of $17,200 at the church's present Brown Avenue site. This facility has been added onto and renovated several times.

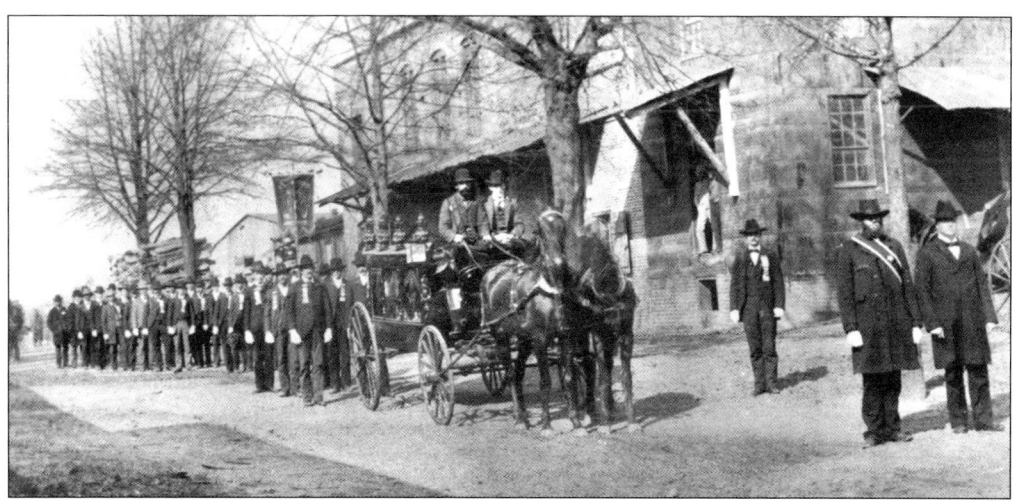

A CITY PATRIARCH LAID TO REST. R.A. Lewis served as deacon and treasurer of First Baptist Church for many years. His funeral was held the day after his death on November 11, 1909. As the traveling caravan made its way to the cemetery, the Rev. W.T. Tate, T.C. Poore, and Frank Robertson, chief of police, led the procession. Floyd M. Cox and J. B. Putman drove the hearse. The body is followed by members of the Woodmen of the World Myrtle Camp.

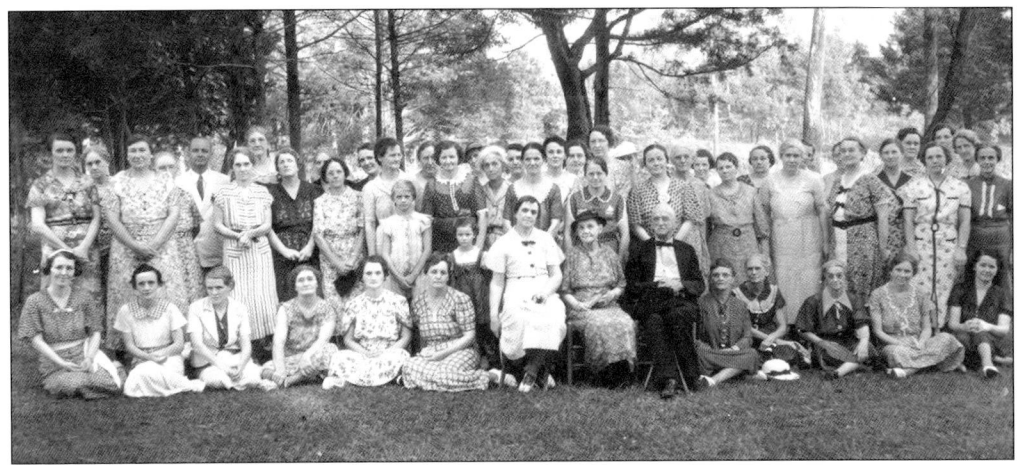

BESSIE RICE SUNDAY SCHOOL CLASS, 1937. Bessie Rice, the second wife of J.T. Rice, was a matchless Biblical scholar and a wise advisor. The following women, from left to right, attended her Sunday School class religiously: (front row) Mrs. Sumner, K. Hanks, Mrs. J. Anders, R. Green, F. Pinson, M. Boyce, Mrs. J.M. Burnett, B. Rice, J. Rice, I.G. Haynie, S. Willingham, M. Balentine, L. Ellison, and unidentified; (middle row) Mrs. W. Madden, P. Campbell, N. Henderson, Mrs. M. Rice, Mrs. J.D. Hunter, Mrs. B. Hanks with granddaughter M.J. Burris, Mrs. H. Meeks with daughter B. Meeks, Mrs. E. Stansell, Mrs. C. Campbell, Mrs. F. Ellison, R. Owen, B. Campbell, Mrs. L. Shirley, Mrs. F. Horton, M. McCuen, C. Murdock, and unidentified; (back row) E. Goodman, L. Kay, M. Rice, M. Willingham, unidentified, J. Haynie Rice, S. Poore, M. Gambrell, R.M. Bowie, Mrs. R. McMahan, M. Cox, L. Banister, unidentified, N. Moorehead, Mrs. B. Black, M.G. Whitlock, unidentified, Mrs. W. Cobb, J. Rice, E. Tollison, and E. Warnock.

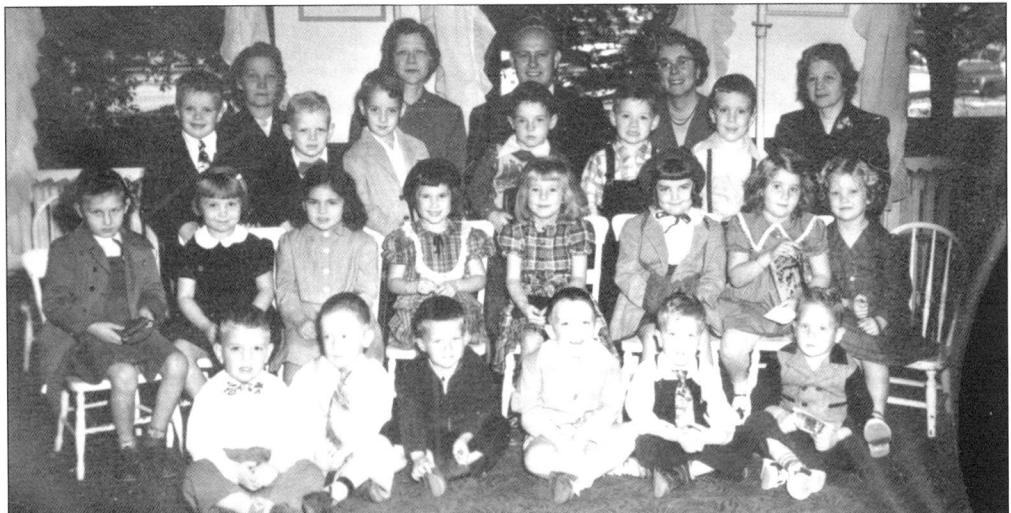

SPREADING HOLIDAY CHEER. The preschool department sent holiday greetings in 1951 to community residents. Featured on the card, from left to right, were the following children: (first row) Rex Maynard, Brooks Marshall, Carey Ellison, Jim Garrett, Ronnie Cox, and unidentified; (second row) Gale Smith, Pat Campbell, Nancy Haynie, Dianne Gambrell, Dawn Robinson, Elaine McClellan, Patty Anderson, and Linda Davis; (third row) Dickie Kay, Tommy Green, Van Chapman, Dave King, Billy Clinkscales, and John Keys; (fourth row) Edna Haynie, Mary Harris, Rev. D.H. Daniel (pastor), Irene Elgin, and Ruth Drake.

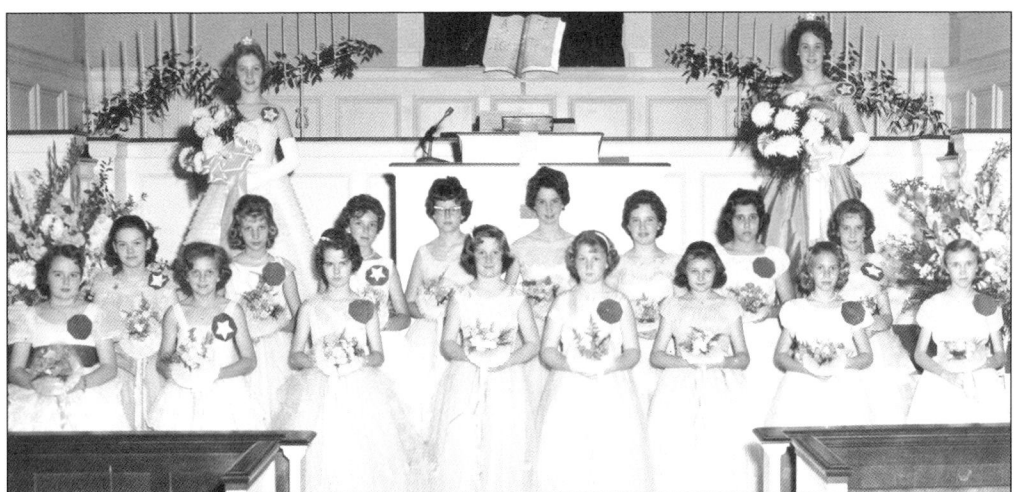

QUEEN AND COURT. The Girls in Action group, a missionary organization for young girls, held a coronation in May of 1962. Those attending were, from left to right, (first row) Becky McMahan, Jenny Cox, Joyce Major, Caroline Marshall, Mary Elizabeth Garrett, Charlene Smith, Margaret Lynn West, and Linda Murphy; (second row) Elizabeth Clinkscales, Barbara Newman, Martha Kay, unidentified, Jeanne Rice, Nancy Gambrell, Chris Annese, and Kaye Smith; (third row) Mopsey Marshall and Paula Rice.

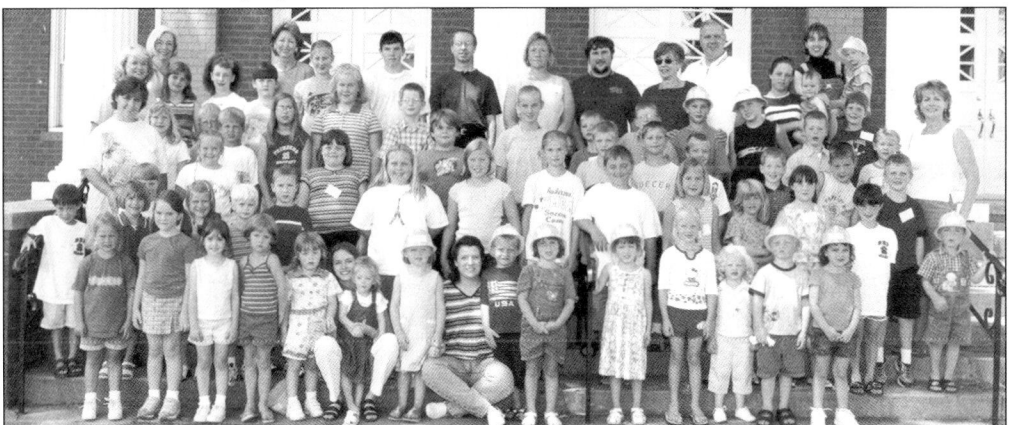

VBS CONSTRUCTION, JUNE 2002. Vacation Bible School is usually held the second week in June. Children from other area churches are welcomed. Assisting with the Habitat for Humanity project in conjunction with the Belton Presbyterian Church, the children who attended VBS raised over $1,000 to buy the studs to build a house for a needy person in Belton. Pictured here, from left to right, are (first row) M. Haynie, A. Gilreath, N. Gilreath, M.M. McCollum, D. Gambrell, K. Heller, unidentified, B. Wilson, A. Vaughn, P. Darby, unidentified, M.K. Holliday, S. Clinkscales, S. Darby, A. Darby, and M. Gravina; (second row) J. Sherard, J. Wilson, B. Butler, C. Meeks, J. Greer, K. Clinkscales, E. Meeks, D.J. Smith, M. Wilson, L. Eidson, L. Vaughn, E. Sherard, and C. Green; (third row) T. Sicard, C. Dixon, R. Carwile, L. Gambrell, J. Sicard, J. Darby, A. Darby, J. Clinkscales, S. Eidson, C. Kay, and C. McCollum; (fourth row) E. Beeks, J. Dorn, T. Haynie, unidentified, M. Greer, D. Eidson, A. Foster, Z. Farmer, R. Dorn, J. Smith, Z. Wilson, D. Epps, A. Green, C. Boatwright, and L. Boatwright; (fifth row) A. Darby, A. Burriss, K. Hoover, E. Lollis, unidentified, B. Locke, A. Meeks, M. Foster, E. Fort (minister of music), J. Green, J. Marshall, L. Nation, D. Tadlock (minister of youth), E. Player, B. Wilson, J. Rice, and B. Rice.

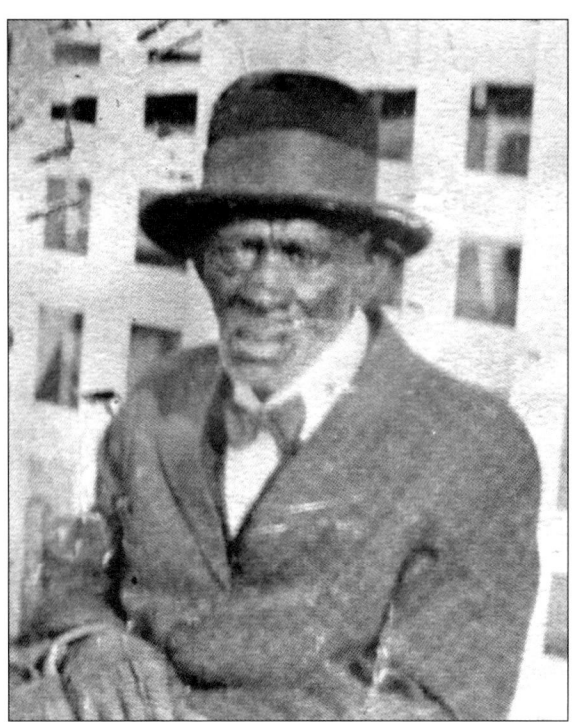

REV. STEWART OLIVER, C. 1910. Denied membership in the First Baptist Church by a formal resolution in 1866, the black members, with the aide of the mother church, formed a separate congregation, and Mt. Zion was born. The members met in a brush arbor under the guidance of the Rev. Peter Walker (a white pastor) until the Rev. Frank Morris became the unanimously elected pastor in 1868. In 1886, the Rev. Stewart Oliver, shown here, was called to fill the pulpit. Under his guidance, a third church structure made of brick was built to house the growing congregation, and Sister Corrie Watkins formed the Woman's Missionary Society. The Rev. Oliver continued in his undying devotion to the spiritual growth of his people until he left the pulpit in 1933.

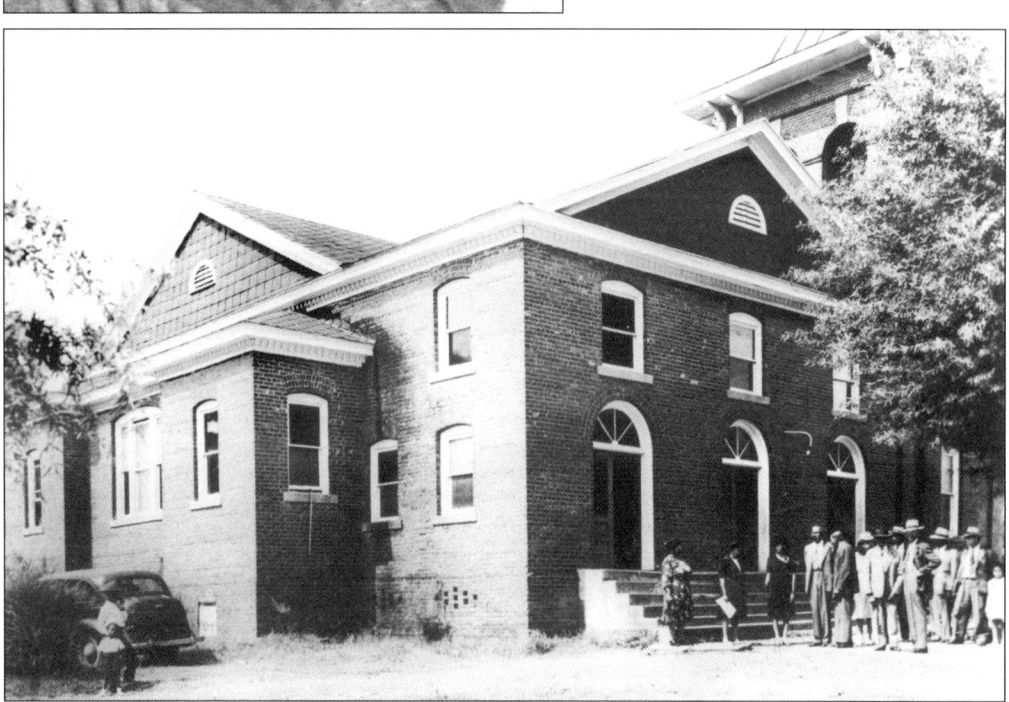

A HOLY PURPOSE. On August 11, 1911, the first brick sanctuary was completed at a cost of $3,000. This building served the congregation until 1977, when a modern brick building with Sunday School rooms was erected on the same site as this edifice. Mt. Zion is a member of the Rocky River Baptist Association. The church takes the Great Commission (Matthew 28:19–20) as its statement of purpose.

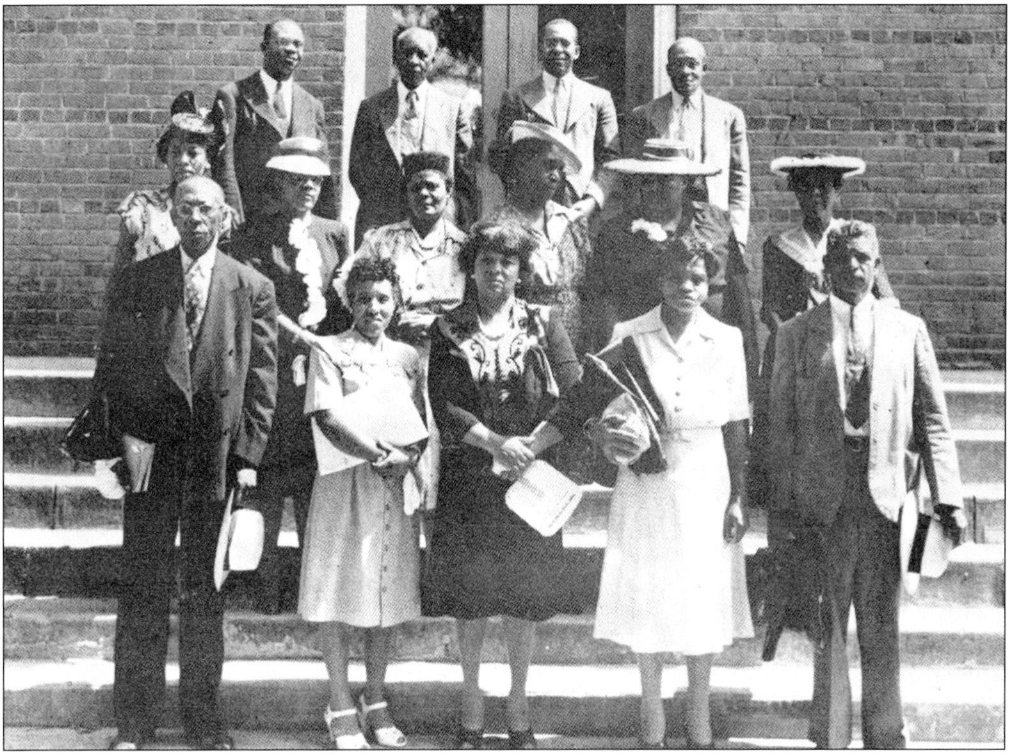

MT. ZION CHOIR, 1958. Choir members included Fred Mattison, I.B. Bradley, Louise Bradley, Rosena Greelee, Leila Anerson, Foster Palmer, Addie Brazeale, Lucia Brown, Melrose Best, Matie Green, Thomasina Alexander, Robert Keith, Mozelle Payton, and Maud Cox. Ed Jefferson fondly recalls Foster Palmer, a talented reed player, lifting up songs of praise on his clarinet during services.

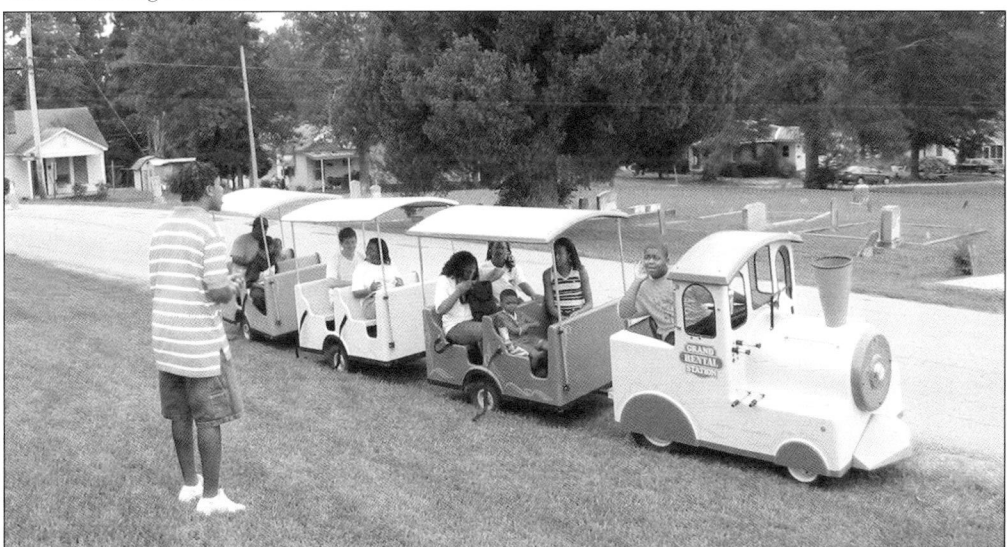

REACHING OUT TO THE COMMUNITY. For three years Mt. Zion has sponsored a free multiracial, community-wide festival complete with games, prizes, delicious food, singing, and fellowship. Church members distribute religious tracts and witness to those who attend.

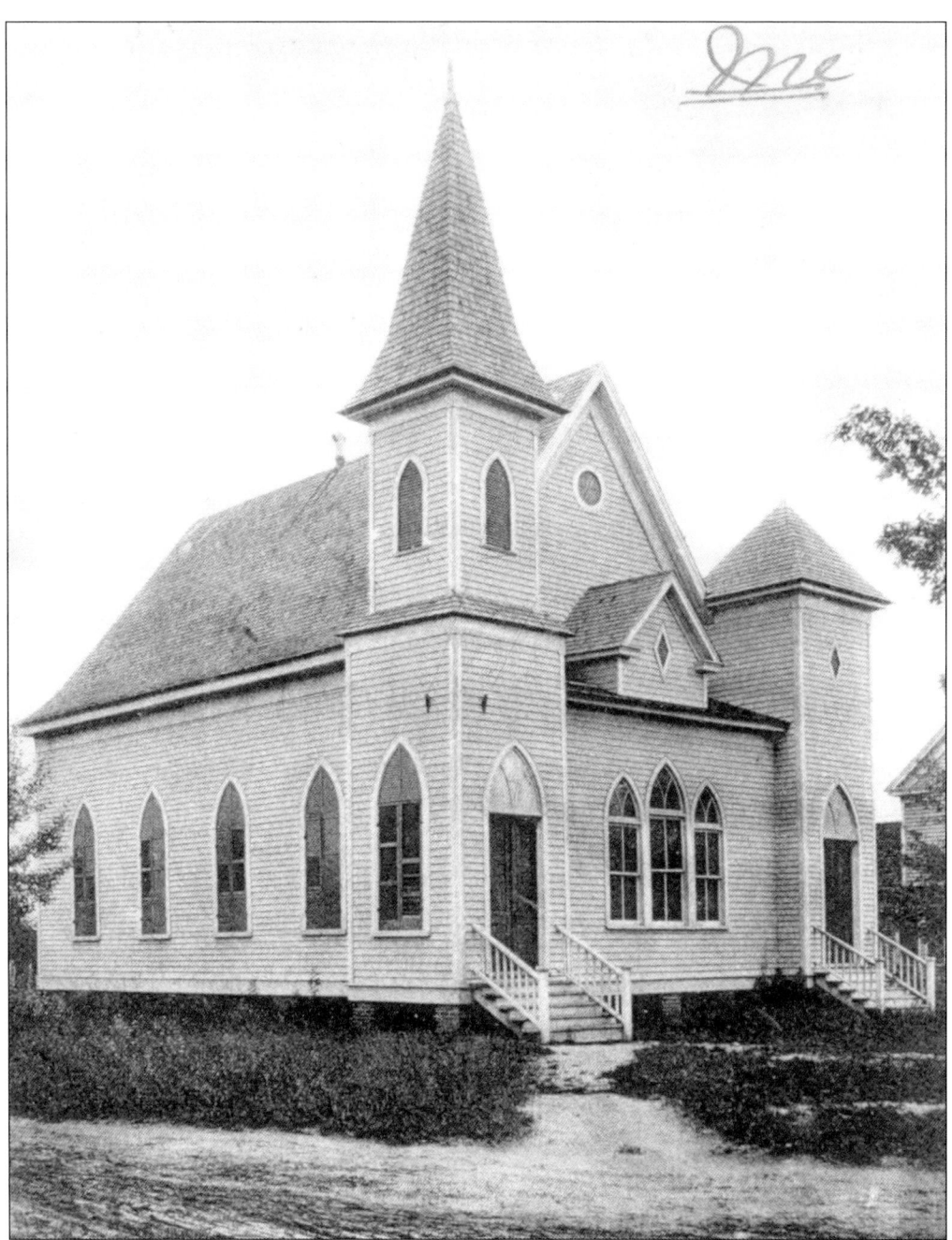

THE LITTLE BROWN CHURCH IN THE VALE. In 1876, Rev. John Attaway organized the Belton Methodist Episcopal Church South. The congregation met at the Presbyterian Church until 1882, when this frame meeting house was built at the corner of River and Green Streets. In this c. 1910 picture, the original structure has been enlarged, and two separate entries are provided for men and women. The church was renamed in 1911 in honor of Sen. Asbury Churchwell Latimer, who was a faithful member, teacher, and benefactor. The church was extensively renovated in 1942, with brick added to the exterior and new stained glass windows. A steeple was added in 1992.

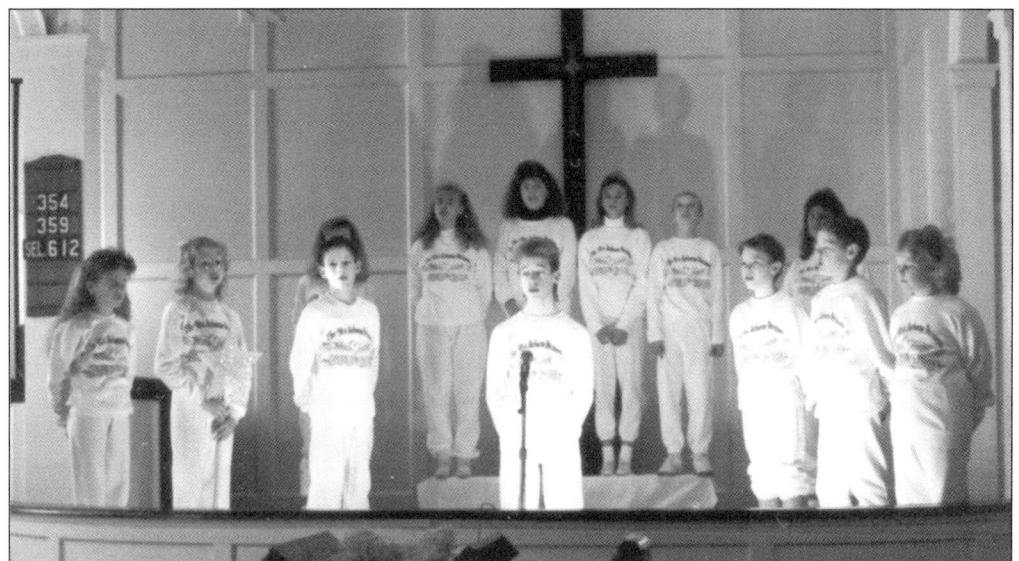

CHRISTMAS ANGELS. The youth choir of Latimer Memorial Methodist Church produces and performs a play each Christmas season. This picture shows, from left to right, (front row) Elizabeth Dial, Leona Walfield, Andy Burleson, Bud Smith, David Burleson, Allen Ferguson, and Janet Pinson; (back row) Jane Walfield, Jill Minton, Kelli O'Cain, Ellen Eaves, Alan Walfield, and Kerry Anderson. The musical was staged on December 17, 1989, and was entitled *Arch the Angel: Angels of the 91st AirBorne*.

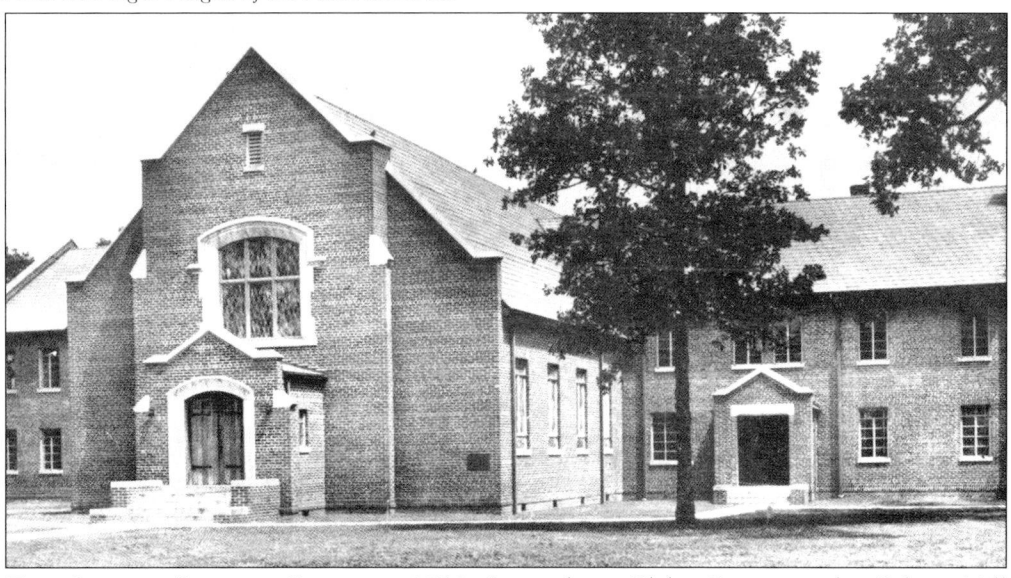

THE SECOND BAPTIST CHURCH, 1956. Located on Blake Street in the Belton Mill community, the Second Baptist Church was organized in 1901 and had a congregation of about 750 members by the mid-1950s. The Rev. Harold E. Cunningham was pastor, and Jimmie Mize was the Sunday School superintendent. Constructed in 1947 at a cost of $130,000 with the financial backing of the Belton Mill, this building replaced the wooden structure that had housed the congregation for over four decades. The old church building was renovated and used as a recreational center for the young people of Belton. In 1996, the church moved to its present site on Anderson Highway and has a current membership of 1,005.

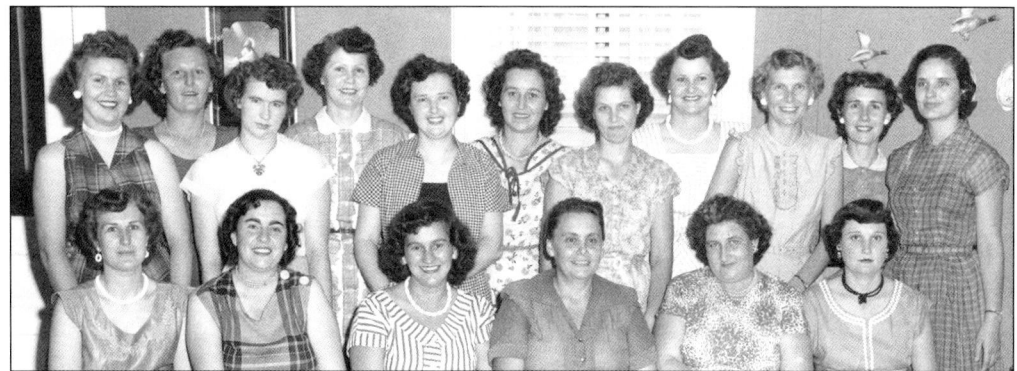

SUNDAY SCHOOL CLASS, 1960S. Ruth Silvers' Sunday School class met for an after-church social at their teacher's home, c. 1965. Members included, from left to right, (front row) Christine Oates, Emma Lee Shaw Lowe, Helen Hawkins Finley, Ruth Silvers, Louise Mattison Snipes, and Sara Faye Bruce Timms; (middle row) Allie Sue Escoe Sellers, Jeanette Ashley Rice, Ann Lawson, ? Edwards, ? Rentz, and Betty Shaw; (back row) Jenette Reeves Strickland, Ruth Escoe Madden, Meleeda Wilson, Lovelle Escoe Knight, and Mae Snipes Minyard.

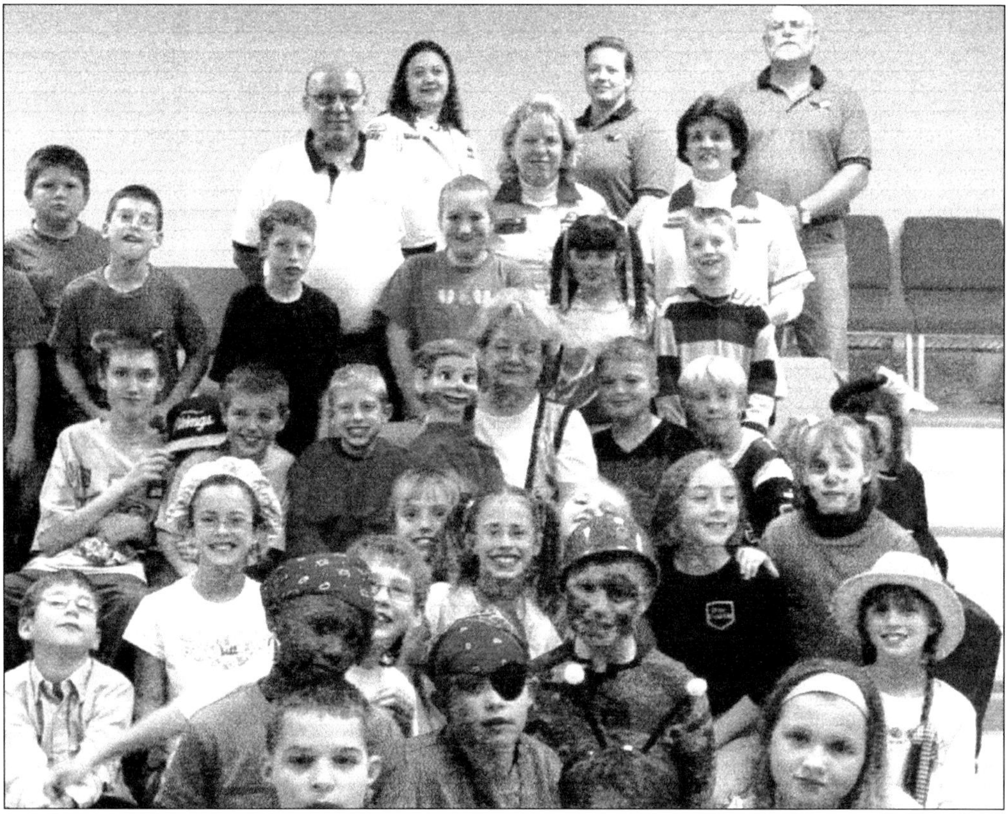

YOU'VE GOT A FRIEND IN ME. Linda Brooks (center), wife of pastor Mitch Brooks, performs her ventriloquist act with her friend Lonnie, much to the delight of the children in the Awana program. The children meet each Wednesday and memorize Bible verses to earn badges, play games, and compete for points to redeem for Awana Bucks. Some of the leaders pictured with this group are Danny Whitt, Becky Holloway, Patti Campbell, Beth Lindsay, Cynthia Ellison, and Commander Neil Ivester.

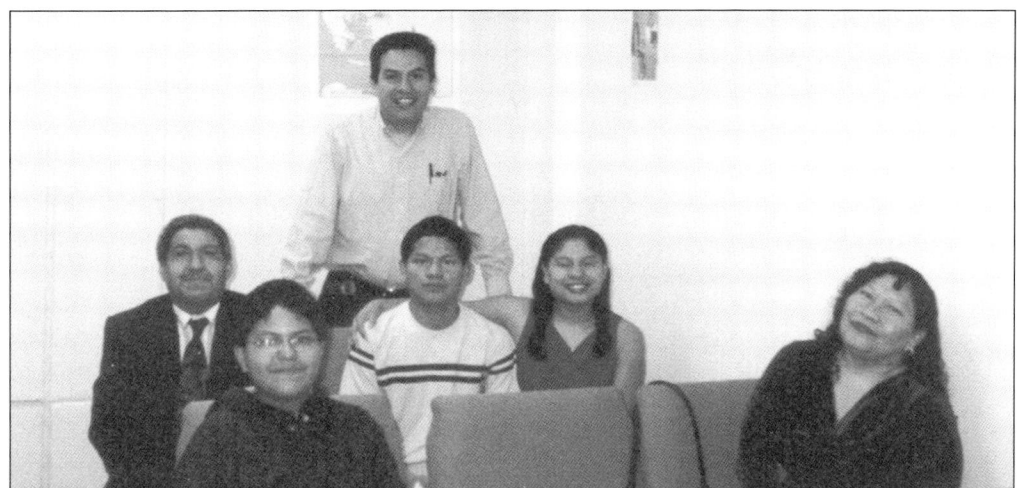

PALABRA DA VIDA. The Second Baptist Church began a Spanish-speaking ministry in 2000, and with the help of Ricardo Benitez, the church is reaching out to the Hispanic community in Belton. Thirteen Hispanic neighbors are part of the class, whose title means "Word of Life." Pictured here, from left to right, are a few members: (front row) Joshua Montaya and Catalina Montaya; (middle row) Geronimo Montaya, George Montaya, and Ruth Montaya; (back row) Ricardo Benitez.

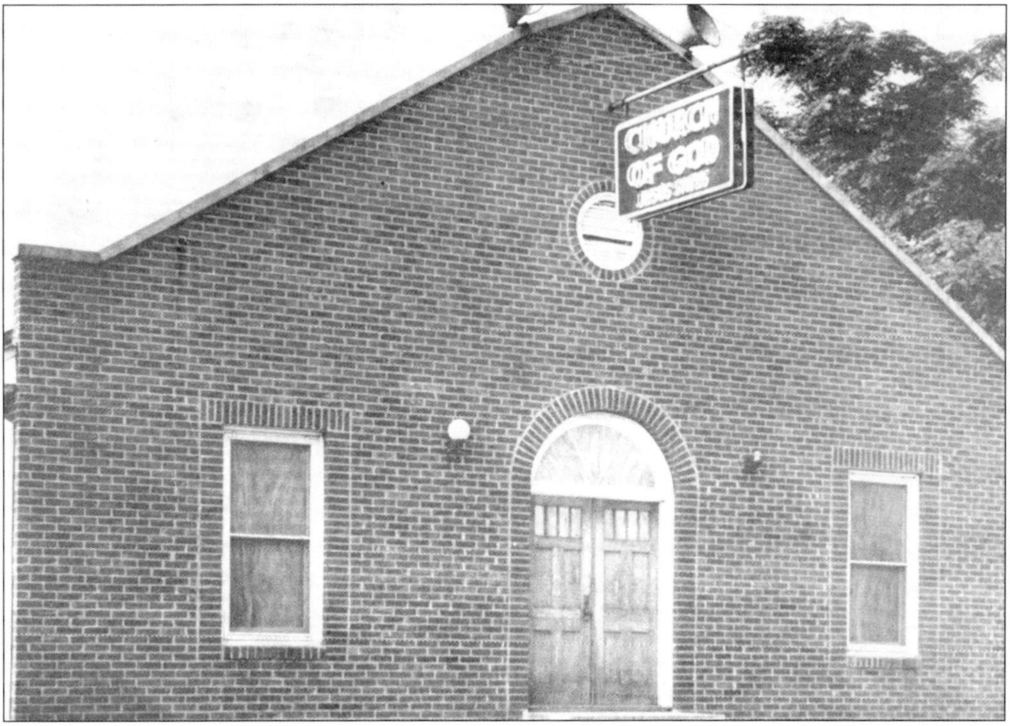

ATTENTION-GETTING SIGN. In 1955, the Belton Church of God was located on Shirley Street. At that time the church, which was organized in 1924, had a membership of over 200 and an average Sunday School attendance of 250. The church moved to its new facility on North Main Street in 1964. Approximately 100 to 150 teenagers participate in the church's youth group activities each Wednesday night.

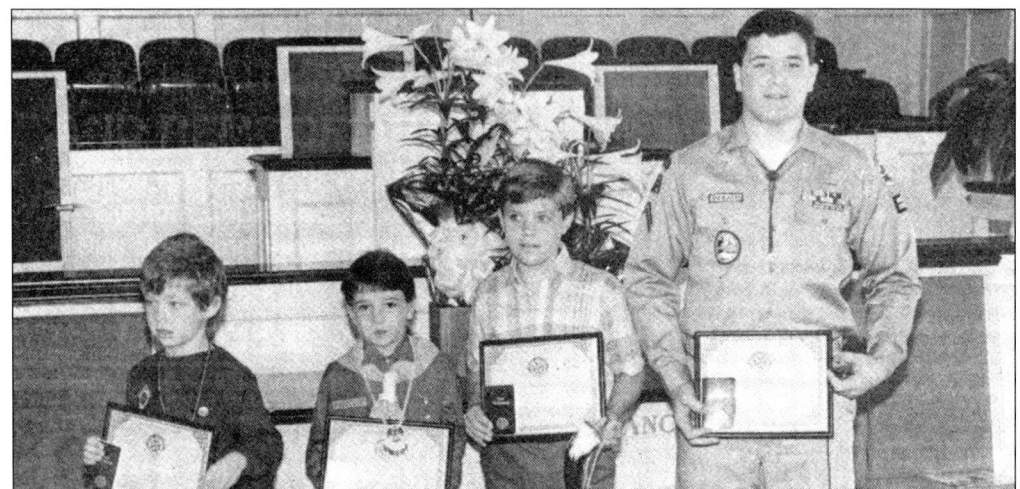

ROYAL RANGERS OF THE YEAR, 1991. Nick Frye was selected Royal Ranger of the Year, Straight Arrow Division; Christopher Cooley, Buckaroo Division; Joshua Hawkins, Pioneer Division; and Matt LeCroy, Trailblazer Division. The official boys' ministry of the Pentecostal Holiness Church, the Royal Rangers meet every Wednesday night and plan outings, develop personal skills, and participate in Bible studies. The Belton Pentecostal Holiness Church, organized in 1904, worships in a large structure on Calhoun Road, which was built at a cost of $500,000 and dedicated in June of 1980.

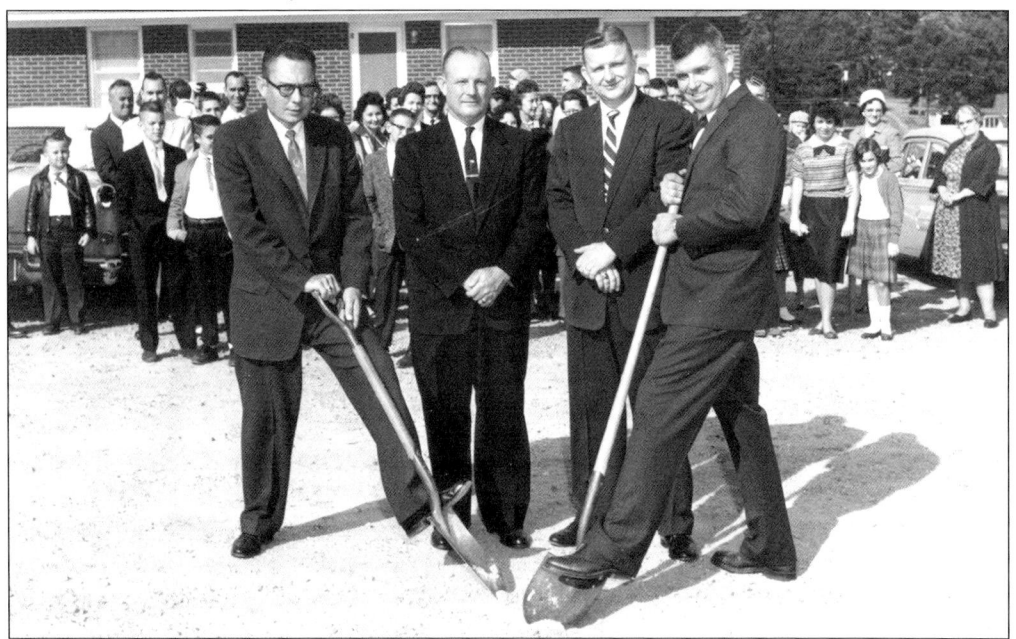

A NEW BAPTIST CHAPEL TO BEGIN IN JANUARY. James Mitchell, Bill Allen, Frank Shirley, and Julius Cox break ground in October 1959 for the structure that would eventually become Eastview Baptist Church. Members of the chapel committee were Clyde Cox, Bill Allen, Marvin Kay, Stanley Wilson, and Max M. Rice Jr. Sponsored by the First Baptist Church, the chapel was constructed on Meeks Drive and completed for opening on January 24, 1960, with 121 persons present for worship. Four old buses were purchased to provide Sunday School and nursery space. The sanctuary built in 1968 can hold 800 people.

Eight
MILL LIFE

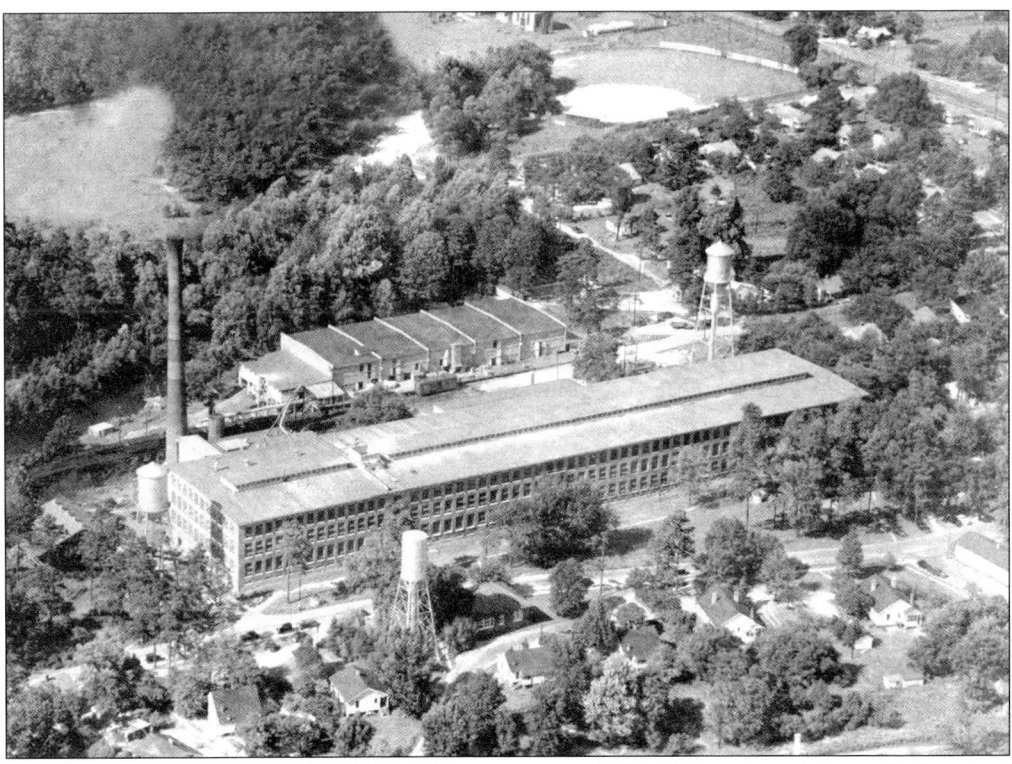

A MILL IS BORN. Through the efforts of R.A. Lewis and W.B. West, Capt. Ellison A. Smyth of Pelzer was convinced to begin a mill in Belton in 1899. With Captain Smyth, president, and Lewis D. Blake, secretary and treasurer, the first board of directors included F.J. Pelzer, R.A. Lewis, R.T. Woodward, J.T. Rice, A.L. Kelly, and J. Adger Smythe. In July 1900, operations began with 88 cards, 27,272 spindles, and 600 looms. In 1940, J.P. Abney of Greenwood acquired the controlling interest in the plant. By 1952, Belton Mill had 63,000 spindles, 1,650 looms, 1,000 employees, and produced 47 million yards of cloth annually. The mill manufactured sheetings, printcloths, three-leaf twills, and polyester/cotton blends until 1977, when the plant was shut down. This picture shows the plant and surrounding property in 1952.

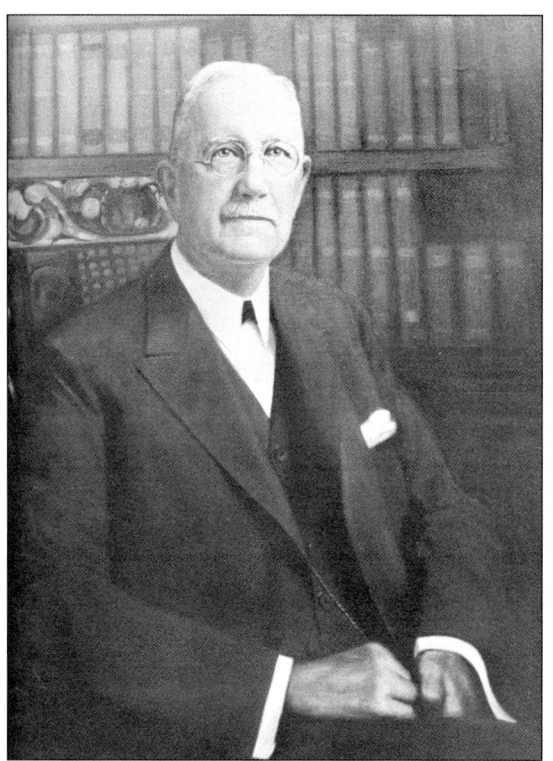

ENTREPRENEUR, CIVIC LEADER, AND SOLDIER. Entrepreneur and president of the Belton Mill, Ellison A. Smyth is pictured here as he appeared c. 1910, at the height of his career. A native of Charleston, he enlisted in the Civil War when his schooling was interrupted and served in the last battle on South Carolina soil near Williamston. After the armistice, he traveled by foot back home, and on his way he recalls thinking that the potential water power of the untamed rivers of the upstate should be developed. After selling his business ventures in Charleston, he struck out to build a mill, first in Pelzer, then in Belton, and then again in Greenville. He loved the mountains and owned a North Carolina estate he named Connemara, the home that is synonymous with Carl Sandburg today.

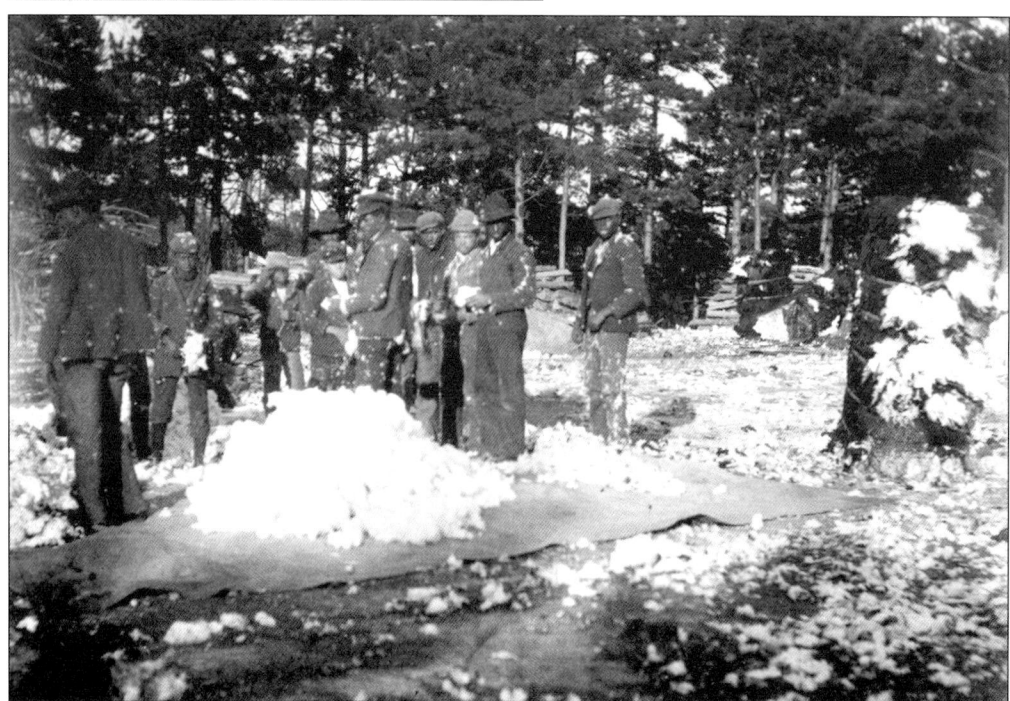

SORTING COTTON, C. 1905. When cotton was brought to the plant, black workers called "lint heads" took on the task of sorting the various grades of fibers. It was a messy job and the cotton fibers would stick to clothing and hair, thus the nickname was coined.

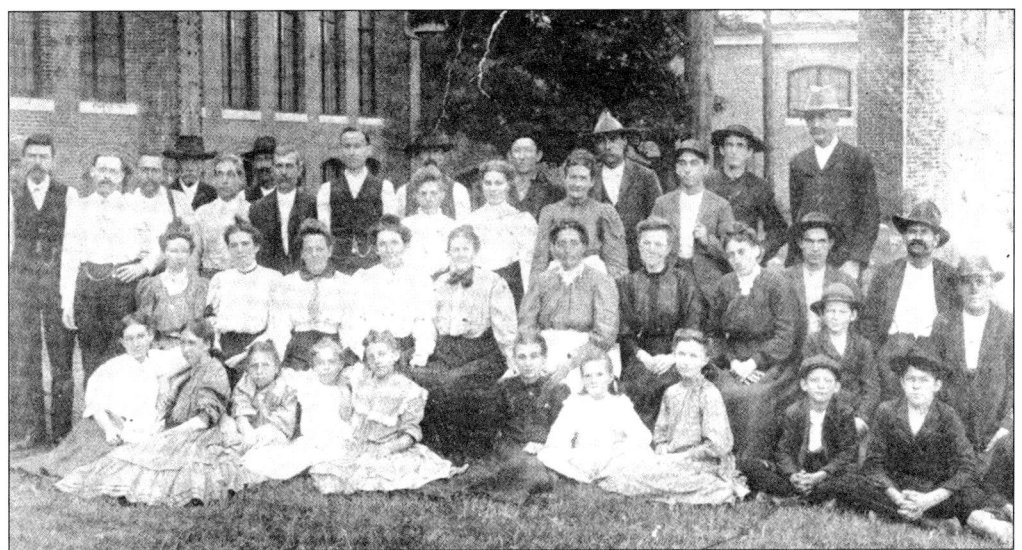

BELTON MILL, 1908 CLOTH ROOM EMPLOYEES. Before child labor laws were enforced, children as young as eight could be found working in the mill. Charlie Thompson recalls his daddy Hentz Thompson saying that when he first started working at the mill at eight years old, he would be forced to hide when the inspectors came to audit the employment conditions.

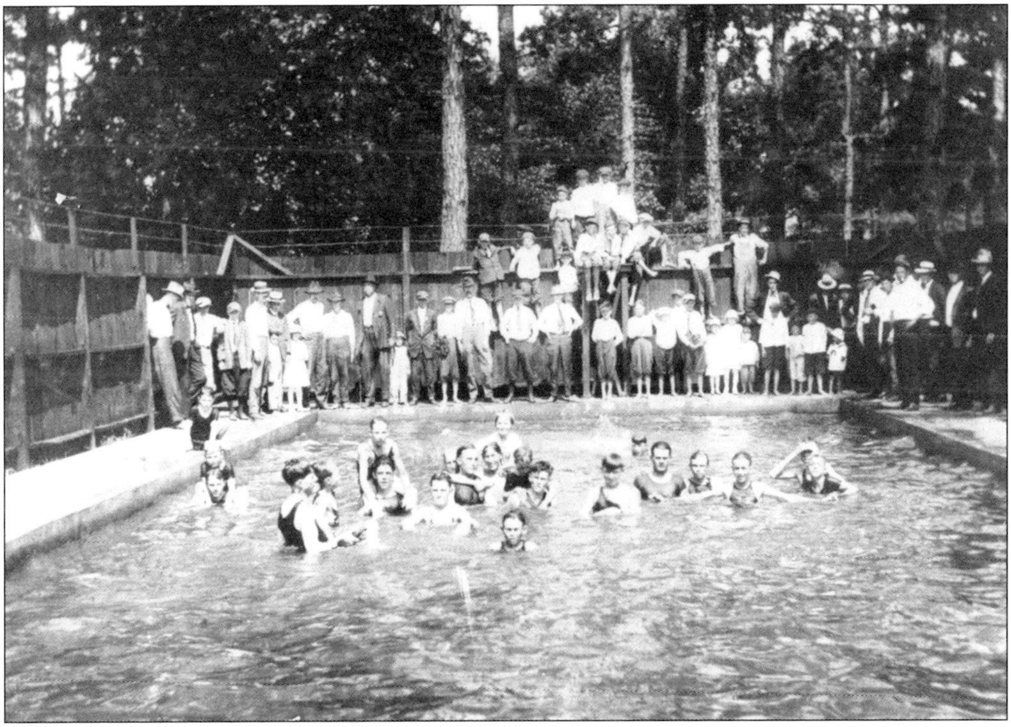

OPENING OF SWIMMING POOL FOR BELTON MILL EMPLOYEES, C. 1920. Managers at Belton Mill were always trying to improve the lives of their employees. In addition to a community house where games and activities were scheduled, the mill built a swimming pool for the enjoyment of its workers. Unfortunately, decorum dictated that only men and boys could use the pool and they must be clad in full dress (note t-shirt tops as part of bathing suits).

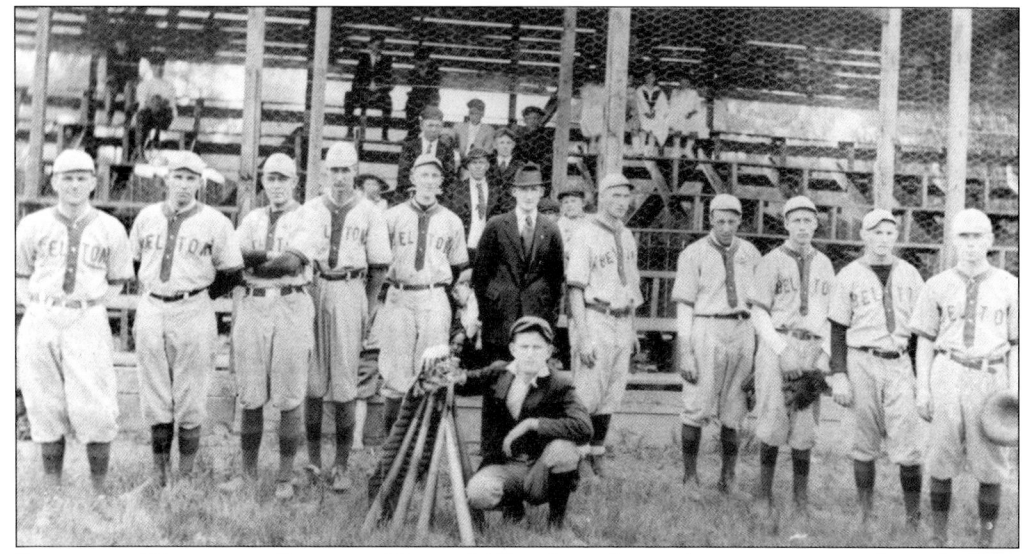

BASEBALL WAS THE COTTON KING. Mills throughout the state engaged in healthy competition when their baseball teams hit the field. As the only entertainment during the first half of the 20th century, mill baseball attracted townspeople and mill employees alike to the games. Belton Mill began fielding a team in 1905. Two former Belton Mill players went on to the majors: Leroy Mahaffey to Pittsburg in 1926 and Flint Rhem to St. Louis in 1924. This picture shows the 1920 baseball team, from left to right, with the mill stadium stands behind them: John Thomas, unidentified, "Bus" Bannister, James Clement, Eugene Snipes, DeWitt T. Snipes (manager), Clyde Snipes, John Campbell, unidentified, Bill Stephens, unidentified, and bat boy Ray "Pig" Snipes.

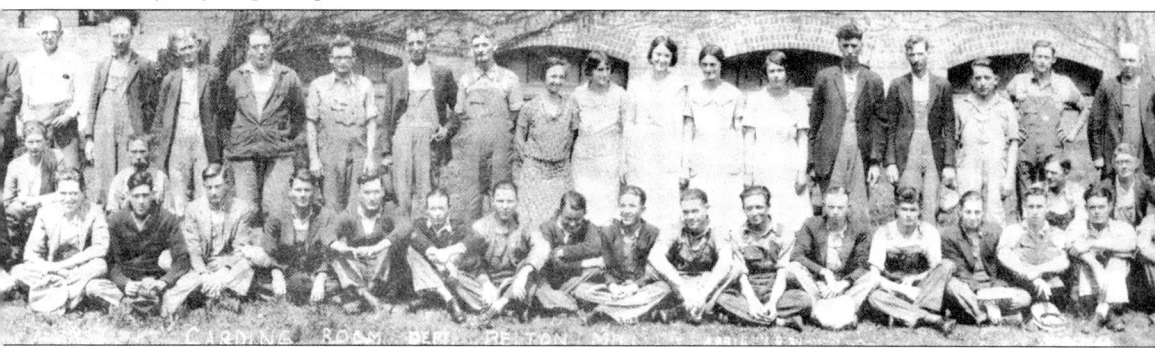

1931 CARD ROOM, BELTON MILL. Identified in this photograph are ? Carter, Gene Holtzclaw, Ike Allred, Monk Madden, Henry Shaw, Silas Smith, Sam Allred, Jack Allred, Kent Kelly, ? Nelson, ? Nelson and ? Cummings. Most of these employees were working when the first strike occurred on May 29, 1933. The employees closed down the mill by pulling switches. No union existed at this time, but the workers' demands included a 15 percent pay raise and a few minor workload adjustments. The strike was settled by the offer of a 10 percent increase in wages and a compromise on the workload of weavers and loom fixers. The mill started operation again on June 6, 1933. The next year, workers pulled the switches again on May 31, 1934, shutting down the mill. No demands were brought to the attention of the management, so in September someone conceived the idea to write the president a postcard requesting that the mill be started back up. The first card was received on Sunday, September 16, and two days later 81 percent of the workers had sent in a card. On September 20, 1934, the employees reported to work for the same pay and under the same conditions as previously.

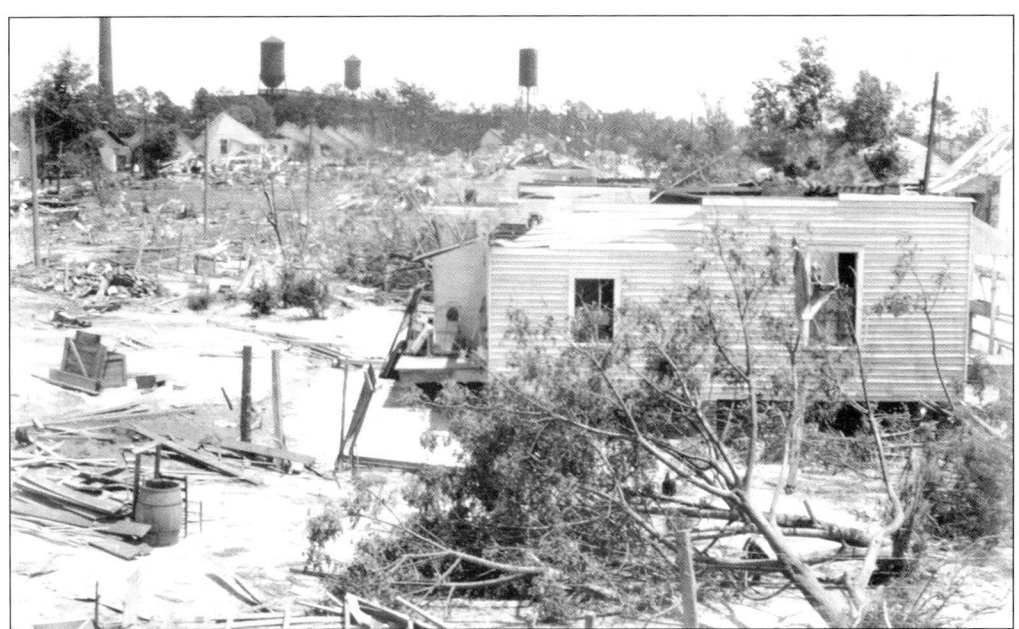

DEVASTATION. This view shows the damage done to the Belton Mill village after a tornado ripped through the town on May 5, 1933. About 2:00 p.m. on a Friday afternoon, employees were busy doing their jobs when all of a sudden the power went out and the windows of the mill were blown out. The mill suffered no more damage than the broken window panes. DeWitt Snipes was told by his supervisor to run home to check on his family since the tornado had blown away most of the houses on his street. Being careful not to step on any loose wires, Snipes found that indeed his house had been demolished, but his family was safe. Thirteen people had gathered at a neighbor's house in a room left standing when all others had been peeled away. This miraculous story and many others like it were told subsequent to the damage done that day.

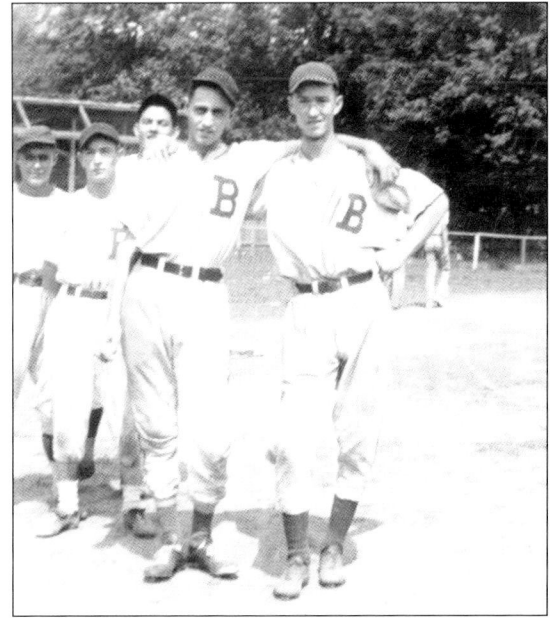

BATTER UP! By 1936, Belton Mill's baseball team had taken on the name the Belton Athletics. The team participated in the Anderson County League. Players listed that year included Bumgardner, Minyard, Willingham, McAllister, Deanhardt, Gunn, R. Owens, Nelson, Glenn, D. Owens, Shirley, Hogg Vost, Cummings, Shockley, Best, Carlton, Warnock, Haynie, Ellison, Hopper, and Shirley. Here, "Cotton" Nelson, Walter "Fat" Nelson, unidentified, Sherman "Lefty" Carlton, and Charles Minyard strike a pose before their next game. They had a 5–9 season that year.

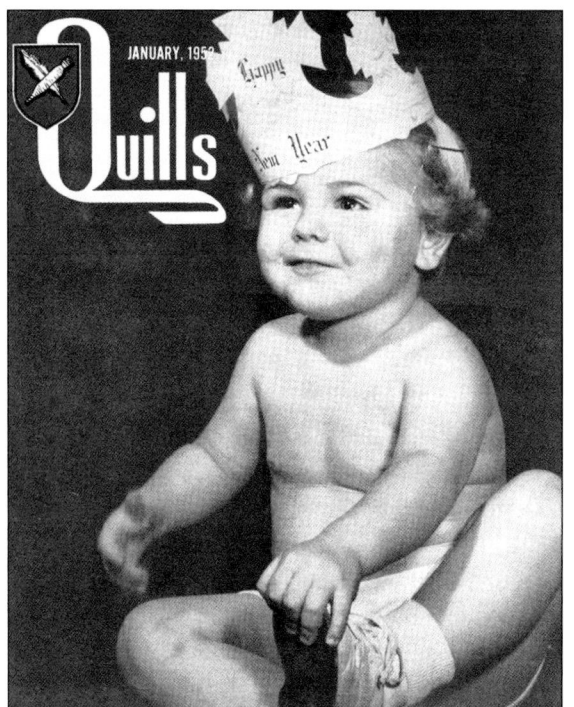

CUTE AS A BABY. *Quills*, the official magazine of the Abney Mill family, featured articles about safety, events at the different mills, and informative pieces. On the January 1952 cover sits a Happy New Year baby, June Madden (Horton), who was born on December 12, 1949. June's crown was made and lettered by Mrs. Talmadge Embler, wife of the assistant superintendent at Anderson Mill. June is best known as a dance instructor for many a Belton girl.

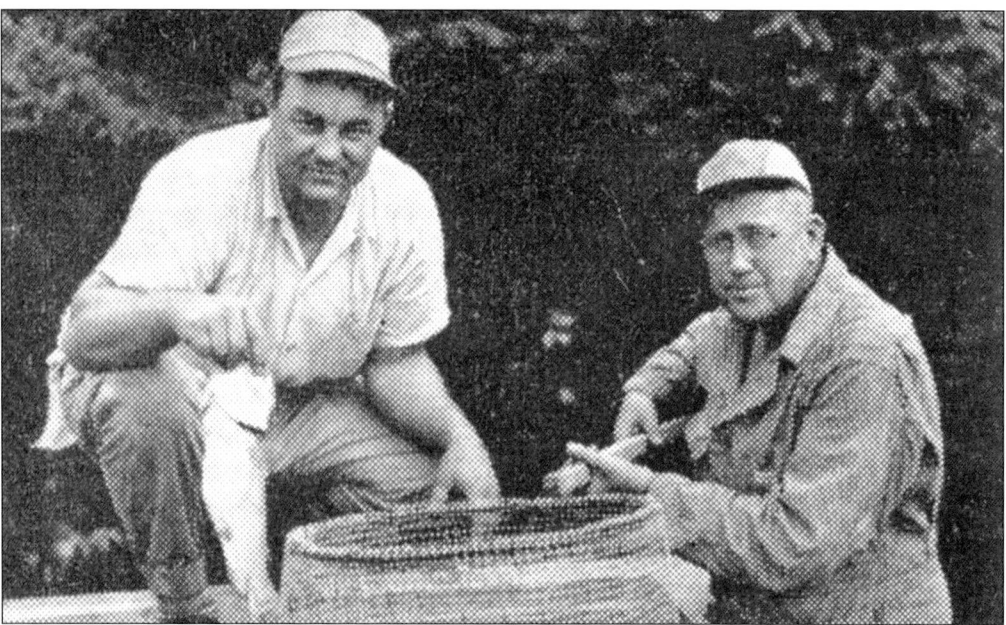

A FISHY STORY. The Belton Mill Fishing Club was organized in January 1952. In 1953, the Belton Mill pond was turned over to the club. Club members sponsored a community carnival, which cleared some $200, and the money was used to stock the pond with 1,500 pounds of catfish brought back from Santee Cooper. The pond already had been stocked with bream and bass. Any Belton Mill employee was allowed to fish at the pond on Wednesday afternoons. Ten fish was the limit. In this picture, Fishing Club president Ralph Woods and weigher Gene Holtzclaw prepare to stock the pond.

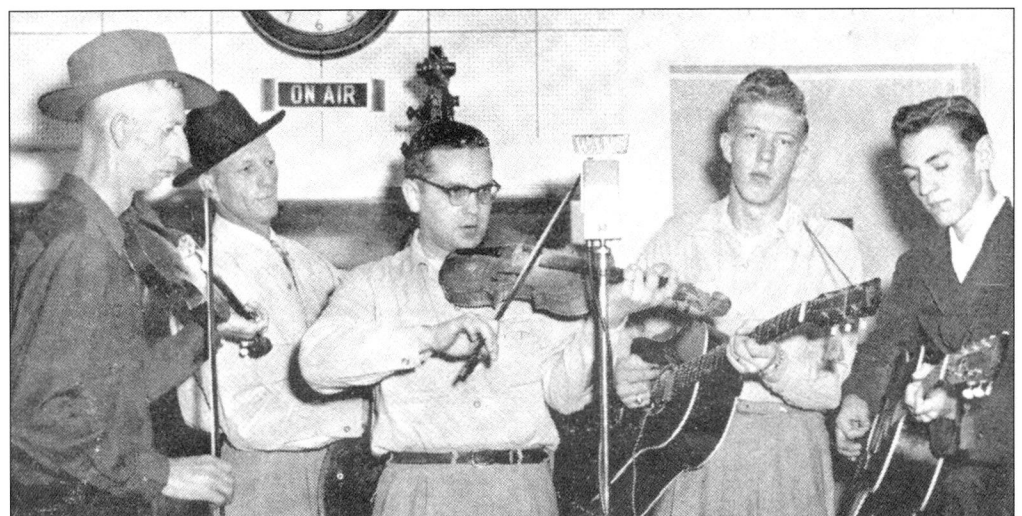

WATERMELON ON THE VINE. When mill employees turned up the volume on their radios and captured the Saturday morning broadcast from WANS in 1952, they heard a little bit of home on the waves. Lonesome Luke and his string band had been fiddling their way into the hearts of Beltonians for a decade before they got their music show on the air. Famous for their songs "The Soldier's Last Letter," "Down Yonder," and "The Wild Wood Flower," the 11-piece band whipped out one witty remark after another in between singing their favorite tunes. "Fiddling Judge" (Bob Thompson), "Lonesome Luke" McKee, "Poke Salad John" (Carroll Lee), Dickie Lloyd, and Little Jimmy Lowe tune up before a show.

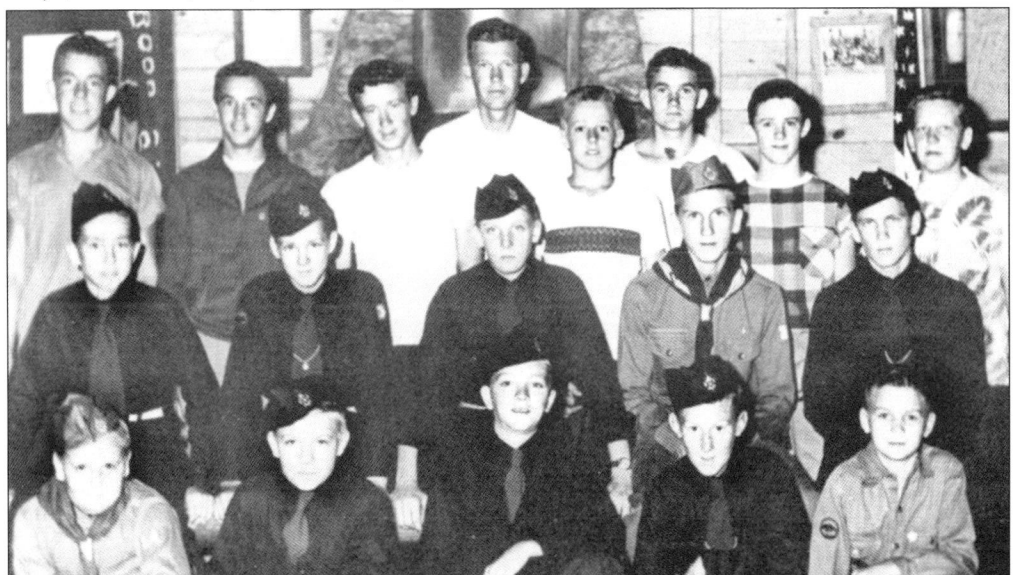

BELTON MILL SCOUT TROOP #34. In 1951, the Boy Scout Troop of Belton Mill posed as follows, from left to right, at the troop's scout cabin: (front row) Wilton "Buddy" Johnson, David "Duck" Shirley, Doug Broome, Doyle Martin, and Billy Dunlap; (middle row) Jimmy Bannister, Randy Campbell, John Hawkins, Joda Snipes, and Randolph Snipes; (back row) James "Moose" Philyaw, Dink Malone, Billy Lowe, Luther Rentz (scoutmaster), Jimmy Larry Lowe, Charlie Thompson, Jimmy Nelson, and William Shirley. The troop went on camping trips and earned badges for community service.

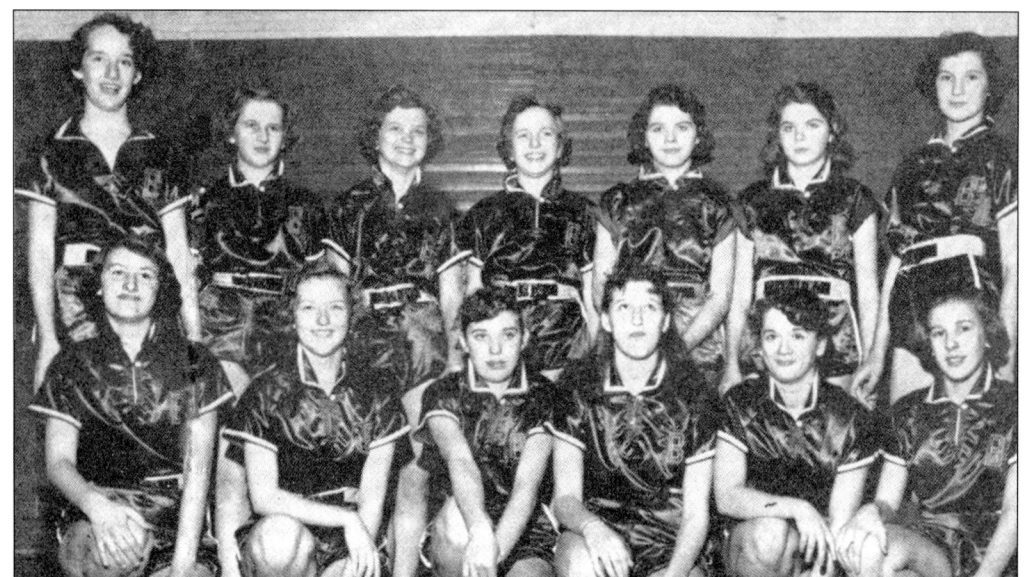

HOOPSTERS, 1956. Archie Morgan organized this girls' basketball team to play in the Christian Youth Fellowship League. The girls won nine games played in their age group. The team won the sportsmanship trophy during this season. Pictured here are, from left to right, (front row) Reba Crawford, Dianne Moore, Linda Adams, Jo West, Faye Irby, and Brenda Lowe; (back row) Iris Ann Thompson, Caroline Hembree, Sylvia Clayton, Nancy Malone, ? Elrod, ? Elrod, and Betty Fant.

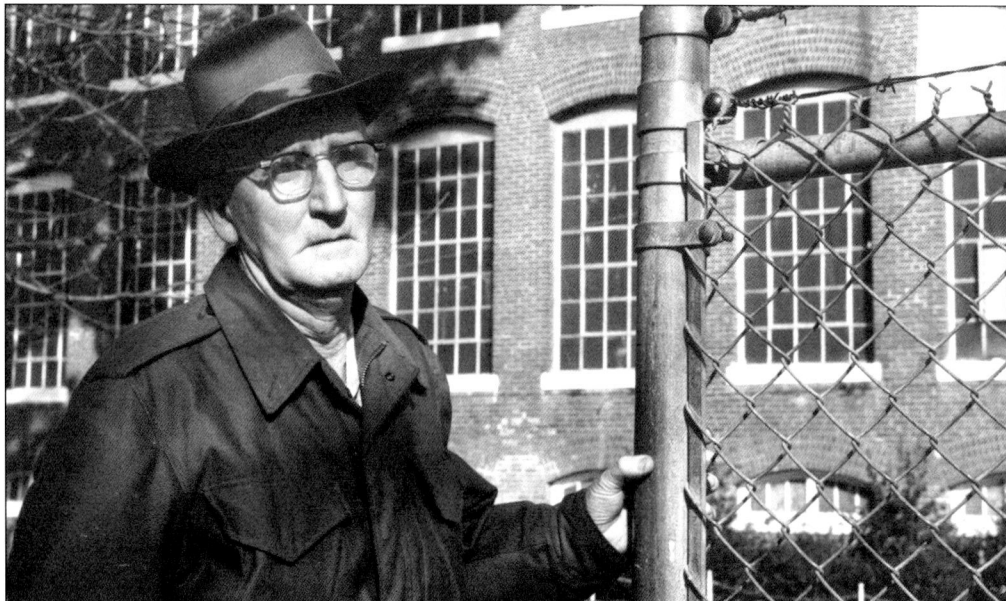

A TRIBUTE TO SERVICE. DeWitt Snipes began working for Belton Mill in 1917 and worked continuously at the plant until his death. For a time he worked as a doffer; he was later advanced to section hand and still later to second hand. He served in the latter capacity until he was made the gate watchman. According to his daughter, Mae Minyard, Snipes' health began to deteriorate in the 1950s, but instead of putting him out of a job, the management created the gate watchman's job just for him in honor of his long and useful service to the mill.

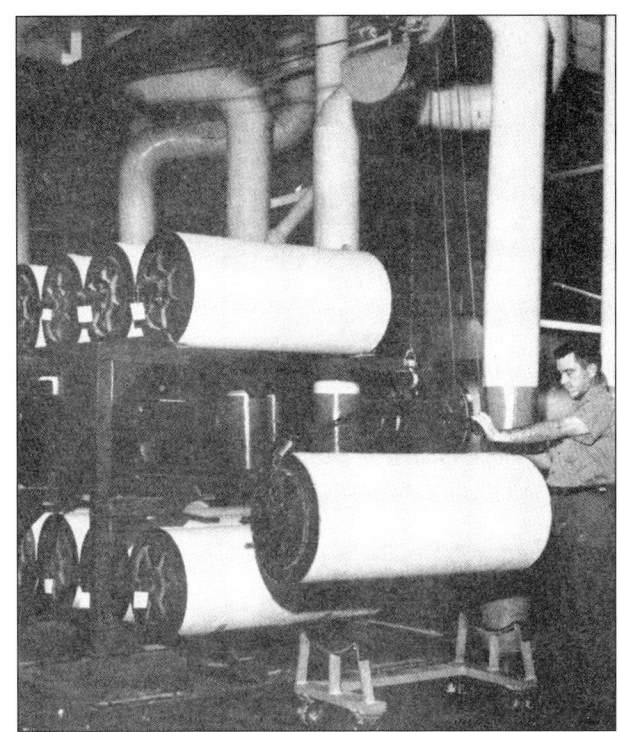

INNOVATIONS PROTECT WORKERS. Since slashing departments presented lifting hazards, the Belton plant made improvements in the slashing operation in 1958 so that the storage of warps, the doffing of slashers, and the loading and unloading of the tie-in machines are all accomplished without any lifting being required of the employees. Specially designed trucks were created to help transport the warps but still keep the floors in good condition and the warps free from damage. Here, J.M. Cason, slasher tender, operates the electric hoist at a storage rack.

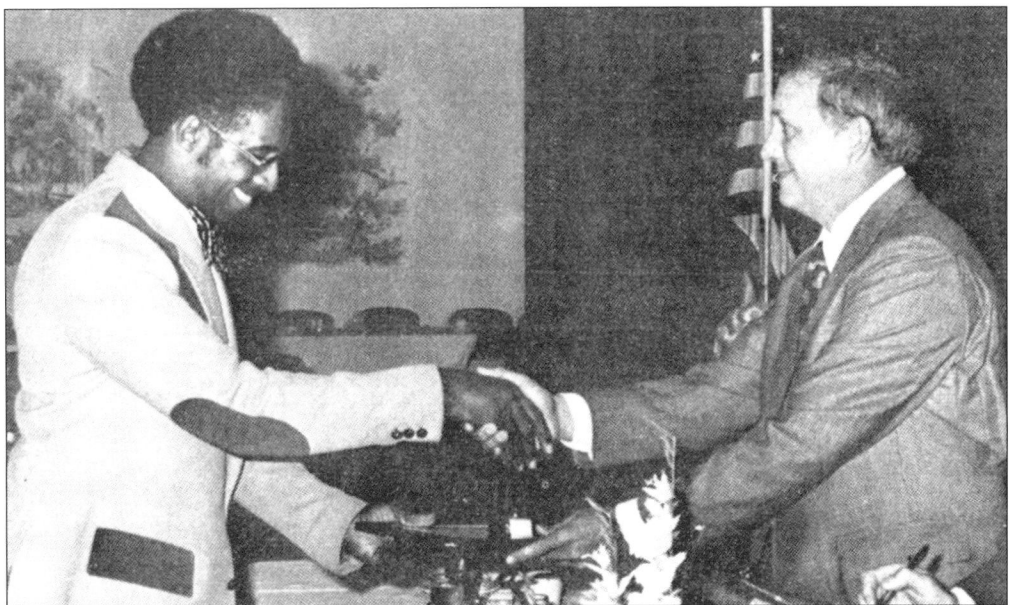

INTEGRATION OCCURS TWO DECADES BEFORE THE 1960S. Fleet Clinkscales, a press operator in the cloth room, accepts congratulations for his 30 years of continuous service in 1974 from Jimmy E. Jones, division manager for Abney Mills' Belton and Toxaway plants. When so many soldiers left for World War II service, vacated jobs were taken on by women and blacks. When the veterans returned, blacks had already made such an impression on the mill supervisors that they were able to keep the jobs they had been doing during the war. Thus, the mill paved the way for integration.

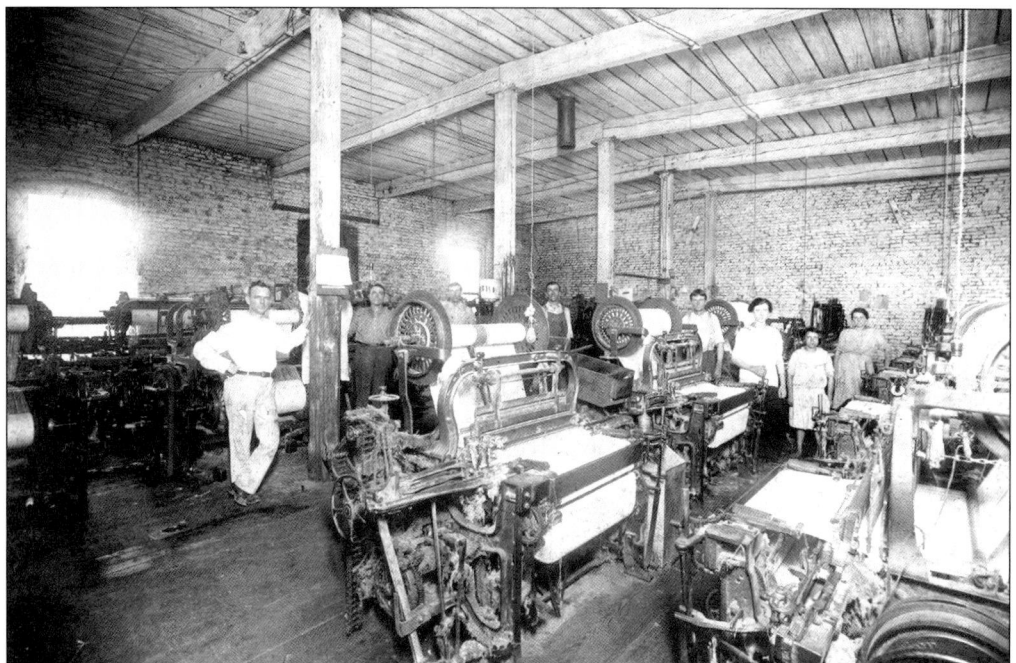

BLAIR MILLS, C. 1910. In 1908, E.B. Rice Sr. started a tiny textile operation with one loom he had purchased in Pelzer and hauled by wagon to Belton. To drive his loom, he cut holes through the floor and connected the loom to the motor, which also ran the bottling works downstairs. His first manufactured product was in the form of damask napkins, which were sold to New York commission houses. This old photograph shows his "mill" over the Belton Bottling Plant in 1914. Today, Blair Mills is a flourishing operation.

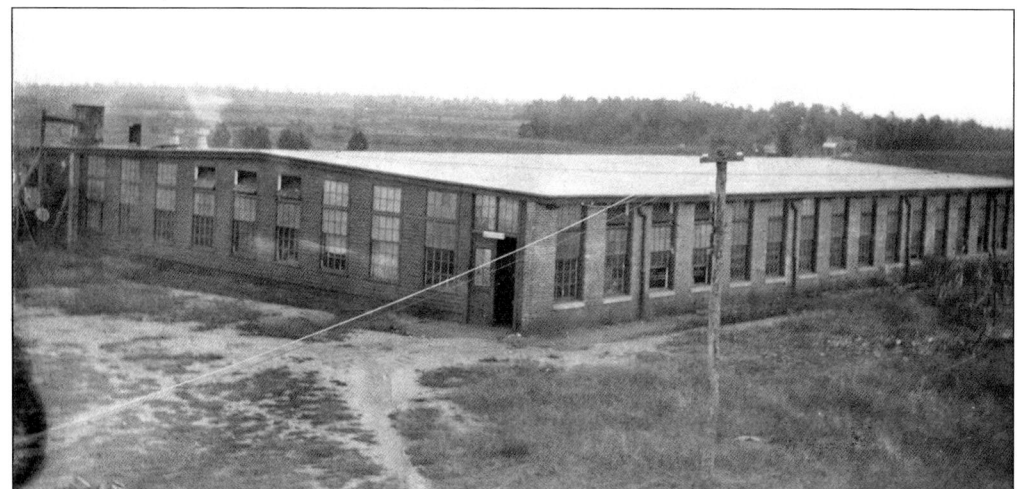

EXPANSION. With 12 looms and seven employees, E.B. Rice Sr. built his first building in 1916 on the present site of the mill. In addition to his original product, he took on the manufacture of Turkish towels and added a bleachery and sewing room. By 1932, his plant had increased to 164 looms with 150 employees. The mill was set up to take the raw cotton through the various processes to produce the finished products of Turkish towels and terry cloth. The mill has undergone extensive modernization programs. The first was in 1950, when new machinery was purchased for the entire mill, and the second in 1967, with a $700,000 expansion.

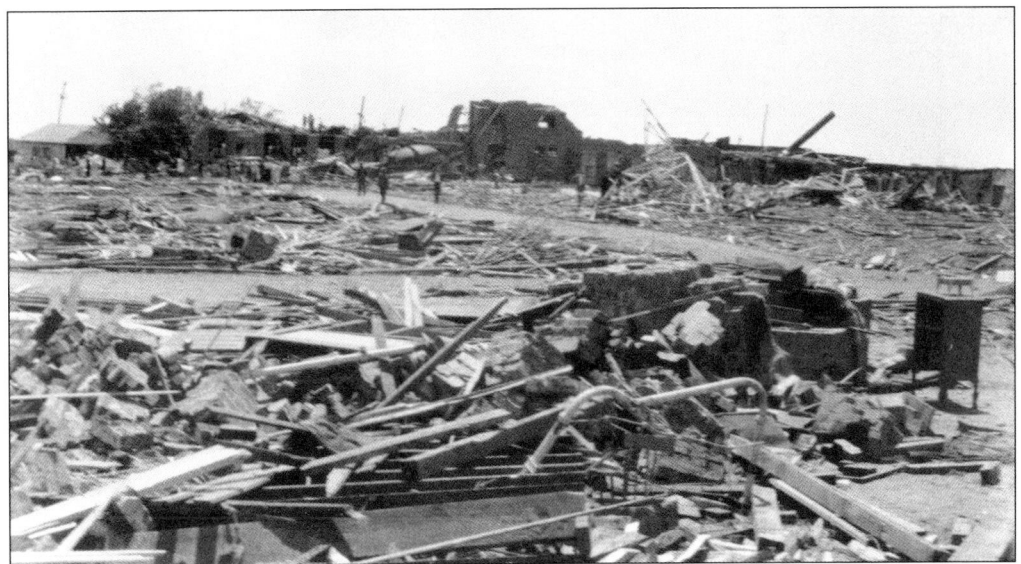

DESTRUCTION OF BLAIR MILLS BY THE GREAT TORNADO OF 1933. Blair Mills and its mill village was struck by an unexpected tornado on May 5, 1933. The nearly 20-year-old building was completely demolished, causing $100,000 in damages and the loss of nine lives. Frank Little, superintendent of Blair Mills, is credited with keeping the death toll to a limit. When he saw the twister coming from a distance, he rang the alarm and then ran to the plant to vacate the workers. The last of the sewing ladies from the second floor had just gotten down from the stairs when the tornado slammed into the building, taking the entire top story with it. Within four months, the mill was rebuilt on a larger scale and employees were once again producing Turkish towels.

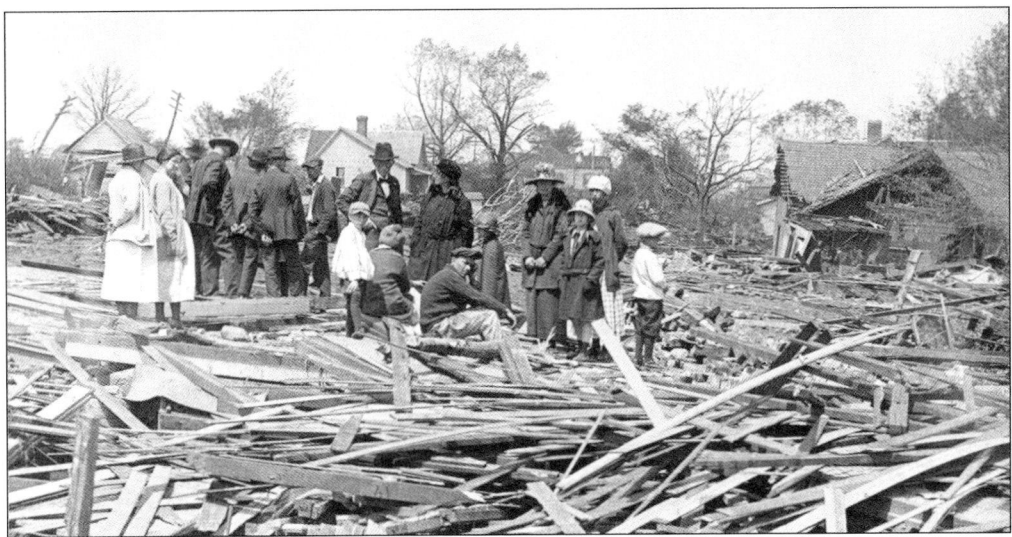

CURIOUS ONLOOKERS. The day after the tornado when a little of the shock and weariness had faded, townspeople and curiosity seekers from all points arrived to survey the damage. The Red Cross and R.F.C. fund quickly organized to provide food and shelter for the destitute and homeless. And the work of clearing the damage began. Houses in the Blair Mills village were rebuilt in brick instead of clapboard, at personal expense to the Rice family, since the plant did not carry storm insurance.

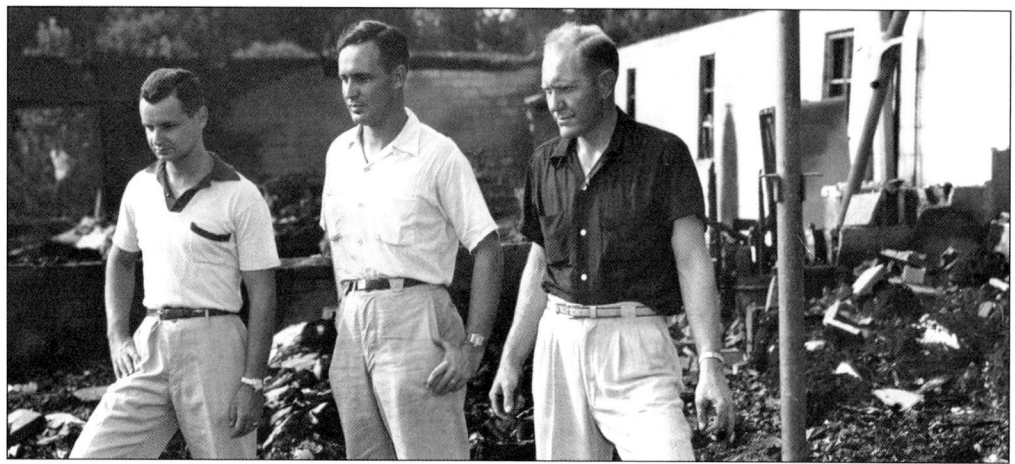

EVERYTHING LOST. Rice Mills was founded in 1947 by Will Rice. Originally, Rice would travel to New York and sometimes wait all day to receive two or three minutes of a buyer's time. If he succeeded in getting a small order, he would rush back to the mill, lay the pattern out himself, and have his operators stitch, finish, and ship the order. Time and again he had to prove that his mill could produce the best quality product for the target audience, and he eventually won some large retailers over with his persistence. The mill suffered a temporary setback on July 27, 1955, when the factory on Anderson Street caught fire in a lightning storm. The building burned to the ground, but the next day Will and Max Rice rented the cotton warehouse on North Main Street and went looking for sewing machines. Only 11 days after the disaster, partial operation resumed. Here, Max Rice, Will Rice, and Stanley Wilson survey the damage.

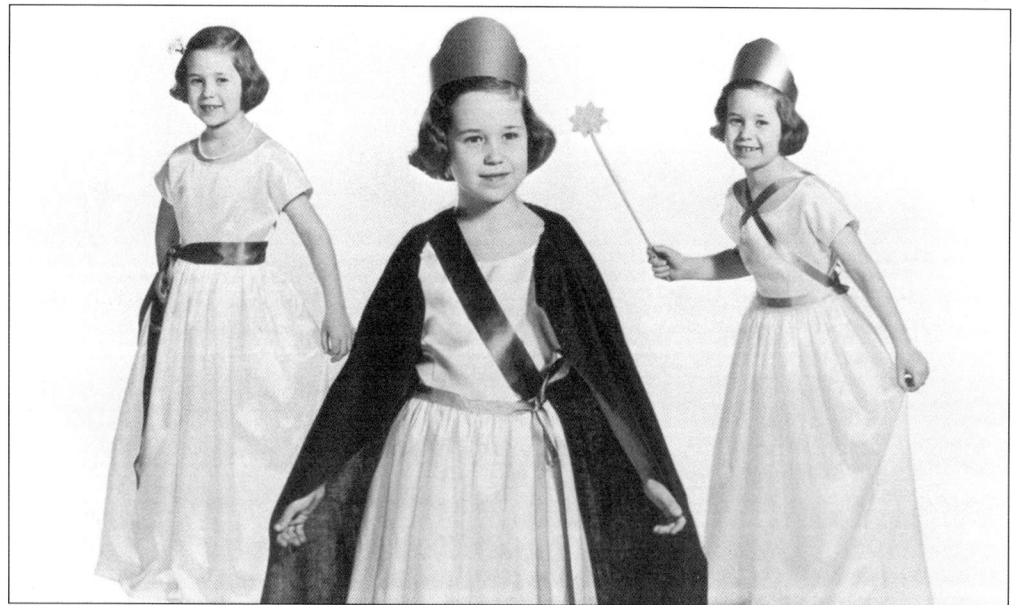

THREE IN ONE, 1956. Paula Rice (Blake) demonstrates the various uses of the three-in-one costume produced of sturdy materials at Rice Mills. An imaginative little girl could become a queen, a fairy, or a lady out for the evening in this costume. Other variations were the Bo Peep-Red Riding Hood-Alice in Wonderland combination, the pirate girl-masquerade girl-gypsy switch, and the bat girl-party lady-witch costume. The original patterns were cut by Paula's mother Pauline and then mass-produced at the plant.

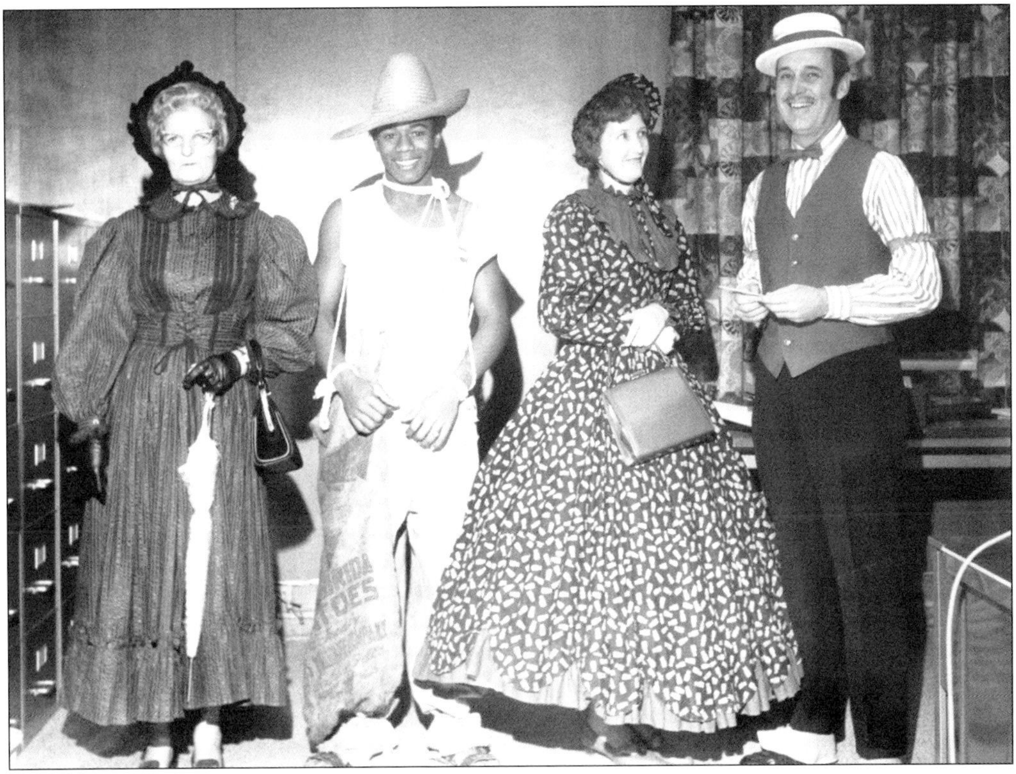

MOONLIGHT AND MAGNOLIAS. To improve employee morale, Christmas was celebrated in quite some style at Rice Mills. Each year, a themed dress-up day was announced and the employees were encouraged to come up with imaginative costumes. The employees would vote to determine who had come up with the best costumes, and the winners would receive prizes. In 1970, it was Antebellum Day, and employees Euzelia Fields, Queenie Sloan, and Shirley Sanders were declared the winners and received a gift from President Will Rice.

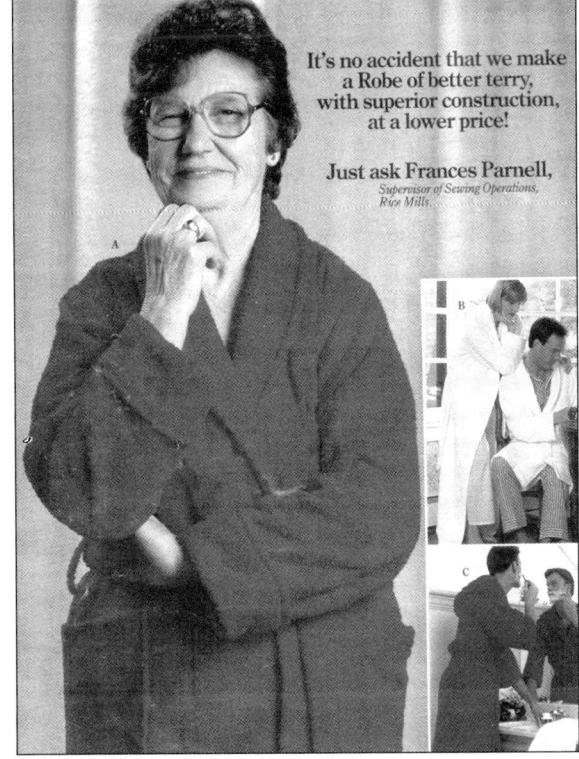

IS IT TOP QUALITY? ASK FRANCES. Frances Parnell poses for a Lands' End advertisement in the 1990s describing the process that the luxurious terry bathrobes go through before reaching a Lands' End customer. Parnell has worked at Rice Mills for 47 years.

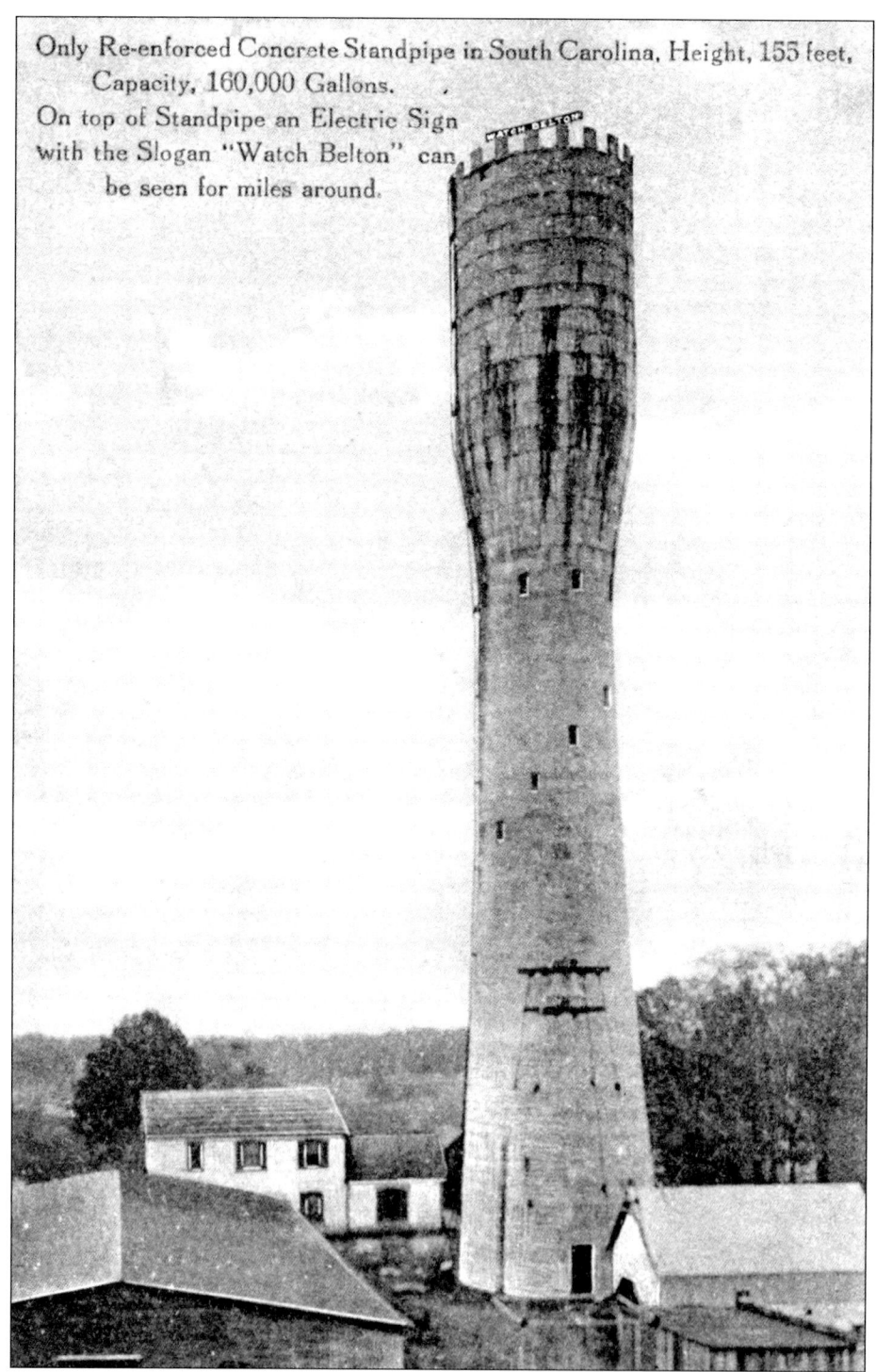

WATCH BELTON. In 1912, an electric sign was placed atop the newly constructed Standpipe. "Watch Belton," it read, and for years people were encouraged by the progress occurring in the city. On the eve of its sesquicentennial, again we challenge, "Watch Belton."

ACKNOWLEDGMENTS

A work of this magnitude cannot be accomplished solely by one person. Many people have painstakingly recorded our history and preserved our heritage through their efforts. I owe a tremendous debt of gratitude to these people: Dr. Don Herd, Prof. Max Grubbs, Max Williams, Judge William Kay, Luther Cox, and Ruth Cox Drake. I have relied heavily on their work in both print and on display in the museum.

I truly appreciate the support and enthusiasm of the Belton Area Museum Board members (Dick Gaillard, Joe Greer, Mae King, Lucille Mattison, Charles Martin, Margaret A. Cole, Bill Thomson, Linda Bradshaw, Hattie Green Ligon, Bonnie Fleming, and Sadie Rice Maynard) and the WebbCraft Family Foundation, Jerry Craft, CEO.

Thanks to the following people who welcomed me into their homes or businesses and generously opened their scrapbooks and photo albums: Loretta Holloway, Sadie Rice Maynard, Lyn Crayton Griffith, Carroll Hart, Henry Clinkscales, Judy Fisher Harris, Wallace and Linda Locke, Buddy and Charlene Minyard Ferguson, J. Allen Wilson, David Ellison, Mae Snipes Minyard, Stan and Mosie Rice Marshall, Dr. Don Kay, Judith Anderson McDowell, owner of McDowell's Emporium (the absolute finest new and used book store in the state), Butch Allred, Joe and Donia Campbell Coward, Jean Crawford Martin, Jukie and Paula Rice Blake, Rick and Jeanne Rice Henderson, Debbie Rogers, DeWitt Ledbetter, Martha Ledbetter Daniels, Ann Marshall, Bobby Johnson, James Ledbetter, Glenda Coward Conley, Charles Martin, Joe and Elva Simmons Park, Faye Barras, Marguerite "Punkie" Rice, Miriam Grubbs, Buddy Warnock, Tecie Bryant, Florence Cox, Shirley Cox Grant, Bill Smith, Clara Hawkins, D.K. Acker, Henry Hester, Dean Bannister, Hattie Green, Henry Norris, Martha Pinson Manry, Jan Moore Meeks, Sam and Ruth Driver, Judy Kelly, Dr. Dwight McBride, Carol Martin Brooks, Glenn Locke, James B. Mattison, Janice Ruth Edwards, Maj. Roger N. Anderson Sr., Lucille Vaughn Mattison, Bob King, and Bill and Margaret King.

I owe appreciation to those who showered me with information, solicited pictures, or helped me identify people in the photographs: Hattie Green Ligon, David King, Rufus and Grace Callaham, Wallace Shaw, Elaine Ellison Ryder, Sara Norris Sharpe, Molly Cheshire, Rev. Kenneth Dean, Vivian Buchannan, Sam and Carol McCombs Anderson, Cheryl Dooley, Dan Harvell, Christy Hannah Minor, Rev. Ronnie Grant, Dan Harvell, Jim and Frances Mattison Russell, Charles Cox, Fred Norris, Linda Ford, Emily Peeples, Lewis and Sherry Mattison Haynie, Wilson and Karon Wilson Ledbetter, Connie Whitten, Skipper Maynard, Rex Maynard, Mitchell Cole, Jim and Debbie Anderson Culwell, Becky Holloway, Rev. Dwight

Green, Jim and Jane Martin Woodson, Ed Jefferson, Lt. Col. Roger N. Anderson Jr., Rev. S.E. Neely, Linda Hill Ligon, Ed McHugh, Camilla Richey, Jeanette Land Eskew, Charles and Martha Meeks, Norma Hughes-Smith, Patsy Martin, Marlee Gambrell, Gale Pruitt, Theresa Buchanan, Terri Miller King, Linda Anderson, Elaine Marcus Long, Betty Burton, Jennifer O'Barr, Connie Vaughn Caldwell, Steve Sylvia, Don Trioni, Homer Booth, Roger Bolt Sr., Jack Oates, Sarah Willingham Thompson, William Henry and Ruth Ann Norris, Rufus Gambrell, Ella Mae Johnson Gambrell, Andrew Norris, Larry Gambrell, and Lila Mae Hand Lindler.

Many pictures would have gone unidentified if not for the sharp memories of the boys at Rooster's: Butch Allred, Dan Sellers, Roy Mac Haggard, Marvin "Doc" Holliday, Bud Hiott, Tony Buffington, Bill Dunlap, Dave McKee, J.T. Hanks, James "Red" Thomas, Jack Taylor, Terry Thompson, Harold Arflin, John Sanders, Donnie Ray Cooley, and Hank Arflin. The coffee's on me, guys.

To my First Buddies, thanks for your coveted prayers, your calm reassurance, and welcomed childcare during these harrying months: Barbara Locke, Sadie Ellen Maynard Blake, Jennifer Gilreath Wilson, Paula Gilreath, Laura Tadlock, Polly Blake Gilreath, Gale Clinkscales, Amy Fassett Vaughn, Lib Nation, Mary Rickenbaker, Jan Clinkscales, Jan Chastain Holliday, Jill Allred Sorrow, Tina Ehlies, and Jeanette Baylor. You've helped keep me sane and grounded.

To Kristy Williamson and Barbara Mickelson Erwin, a special thanks for opening the doors of the Belton Center for the Arts for picture-gathering sessions. I won't touch your computers again; I promise.

To my editor, Laura New, I thank you for the privilege of pursuing this project. Your encouragement and incentives have urged me on when I thought the project couldn't be accomplished in such a short time.

And I would especially like to thank my family: my mother, Troyce Anne Ashley, and my mother-in-law, Elizabeth Darby, for keeping the children entertained while I worked on this project, and to my husband, Steve, and children, Philip and Sloane, for putting up with cold sandwiches, unwashed laundry, and gritty floors. I love you all the way to Pluto and back!

AAD